A Way of Happening

Books by Fred Chappell

NOVELS

It Is Time, Lord
The Inkling
Dagon
The Gaudy Place
I Am One of You Forever
Brighten the Corner Where You Are
Farewell, I'm Bound to Leave You

SHORT STORIES

Moments of Light
More Shapes Than One

POETRY

The World Between the Eyes
River
The Man Twice Married to Fire
Bloodfire
Awakening to Music
Wind Mountain
Earthsleep
Driftlake: A Lieder Cycle
Midquest
Castle Tzingal
Source
First and Last Words
Spring Garden: New and Selected Poems

ANTHOLOGIES

The Fred Chappell Reader

ESSAYS

Plow Naked

A Way of Happening

Observations of Contemporary Poetry

Fred Chappell

Picador USA
New York

Production Editor: David Stanford Burr

Design: Nancy Resnick

Library of Congress Cataloging-in-Publication Data

Chappell, Fred,
    A way of happening : observations of contemporary poetry / by Fred Chappell.—1st ed.
        p. cm.
    Includes bibliographical references.
    ISBN 0-312-18033-0
    1. American poetry—20th century—History and criticism.
2. Criticism—United States. 3. American poetry—Study and teaching (Higher)—United States. 4. Poetics. I. Title.
PS325. C48   1998
811' .509—dc21   97-33375
                                              CIP

First Picador USA Edition: April 1998

10 9 8 7 6 5 4 3 2 1

for
Stan and Jeannie Lindberg

Contents

Acknowledgments

"First Night Come Round Again" appeared in very different form in *The South Atlantic Quarterly* 84:1 (Winter 1985).

"Attempts upon Delight: Six Poetry Books," *The Kenyon Review* n.s. 12:3 (Summer 1990).

"Brief Cases: Naked Enterprises," *The Southern Review* 28:1 (Winter 1992).

All the others, except for the new introductory piece, "Thanks but No Thanks," appeared in *The Georgia Review* as herewith, following the table of contents:

The Georgia Review 43:1 (Summer 1989); 45:4 (Winter 1991); 45:2 (Summer 1991); 46:4 (Winter 1992); 50:1 (Spring 1996); 44:4 (Winter 1990); 48:2 (Summer 1994); 47:2 (Summer 1993); 46:2 (Summer 1992); 50:3 (Fall 1996); 51:1 (Spring 1997); 47:4 (Winter 1993); 48:4 (Winter 1994); 49:3 (Fall 1995).

A Way of Happening

Thanks but No Thanks:
An Introduction

Poets, the adage claims, are born, not made. And while it does not then follow in course of logic that critics are made, not born, there is a noticeable aura of "made" about the critic. Poetry, we might propose, arises from the spirit; criticism is committed by an intellect which has had to will itself to perpetrate the act.

But if that is true, why is the world so flooded with criticism over which the least breath of intellect seems never to have passed? I would submit three reasons:

1. Criticism is a more difficult art than most readers suppose, than many critics have recognized;
2. Much of it—especially the output of the breed known as "reviewers"—is produced under pressure of deadline constraint and subject to the selective claims of editors;
3. The influence of literary politics is so pervasive as to be inescapable, even in the most conscientious and least partisan of writers.

To these reasons I would add a fourth not unique to the situation of literature: It is difficult to train oneself to listen to what someone else has to say, in print or in person, without interposing the force of one's own personality and permitting the tinctures of one's own prejudices to color responses that ought to be spontaneous though gravely considered, genuine though well-informed, unique but rarely cranky.

The poet's responsibilities are large and the critic's correspondingly are almost as large, and this is true even if the versifier is only a maker of graceful trifles and the critic is only an infrequent reviewer, a friend whom the local newspaper's book editor has cajoled into doing a job of work. For what is said in print can never be unsaid, no matter how thoroughly it may later be altered, regretted, deplored, or retracted. An unfavorable review stings the poet, but an unjust review smirches, however temporarily, the work itself and mars the fair face of truth. It is a happiness that such injustice is its own avenger. The victim of an unjust review may suffer diminished sales and the desultory sneers of passing strangers who will never trouble to investigate the volume for themselves. But the author of the unjust or obtuse review is shown over time to be a fool or a knave, a toady or a cynic—and this is true even when the hapless man or woman has undertaken comment in the best possible faith.

So why do some writers consign themselves to this hopeless, confused, and sometimes dangerous task? Why do not all of them always say, as I have often said when presented the opportunity to review a book or stack of books, "Thanks but no thanks"?

Even the obvious motives are suspect.

"If I don't do it, then it will be done by those whose opinions I cannot respect." This reason would be legitimate, except that the result will obtain anyhow. No reviewer can write broadly enough, or vehemently enough, to muffle disagreeing voices. Until they are all assassinated, rival critics will continue to criticize.

Or perhaps our reviewer has urgent axes to grind, perhaps he or she is a Neo-Objectivist, or an Anti-Authoritarian or a Radical Nonfeminist or a Neo-Marxist Miscegenarian and feels that the purposes and principles of a certain school of critical philosophy need to be brought to bear upon the contemporary scene, to reward the poets who adhere barnacle-like to the received system of thought and to chastise severely those who attempt to swim on their own the uncharted seas of inspiration. This motive seems legitimate, though circumscribed, since the critic believes that the truth is on his side and makes him mighty. Its drawback is its pro-

crustean tendency, its inability to judge fairly works that do not belong to
its school of influence. Another licit motive for criticism might be protest. A faithful reader
of poetry looks about her and finds that, according to her lights, the
state of poetry criticism is abysmal. The reviews she reads are mere
logrolling or personal feuding, the critical pages are couched in jaw-
breaking jargon or are mincing in style and pallid in content. Or they are
vitiated by political prejudices of various colors. Firmness, levelheaded-
ness, and even attentiveness seem lacking—and so this faithful reader
decides to become a faithful reviewer. She is trying to make up, she
believes, some part of a large critical deficit.

Though there may be a tinge of messianism in her decision, it is an
honorable one. Perhaps she is mistaken; maybe her standards of fairness
and her attempts to reach it are no stronger or purer or better informed
than those of the critics she so despises. But she has discovered a vision
for her criticism and thus has taken the first step toward producing judgments that are well meant, however erroneous they may prove in the
long run.

But a critic needs a strong motive, for the troubles are many and the pleasures are few. The critic makes no friends among poets, not even among
those he or she praises. Poets are famously a vain race, though perhaps
their skins are not measurably thinner than those of most other human beings. Yet the number is legion for whom a mountain of praise will not suf-
fice and the slightest hint of censure will wound like an assegai. The
slimmest passing adverb in a review may serve to make its author a blood
enemy of that poet until Gibraltar melts. Even graceful praise can make
the critic an anathema to a rival of the poet being praised.

And if the critics happen also to write poetry, then they can bid a glum
farewell to the possibility of calm judgment of their own work. The literary world is a sensitive web, and when one strand trembles others tremble in sympathy. Poet-critic Robin is bent on avenging the injuries
poet-critic Sparrow visited upon his friend poet-critic Waxwing, and
Sparrow's new book, *A Diet of Worms*, gives him plenteous opportunity
for close analysis with scalpel, drawknife, electric drill, chain saw, and
jackhammer.

The reviewer or critic desiring to acquire a reputation for the excellence of his prose and the steadiness of his judgments had better be a canny animal, for these two virtues are among those least likely to be remarked in his pages. It is more useful to know, if you are trying to make a name, which poets to review and which to overlook. The brightest and most articulate critic practicing will gain little credit by comprehending the work of Marilyn Nelson or Al Young or John Morris and writing brilliantly about it. No, he must go to the familiar names and rack his brains for something fresh to say about John Ashbery, Anthony Hecht, Jorie Graham, or even—Lord forgive us!—Allen Ginsberg. He must choose publishing houses as meticulously: Ecco, Knopf, Random House—okay; Coffee House, BOA, Copper Canyon—maybe; Asahti, Crosshairs, Singing Horse—dubious.

There is one excepting factor in this game of Who's Hot & Who's Not: the pet. Critics are usually allowed to have one or two poets to favor against general opinion. But here too a rule is in force. If you decide upon a pet, a poet unfashionable or out of fashion, you are supposed to choose one whose work is difficult—obscure in subject matter, eccentric in format, abrasive or wispy in tone. Your pet is one of your credentials, living proof that you do not always make safe choices, that you support the vanguard of the art, even at the cost of being suspected of a blind spot. But if you have more than two or three pets you are known as a crank and will not be consulted in the production of textbooks and popular anthologies or invited to international conferences on Postmodernism in the Post-Saussurean Universe.

Perhaps that is not such a bad thing. If a poet too habitually in the company of other poets may run the danger of making her work derivative, then may not a critic too often surrounded by other critics risk being faddish? I would count the peril a genuine one and might even point toward the alarming amount of consensus among critics as evidence. People, even critics, like to hop onto a bandwagon and if the vehicle is flashy enough may well be convinced it is taking them in the right direction.

We all know better, of course we do. Critics are required to be aware of literary history, and many pages remind them of the sorry figures they are likely to cut in course of time. If it was not a critical article that doused the fiery particle that was John Keats, it may as well have been, for that became the poetic truth. Even the most celebrated critics turned out to be weak soothsayers; few of the authors who drew Sainte-Beuve's perspicacious comment attract modern notice. Edmund Wilson is known—or ought to be known—for his entertaining book reviews and his brilliant intellectual history, *To the Finland Station*, but he is also known for his curmudgeonly blindness toward genre fiction and the silliness of much of *Axel's Castle.*

Wilson also produced two novels, *I Thought of Daisy* and *Memoirs of Hecate County;* they are worthy efforts, though probably less well thought of now than when they first appeared. Most critics whose reputations have endured were also poets or fiction writers or historians or familiar essayists; their pages were informed by their knowledge of the inner parts of writing. Dr. Johnson and Coleridge, John Dryden and William Hazlitt, Victor Hugo and Ezra Pound, Malcolm Cowley and Kenneth Burke, and a bibulous host of others sit at the winestained table in the convivial Poets' Pub. In the hushed formal saloon upstairs Aristotle and John Dennis and Helen Vendler—they who never published poetry—are taking a sober tea.

I think it is important for a critic or reviewer to understand writing on its day-labor side. The poet may or may not be an artist, but if she is worth the ink she expends she had better be an artisan, concerned not only with what she says and how she says it, but also with what kind of object she is making, the probable uses it can be put to, its cost to her in terms of economics, emotional tear, social status, and personal dignity. You cannot give your all to poetry unless you know what your all is—and then you must decide if you want to risk it. The chances of a poet enduring in this day and time a life as disheartening as that of John Clare or Gérard de Nerval are very good indeed. Amon Liner and Winfield Townley Scott lived obscure lives and died almost unremarked, and I will be surprised if proper critical recognition overtakes the work of either of them.

These are some of the reasons that I have mostly restricted my critical writing to the area of practical criticism, to the nuts-and-bolts of poems. I have nothing against theoretical writing. Let every dogma have its day. Except in academic circumstances a literary dogma can do little harm, and the harm it does in universities affects only pedagogy and the personal careers of teachers. Literature itself is hardly affected, for though it welcomes the patronage of the university it does not depend upon it.

Criticism is direly affected by academic fashion, however. The academic critic must at least pretend to a knowledge of prevalent intellectual fashions. It was once necessary for an academic critic to claim to know the ideas of Suzanne Langer, Maud Bodkin, and John Crowe Ransom. Now he had better bow toward Derrida, Lacan, and Anna Freud. All these thinkers are heavyladen with merit and all of them are worth the time it requires to become acquainted. But when the critic decides that any one of these philosophers—or any other—holds the single key to the comprehension and insightful explication of literature, then he or she has struck an eye out, so to speak. The programmatic point of view is very attractive; neo-Marxist or neoconservative or Derridean ideology gives one something to say that is likely to sound valuable whether it is much to the point or not.

And the temptation to ideology is not only in the eased access it promises to offer to new works of art but also in the cachet it confers upon the critic herself. If you have adopted a point of view—if, say, you have decided you are a Lacanian critic—then you have gained importance in the eyes of an academic audience. It can be taken for granted that you have points to make and if what you say is rather predictable, so much the better. For that means that you can be invited to attend symposia, to contribute to critical anthologies and special issues of journals, to address learned conferences, in full confidence that your one message can be squeezed to fit under almost any rubric and that it will complement the other single messages that can be called forth in Pavlovian fashion. A professor saddled with the task of gathering members for a panel on "Lesbian Subtexts in the Poetry of Emily Dickinson and George Herbert" will strategize in this manner: "Let's see now . . . I've got two brands of feminists committed to show up, one poststructuralist, one neo–New Critic—what else do I need? Ah, a Lacanian! Why don't I invite Smith Smithson? He will pair off well with Joan Johnson, who hates everything he stands for. That will give us balance."

In a similar manner, perhaps, the Smoked Trout Salad with Bitter Chocolate Dressing was conceived.

Should the critic then subscribe to no beliefs? Should she strive to possess that famous sensibility so fine no idea can violate it?

Such a prize is devoutly to be desired, I'm sure, but it is unlikely that many critics now will closely resemble T. S. Eliot's description of Henry

James. We had better recognize that fact, all we scribblers about poetry, and prepare for our jobs with frank self-examination, discovering our predilections and prejudices and admitting to them with whatever equanimity we can muster. After we have performed this difficult exercise, we may have some notion where each of us stands in relation to new poems, new books of poems, new schools of poetry, and what we know of contemporary literature as a whole.

I wish I could say I'd performed this duty which now presents itself so palpably before me. I did not, but I like to imagine that if I'd known beforehand how much critical comment of one sort or another I was going to produce I would have prepared myself in this obviously fitting manner.

But I came into the task of reviewing poetry so casually and gradually that I hardly remember how it happened. The sequence—as best I can now piece it together—was something like this: A poet myself, with one or two volumes in print, I was sometimes asked to give readings with other poets at universities, colleges, community colleges, civic societies, library groups, and other cultural conclaves. These were frightening but happy affairs for the most part, and they often ended with a shared nightcap between my comrade and me in the sullen dank basement lounges of Holiday Inns or with a private jug passed back and forth in room 321 of a Comfort Inn. In a while, the conversation would settle upon poetry and the situation of poetry and upon literary politics. I began to notice that a common complaint of the poets I encountered was the lack of critical reception their work received. They decried especially the fact that newspapers—sometimes even their hometown newspapers—declined to review their books.

I fancied that in a very small way I might do something in the way of a remedy. In those days I could count a couple of book-page editors as personal friends and I struck a deal with them: I would review any book they desired at whatever nominal fee they could pay if they would also allow me to review, at some later date, a book of poems. The latter would be their choice; I had no desire to infringe upon their prerogatives, only to add the luster of poetry to their verseless pages.

That was how I got into the avocation, and later on when the rules changed so that I was asked to review two and even three books of prose in order to earn my chance with a poetry book, I agreed. I was assured that this new wrinkle was not suggested by the helpless editors but by the publishers, who were themselves pressured by the managements of the huge business conglomerates that owned the newspapers. This explanation conjured the image of an expensively suited corporate board of Dutch and Swiss businessmen sitting around an immense mahogany table, relinquishing their Havanas to ashtrays for a moment in order to raise their fists and shout in thick, rich accents, "These poetry reviews in the Greensboro, North Carolina newspaper are ruining our whole international balance sheet!"

That was but a local hint in the 1960s of the general ruin that was to overtake newspaper book reviewing. Nowadays book-page editors may refuse to review any book that is not a best-seller, or may insist upon reviews being tied to advertising of different sorts, or attempt to make reviews concurrent with hot news topics. Perhaps only writers and book editors have remarked and regretted the decline in the integrity of reviewing, but I cannot think it a good thing, no matter its relative unimportance in the largest scheme of things.

At any rate, my newspaper writing caught the notice of a few editors of literary magazines. I was asked to do a piece for *Western Humanities Review* and then for *The Georgia Review*. This latter review attracted the notice of *The Kenyon Review*. Then, after some adjustment, I became one of the regular poetry reviewers for *The Georgia Review*. I was proud to be listed on the masthead and happy that my counterpart reviewer was the bright, serious, insightful Judith Kitchen. She wrote two essay-reviews a year; I wrote the other two.

That is how these pieces have been listed on the journal's contents page—as "essay-reviews." After my initial efforts—the ones that follow this present introductory essay—I began to emphasize the first term of that compound noun. I decided the assessments of books would have more point and cogency if they were organized around a single topic common to all of them. There was a clear danger that I might write a little like the theoretical critics I have decried, attaching some books to topics with which they were not entirely consonant, and leaving them awkwardly adangle from the main body of the piece. In some cases I might have to overlook a large number of poems in a collection because these did not fit into my chosen topic.

I have to admit that I have been guilty of both of these faults and, though I tried to indicate in my paragraphs where I was stretching my limits, I have regretted some injustices I committed. I do believe them to be minor, and have pointed them out when I recognized them. Yet I don't wish to excuse myself too thoroughly. It will be hard for any reader to believe me, but when I first set out writing these essay-reviews I felt I could hardly do injustice to poems because I was certain I had no prejudices. Ethnicity was immaterial to me: if a poem was Native American, African American, male, female, Eurocentric, Asiacentric, Oceanocentric, or Neptunian in outlook, I didn't care. The only important considerations were that it be beautiful, honest, and interesting—that is, that it intrigue the mind or affect the feelings. Nor was I a partisan of form: sonnets, ballades, prose poems, free verse, syllabics, computer-designed chunks, aleatory concatenations—anything suited me, I thought, as long as it was *good*. As for politics, who cared? Let the poet be the nastiest Nazi, or the bloodiest Stalinist, let her be Saint Catherine or Messalina, only her poem counted. I imagined myself as being as open to a poem as to any person I might meet for the first time, offering a friendly handshake.

In fact, that was the image I presented to myself of my reading—encountering a poem as if meeting a person. I would be open and easy of mind, I would be a pal of the poet—until his lines betrayed me aesthetically.

And to think a grown man might harbor such callow fantasies!—Yet I did so and, to tell the truth, mostly still do, even though I came to recognize soon enough that I did indeed possess prejudices I had been coolly unaware of.

It turns out that I prefer a clarity of intention in a poem; I like to think I know where, as a piece of speech, it is supposed to be pointing. I embrace as a sister the "intentional fallacy," for I discovered that if I cannot guess what goal a work of literature is aiming at, then I will never find out what it says. In other words, I make hypotheses—not very scientific ones—about the phenomenon in front of me. These hypotheses are provisional, and I am ready to transform or cancel them when any bit of evidence in the text at hand seems to contradict them. I'm sure that a great many of these initial hypotheses are flat wrong; maybe most of them are. But if I must examine work so baffling that I cannot grasp enough of its premises to impute an intention, then there is no hope I will ever comprehend it thoroughly enough to comment. By means of this principle I eliminated from my consideration whole shelves of verse.

One of the troubles with provisional hypotheses is that they are a little stubborn and desire to become fixed conceptions. If the hypothesis is wrong, then the ensuing argument is probably, though not certainly, mistaken. And while such misreading does not invariably lead to erroneous final judgments about quality, it distorts explication into nonsense. As I read back through the reviews contained in this volume, I am convinced that I made several bad hypotheses and stuck with them. But though my instinct whispers that I went astray, my analytical powers have not discerned cleaner pathways. So my original judgments remain.

The drab fact is, a reviewer of contemporary poetry might be defined as an organism that makes literary blunders. Innocent readers may believe that reviewers know their stuff, that their judgments can be so soundly informed that mistakes will be few or minor. But a glance backward at some of the earliest critical receptions of William Carlos Williams, Wallace Stevens, e. e. cummings, and even Robert Frost will destroy this illusion. Even more telling than such ill-considered censure is the largess of praise gathered by such bards as Witter Bynner, Theodore Spencer, and Robert Hillyer. And the critics who committed these errors were not provincial dimwits but highly respected pundits, enthusiastically attended and assiduously lauded.

Yet I believe that my hypotheses about poetic intention—the ones I arrived at finally—were right about as many times as they were wrong, and I believe that my own writing of poetry helped me in forming many of the correct ones. Poets are famously bad critics of their own work—so are dentists, come to that—yet it is more than likely that the practice of an art yields critical insight into it. The woman who has wrestled almost daily with problems of cadence, closure, assonance, transition, climax, rhyme, line breaks, and so forth, will have a better feeling for them than someone who has learned about these things without taking the risks that accompany their employment. My statement is bound to irritate a good many critics—in fact, some of them have communicated their displeasure—but I think it to be the case.

There are other areas in which a practicing poet can enjoy advantages over the reviewer who is purely a critic. A poet whose work has been reviewed in periodicals is bound to have a vivid skepticism about the whole critical enterprise and be less likely to take his own pronouncements as definitive. Reviewers don't get reviewed as often as poets—it can seem redundant to review reviews—so that always getting off scot-free is liable to make them cocksure.

Another advantage accruing to the poet-critic is the respect her opinions may receive from the poets themselves. As much as poets may admire intellectuals (and many of them simply *do not*), they will prefer the opinions of a fellow spirit, someone who has endured the birth pangs of a sonnet or prose poem and suffered the vocal reactions of some of its readers.

There are other advantages too, but I ought to mention one hefty disadvantage in straddling the disciplines: this is the matter of allegiance. A poet may stand too close to the whole idea of poetry, to the phenomenon itself, to be a fitting arbiter of poetic taste. A working nonpoet critic may see poetry as an inevitable part of culture, as an adornment of living, as an important voice of history, as a necessary part of human enlightenment; he may set the highest value upon the art. But will he count it as one of the most important aspects of human life, the thing that makes a person's individual life worth living, that makes breath worth breathing?

If the critic did so, he would be mistaken, for only the poet dare set such an extreme individual price and only for the poet will the art be worth such a price. For the majority of people to whom poetry is available, it will and should remain an ornament of existence. It must be there for them as a form of pleasure, an activity that adds resonance to dreams and daydreams, that increases the lilt of a joyous hour and the depth of a sorrowful one. It can say for them what their hearts remember or feel or desire to feel and, once it has said its say, it is proper for poetry to disappear from view until inevitably called forth again.

But for the poet such willed absence of poetry is unlikely, perhaps unthinkable. Poetry is with her always, waking or sleeping, in sickness and in health, in calm reflection and furious activity. It is so much a part of her life it *is* her life and at last all the sadness she experiences, all the vicissitudes she conquers, all the triumphs that defeat her become poems or parts of poems or one great poem that subsumes all her life.

So that when she sits down to write dispassionate criticism she may find that her passions will not cool, that Jack Jackson's work is so precious to her simply because it is *poetry* that she cannot see his most egregious solecisms. Or that Anna Anderson's lines seem to her to violate the spirit of poetry so thoroughly that the woman has to be incapable of penning a legitimate phrase. When poetry itself is one's lover, one's feelings in critical writing lie as raw and exposed as a flayed mole. Such supersensitivity is bound to lead to errors of judgment.

But errors of this sort are probably forgivable, however serious they are. They are crimes of passion and it is better to commit these in hot blood than to murder with cool disdain. There is a species of critic who comes to contemporary work already having made up his mind that it is of little importance and minor interest. He believes that genuine poetry died with Theodore Roethke or T. S. Eliot or Tennyson or Byron or Pope or Shakespeare or Homer and that the poets who now make verse are only tedious grubs mining and digesting the noble fallen tree of past literature. The greatness of the Augustan or Romantic or Modernist age can never be recovered because those ideals have disappeared. The ideals have disappeared because society is too weak, nihilistic, confused, and wrongheaded to understand and support them. Society has fallen into such sad disrepair because its leaders and members have strayed from the true intellectual or religious or scientific path. Much of the blame has to be laid at the feet of Richard Nixon or Franklin Delano Roosevelt or Napoleon or St. Augustine or God Himself because none of these figures turned out to be as trustworthy as they were supposed to be.

There is an endless barren Sahara of this sort of critical comment and it is as predictable, as insistent, and finally as vulgar as television evangelism. It may be that our present time is a skimpy one for real poetry; literature goes through periods when only minor lights are shining and no supernovae burst upon dazzled eyes. Yet is it not more likely that these critics are looking at the midnight Milky Way through sunshades? The purblindness of critics is a more frequent occurrence than the disappearance of good poetry from a culture.

I have taken for granted when reviewing books that I was missing the very best there was, that in some corner of the world, published by a press I could never have heard of, the finest poet of our century was flourishing. My limited purview overlooked her by accident. In the year

2150, when her strength, scope, and intensity were obvious to all the poetry lovers in our overcrowded solar system, there would be a literary historian toiling at the minor figures of the late twentieth century, a scholar who wrote this sentence: "Of the work of the superb Bella Bellissima Fred Chappell wrote not a word." And he would add that such oversight was typical of Chappell's criticism.

I don't mind. The important thing is that the great Bella gets the attention she deserves. We sightless critics who are scrabbling so fruitlessly in this the Bellissima Era shall welcome the oblivion we deserve. I am proud of my faith that my opinions will matter little in the long run and that only my embarrassments will be recalled, for this means that the art of poetry will endure and that after the inevitable geological settling of the literary landscape the noblest prominences will stand out sharply limned, the sunshine of time burning away the obscuring fogs that my colleagues and I have exuded.

This cheery fatalism has encouraged me to try my best at the reviewing of poetry—to figure out what I truly thought and felt, to report my feelings and thoughts with as much honesty and clarity as I could muster, to write them out as patiently and strongly and interestingly as I can. A number of editors have helped me in this task. They saved me from many missteps in syntax, diction, and logic, but never attempted to rescue my stupidity. I am grateful for everything they did.

I am most grateful of all to the poets I read. There were few books that failed to entertain and enlighten me. Even when I disliked the work I respected the poet because I know the demands of the discipline and the toll that is exacted in almost equal measure by success and by failure. So I was constrained to do the best I could by the work—in the full and certain foreknowledge that my best would never be good enough.

Purple Patches, Fuddle,
and the Hard Noon Light

I've had difficulty over the past decade in comprehending some of the poems of Alfred Corn. I figured the trouble was all on my side since he receives good reviews, is an intelligent person (his book of critical essays, *The Metamorphoses of Metaphor*, is pallid but palatable), and is published by Viking, a ritzy uptown house. I figured that I was missing something, that lines like those of the second stanza of "Lost and Found" in his new book, *The West Door*, must add up to something more than a mumble of disjointed abstraction. "Surely," says I to myself, "a passage like this one in 'Trout and Mole' is not a sloppy purple patch; it is something rare and finer than I have grasped":

> Now something tugs upward toward the flexible, sunfired
> ceiling, Something; and so with a will, higher,
> a lunge up through warbled mirrorgold
> into searing vacuum, brightness invisible,
> arcing to the top of his bent—and snap go
> the silver shutters as the wingborne prey
> (for once no useless clot of thistledown,
> but a crispy bite) ephemerid! is taken.

The sending up of G. M. Hopkins I allow, but how am I to forgive the television-advertising adjective "crispy" or calling the jaws of a trout "silver shutters" that go "snap" the way the weasel goes "pop"? If I accept the little Miltonic joke "brightness invisible," must I also accept the clumsy pun "top of his bent"? Could it be that what strikes me as being in such dubious taste is actually some avant-garde aesthetic I haven't yet heard about?

Now the jig is up. In the new book appears a thirteen-page narrative poem in workaday iambic pentameter. "An Xmas Murder" is a story of bigoted violence recounted by a country doctor in West Newbury, Vermont. A bunch of "rowdies" kill a man they don't like, and the doctor himself is threatened after his trial testimony because he is suspected of homosexuality. No one is brought to justice, since "if you can say the things people / Want to hear, then you may lynch at will."

It's not that "An Xmas Murder" is such a bad poem, only that it is pedestrian, for all its melodrama. Considering the claims of sophistication that have been made for Corn's poetry, we would think that a narrative poem in blank verse would be duck soup for the accomplished technician. But he makes two elementary mistakes: the poem natters on for at least three pages longer than necessary, and the character of the speaker is convincing neither as doctor nor as storyteller. The description of the murder, for instance, heads the list of Things We Doubt Ever Got Said by a Country Doctor: "Smash of the blackjack / Against his skull, exploding carnival / Of fire-veined shock that flies to the far corners / Of night." That's not colloquial speech; that's poetic diction in the style of Batman comics. And the doctor's self-pitying postscript vitiates his believability as a witness: "If I had had the sense to pitch / Someone unpopular from off a bridge / Instead of enjoying music, chances are / I'd be a favorite son."

There are some good poems in *The West Door*. "Wild Carrot" is especially taking, and "Home Thoughts in Winter, 1778" and "Toward Skellig Michael" and "The Chi-Ro Page from the Book of Kells." If "Naskeag" owes much to Elizabeth Bishop, well, so do other poets nowadays and the poem itself is solid. And although Alfred Corn, I think, has yet to find the kind of poetry that is truly his own, he is talented and often interesting. I mean no condescension when I say that I think of him as a promising poet.

Michael Burkard's *Fictions from the Self* is the writer's sixth book, but it is not promising. It is vaguely threatening, in the sense that there looks

to be no end to the number of versifiers writing this sort of fuddle. Sometimes it seems the shopping malls are infested with them, all muttering
sotto voce like mildly deranged bag ladies:

> I am in a hurry to decide two things: whether my
> amnesia has any color to it, whether the ghastly
> charity of hope is nothing more than that adjective
> I've chosen: ghastly.

The interesting things to observe about this passage and about most of
Burkard's work will belong more properly to sociology than to literary
criticism, but maybe it doesn't hurt to point out some obvious facts.
Burkard's work sounds like the work of John Ashbery and shares the ambitions of that poetry. It seems, of course, a poetry without ambition, but
that appearance is illusionary. This sort of writing desires above all else
to evade critical stricture. Whatever complaint is brought against it is
opted by its partisans as a strength.

"This stuff is boring," you say, and are told that it is meant to be boring; the fact that it is boring *says something* about poetry in our time.
Silliness, lack of logic, disjointedness, sameness of tone—all those qualities ordinarily noted as indices to bad poetry are referred to as symptoms
of social and spiritual and literary conditions. The more sophomoric
these poems are, the more we are expected to admire them. It is the child's
explanation. In his first attempt to roller-skate he wobbles, staggers, slips,
and falls with a thump. Then he addresses his onlookers with solemn tru-
culence. "I *meant* to do that!"

I quoted the first stanza of Burkard's title poem, figuring that he must
count it as one of his strongest pieces. And in fact it is stronger than his
other work. "Eerie" opens with these lines:

> When in my terror I have not given you
> the admiration, when I have not felt the rain
> chilling my body when it chills my body,
> and I have fallen asleep green but in the green light
> which is not the illumination the potato light gives off,
> which is not the corridor leading to a window
> in the middle of the city, in the middle of the room

where the stone drops
but I do not see it.

The sweaty effort here to produce an effect like those of the surrealist
paintings of Magritte, Chirico, Delvaux, and the others does not succeed
because Burkard cannot keep his heavy hands out of the image. "I have
fallen asleep green"—this phrase is jarringly cute and self-conscious and
reminds us that the visuals are not there to be experienced like images in
a real poem but are only the digressions of a fellow with a typewriter.
(Yes, I know. One might instead say something like "Burkard now allows us to recognize the presence of the poet in the poem, the painter in
his painting, by an adroit appeal to the reader's sense of propriety. He
shares with us the joke of allowing his use of 'green' to be felt as 'cute,'
and his knowingness, and ours, invalidate the charge of cuteness at the
same time they produce it." But I try not to write sentences like these and
am a better person for my effort. There is hardly room for two Helen
Vendlers in contemporary criticism.)

Lines like Burkard's are not actually read; they are merely noticed
where they appear on the page. This school of authors has come close to
achieving in writing what Erik Satie desired in music. *Musique démeuble-
ment,* he called it, music that would simply decorate an environment in the
way that furniture decorates a room. Of course, Satie's notion has since
been accomplished in dreadful style with Muzak, and Muzak is the art
form most closely allied to this sort of writing. I prefer to call it "writing"
because it rests on too faulty an aesthetic to be called poetry. The mere
fact that a clutch of lines is savorless, purposeless, and without narrative
interest or logical thread doesn't make it a poem.

Now and again Burkard does make a noise that sounds like poetry—
whether accidentally or not, I can't say. But I found the opening of "Picture with No Past to It" witty, and there is a haunted Edward Hopper
quality to some of the more purely imagist poems like "Little Final Sunlight":

station in Dover
Delaware, mint
green house,
facing it, the white

shade bending in
the little final sunlight
left. Light within
above clock,

people, even a head
or two. Or here
and there, out of time.

But even these few simple lines trail off with a flippant gesture and a flaccid pun.

As I noted with Alfred Corn's poems, the influence of such archimagists as Marianne Moore and Elizabeth Bishop seems to be strongly welcome in current poetry. Elizabeth Spires's title poem in *Annonciade* contains these lines:

An arm throws open a shutter, flooding
the doubting mind with the brilliant
light of the Midi that changes white
shadowed sheets on the crumpled bed
into a still life of desire and absence.

The lines that follow do not waver in their lyricism, and throughout the book this strong pictorial sense brightens the pages. But Spires is not content to draw pictures, she must draw conclusions from them—homilies, metaphysical reflections, drifty musings—and these distractions sometimes lessen the power of her images.

In this same poem which tells of a stay at the Annonciade in Menton, France, the poet begins to muse upon the nature of the illnesses that bring patients (*"we,"* she calls them, "the ill and ill-disposed") to this monastery to recuperate. She comes to a comfortless conclusion:

How can such suffering be chance?
Surely the spirit chooses its affliction
and makes it manifest, watching itself
fall and retreat from the world to atone,
as holy hermits did, for some secret
failing only its own heart knows.

There is a bothersome fecklessness about the lines, which could be written only by a young poet in sound health, and the poem never recovers from them, for all its heavily sentimental ending. I do not think that Elizabeth Spires is unfeeling, only that some of her poems lecture fruitily about themselves instead of closing. Even a fine and lovely poem like "Sunday Afternoon at Fulham Palace" is not unmarred. After showing us the park and empty palace, the fountain and peacock, the band concert and spectators, the poet slides into a reverie about destruction, and imagines, as the band plays "Mood Indigo," a bomber flying overhead, "the gray metal belly opening and the bomb dropping, / a flash, a light 'like a thousand suns,' / and then the long winter." Then she is recalled to herself by the presence of her lover; the band plays a selection by Purcell; and the couple begins to return home.

> All is as it was as we make our way back along the Thames
> to Putney Bridge, the old souls still sleeping unaware,
> hands lightly touching, as the river bends in a gentle arc
> around them. Mood indigo. The white peacock.
> The walled garden and the low door.

This makes a marvelous closure, a calm and sweet walking-away from the subject, a warm inevitable distancing. But the poem doesn't end here, alas: "As if, if it did happen, we could bow our heads / and ask, once more, to enter that innocent first world." The unmusical stutter of that line opening ought to have signaled Spires that the poem was over.

Yet this poem survives its faults—and so do others. The last two lines of "The Little Boys" don't belong there, but it's a memorable poem nonetheless; the last thirteen lines of "Mutoscope" are excess baggage, but the poem remains both wry and wistful, a mixture of tones hard to bring off. Several poems do achieve harmonious natural closures; "The Woman on the Dump" is a striking allegory that allows no room for commentary, and even with its apostrophic *O*'s "Glass-Bottom Boat" holds up in its final phrases. "Patchy Fog" consists of two stanzas, and its last lines bring the poem round in a satisfying circle. But the vivid first stanza is more beautifully quotable, and shows Elizabeth Spires at her very best.

This morning the lilies on Ames Pond,
pink and yellow cow lilies, spoked lilystars,
lie open waiting for the sun, and trees,
or the ghosts of trees, a mild smoky gray-green,
hover and point toward the unseen, heaven
of unbelief, as fog boils and rolls
off the road in patches that come and go,
like the call and its echo of the Great Blue Heron
that lives alone in the pond's long shadow.

The cleanness of Spires's best presentations is matched, or nearly matched, by some of Emily Grosholz's poems in *Shores and Headlands*. Her landscape sonnets especially are lit with a ringing clarity that is both precise and playfully impressionistic, employing a technique that brightly delivers subject matter while also transcending it. "Siesta," in fact, remarks upon the similarities and differences between the visual and the visionary.

All afternoon the heat intensifies
in leaps, like goats climbing the terraced hills;
another fig bursts on the tree; the olives
surrender another cache of livid shadow.
Cicadas transpose their note to a higher key.
As if the ear were the most material sense,
they sing us back to flesh and bone, the steep
rocky quarter acre where we happen to live.

But the eye is aethereal, that watches over
the tranquil cool Aegean, mantle of blue
woven east and west with the stitch of wind.
We see beyond our country into another,
familiar, never attained, where scattered islands
gather like the dream's immortal children.

"Siesta" is perhaps not perfect. The final clause is highfalutin Symbolist gossamer more reminiscent of Herédia than of Valéry. Still, the poem makes an admirable whole shape, its sharply limned details gracefully harmonized within the whole design.

Grosholz is a thoughtful poet, sometimes a metaphysician, and her philosophy can lead her into trouble when she tries to say too many things at once. "Two Variations on a Theme" offers the following difficult formulation, hobbled with a lifeless and puzzling personification:

> I am, I see, but only insofar
> as I have been deceived.
> Ambiguous delight withdraws behind
> the window-screen, inflamed with visible night.

Too much lamplit cogitation will sometimes invest subjects with more importance than they can bear. It is possible that the failure of the poet's brother to receive a grant for his scientific project ("The End of Summer") is not so tragic as it may have seemed, and the humor that Grosholz shows in "The World as Will, Idea, *Grappa,* and Pigeons" and in "Nietzsche in the Box of Straws" would be welcome in other poems as well. "Nietzsche" is especially charming; the veil is lifted from autobiographical material and the personal note is modestly attractive. There is a maturity in the gentle self-irony of "Nietzsche" missing from more portentous performances like "Perpetual Acquaintance." Here are a few lines of amiable apostrophic parody from the former poem:

> Oh, thou dry-footed, ghostly
> children of the earth,
> regret your frail, ill-fitted
> and so inflexible spines,
> learn from me the way
> to be ponderous and fluid,
> like the visionary prose
> of Nietzsche, slipping under
> the surface of the will's
> abyss, its spiraled blue.

Grosholz and Spires are similar in their strengths—fine observation, warm deft renderings of image and small incident, beautiful capacities for enjoyment—and also in a weakness which seems to stem from lack of confidence in controlled presentation, resulting in a sometimes fussy meddling. It's almost as if both poets were not quite sure what to do with their hands while writing a poem.

In the reflective lyric, restraint is power. John Burt has discovered a restraint that allows him to write *sententiae* and invent proverbs without seeming overweening. Of course, the persona poem takes much of the curse off the too-nifty formulation because we attribute the encapsulated wisdom to the speaker rather than to the poet. Burt's *The Way Down* contains a large number of persona poems, including "From the Diary of Willard Gibbs," where we find this couplet:

> We love Theory as poets love pale women,
> For its perfection and its lack of pity.

Gibbs was not the sort of person to think of mathematics in terms of La Belle Dame Sans Merci, but John Burt's metaphor here is so exact, so just, that it gives us a lightning insight into the philosopher-scientist's attitude toward his discipline. Later in the poem there is a description of Gibbs's investigations into the Second Law of Thermodynamics that comes perhaps a little too close to magazine popularizing ("I learned that every order runs to rot, / That every motion must in time be spent"), but the wry humanity of the speaker shines in his conclusion: "I have, at least, survived my theories."

Burt's most ambitious efforts are "Leonce Pontellier," which deals with the characters from Kate Chopin's novel *The Awakening*, and "Plains of Peace," a five-part poem with as many speakers, about Woodrow Wilson, his illness, and the First World War. I admire the genuine achievements of both these poems, and, though their complexities are forbidden to a reviewer with limited space, I shall remark that "Leonce Pontellier" requires the preparation of a fresh reading of Chopin and is worth it. "Plains of Peace" needs as background only Burt's helpful endnote. In this passage, the president's wife waits for her husband to sing a Schubert song:

> This light is from Vermeer, come back to us
> To hurt us with its beauty and reproach;
> When last we sang these songs we were at peace.
> Will we sing again, or will the light

Break and flare at stand-to till night falls?
We will be ghosts, who give ourselves to ghosts . . .

Through all these poems there is nothing unnecessary, nothing self-touting, nothing overdone. Burt grasps the central dramas of his situations, sets them in place as firm scaffolding, then builds his poems upon and within them. "King Mark's Dream" dramatizes the unhappy royal passion for Iseult, who is seen in the poem as a "child he found weeping at his door"; but she is a child whose power "loosened all the knots that held his breath."

In "Rich Blind Minotaur Led by a Girl," the girl loves the monster. Burt draws her as someone born wise; she possesses an innocent wisdom ordinary mortals can never attain:

> Her innocence was never ignorance.
> Love takes us as we are, and at our worst
> Loves us the better as our worst is ours.

Burt has many other strengths besides wise utterance. He can make pictures as well as any other poet writing, and he is, as I say, well aware of the advantages that restraint brings to imagery. In "The Funeral Day" the octave of the sonnet exhibits the preternatural silence of a house in which a father or grandfather lies dead. Birdsong annoys the speaker and he rises to close the window—and sees the Connecticut farmland outside with its gauzy white canvases:

> And there I saw the tobacco-fields
> Moving their shrouds in the dusk.
> The wind came thoughtlessly over the wide cloth
> And lifted the white undersides of leaves.
> I didn't close the window. When I sat back down,
> I didn't say what I had seen.

David Huddle shows even more restraint than John Burt. In both his poetry and his fiction Huddle has faithfully eschewed ornament. Similes and metaphors are rare in his lines, replaced by intense concentration on

the subject and powerful objective presentations of situation. These latter characteristics made his earlier *Paper Boy* pungently memorable, and
now in *Stopping by Home* he has added the usage of traditional forms—
sonnets, syllabics, rhymed quatrains, shaped poems—in order to produce ironic tension and striking formulation. The sestet of "Bac Ha," one
of the best of a series of Vietnam War sonnets, shows Huddle's fine
scorn for adornment:

> Division's garbage dump was three acres
> fenced off from that hamlet's former front yard.
> Black-toothed women, children, former farmers
> squatted in the shade all day, smiled at the guards,
> watched what the trucks dumped out. Walking nights
> out there, you'd be under somebody's rifle sights.

Huddle's spare reportage makes Corn's sensationalized violence look
silly and displays once again the power of understatement. We all learned
about understatement from Hemingway's sweet melancholy, I suppose,
but Huddle's is of a grittier sort. One of his best poems, in fact, is about
the way wars have changed and how the manner of perceiving them has
altered. "Cousin" is dedicated to John H. Kent, Jr., 1919–1982:

> I grew up staring at the picture of him:
> oak leaves on his shoulders, crossed rifles
> on his lapels, and down his chest so many medals
> the camera lost them. He wore gold-rimmed
> glasses, smiled, joked about fear. He told true
> stories that were like movies on our front porch:
> he'd fought a German hand to hand. The word
> *courage* meant Uncle Jack in World War Two.
>
> Ten years from my war, thirty from his, we
> hit a summer visit together; again
> the stories came. He remembered names of his men,
> little French towns, a line of trees. I could see
> his better than mine. He'd known Hemingway!
> I tried hard but couldn't find a thing to say.

Stopping by Home is in large part a farewell to the world of our fathers. After the sequence of tough-minded Vietnam poems comes an equally unglamorous series of childhood poems and after that a longish sequence in various forms about the harrowing death of the poet's father. There is nothing flimsy or arbitrary in the design of the book: each group comments upon and shores up the others, and Huddle never backs off the hard facts of the case, never shirks the weight of his guilt, never fails to confront the depths of his sorrow. His poems are lit with hard noon light; his language is as plain and sturdy and grainy as fresh carpentry. Above all, though, his strength is in intense concentration, in his fixed unwavering gaze that gives him the right to speak of the subjects he chooses in the way that he finds necessary. It is his refusal to prettify, to evade responsibility, to compromise, that lends to the five final words of his book such a feeling of wholesome blessed release:

> He was.
> I say my father was
> here. I say he lived thousands of strong days.
> I know he got sick. My
> father
>
> died. I
> can say that, can walk
> from home to work, can touch my daughter's hair,
> can say anything
> I want.

Attempts upon Delight:
Six Poetry Books

Poetry instructs by delighting. So says our ancient wisdom, and I'm not yet fool enough to attempt contradiction. But there are whole galaxies of ambiguity in those terms, and the sources of delight in poetry are a continual puzzle to me. How is it that some subjects and some emotions that would seem to be the unlikeliest springs of delectation still delight us, while others that ought to be pure delights in themselves bore us or vex us?

It's all in the treatment, n'est-ce pas? In the language, the poetry . . . which is to say delight must proceed from the poet himself, from his art alone when the quality of his mind fails to charm, from the conjoining of his art and character in the best of cases. Collections of personal lyrics—and all the books considered in this review fall into that category—project the lineaments of personalities that may or may not be congruent with those of the actual authors but which must be attractive in some way. There are persons in society with whom we put up and others for whom we pull up a chair by the fire; there are volumes of poetry that we pore through dutifully and others to which we return with a sociable pint of beer and a chunk of Stilton.

Nature is agreed upon as being a respectable source of poetic delight; the nicer parts of Nature are more arable for poetry, but there is also a frisson or two in the corpse of a deer or a groundhog. Even a poet like Jim Simmerman, whose title—*Once Out of Nature*—assures us that he is no

Robert Frost, makes a sardonic obeisance toward the convention. In "Zombies" he admits that he doesn't "even know the name of this plant so common / it must be second nature / to any nature poet / worth his pollen." I take real delight in Simmerman's puns here and in the humor of his sentence; these are so—well, so good-natured.

But I take a sharper delight in his title poem. Here is the second stanza:

> I go up and down the side of the mountain
> With my feet futzing forward like whiz kids on dope.
> I trample through weeds that don't know they're not flowers
> In the foyer of heaven, where nobody smokes.

Objections may be brought: the metaphor in the second line gives no clear image of what the feet are actually doing; the trope in the third line is an utterly silly personification. But here the tone is the main thing; "Once Out of Nature" has zip, tang, and rumble, and the more closely the words approach nonsense, the closer the poem comes to presenting its central emotion, and the dominant emotion of Simmerman's collection, a feeling I will describe as a cheerful disgust. At his dandiest, he sounds like Bertolt Brecht done over by Edward Lear.

Disgust animates some of Simmerman's best and debilitates some of his worst. "Open Season" is funny when it declares war on anything "cute or even / furry"; "let's beat it with a rake," the poet says. But one of the things we might want to beat with a rake is this couplet from "A Rainbow": "Like a poem that didn't know where it was going / we talked fast and drove." These lines are perhaps not very hirsute, but they are undeniably cute.

Every side of a poet has its obverse. The poet who flashes a streak of cruelty to innervate his work or relies upon a tone of disgust will probably turn sentimental when given opportunity. Simmerman mars "Child's Grave, Hale County, Alabama," with a tearjerking fantasy about a father digging his child's grave. And after a telling line in "December" ("The year has turned its pockets out"), we drop rapidly into bathos: "God could finally get some sleep."

One couldn't suppose that disgust always produces the finer poetry. Raymond Carver's volume, *A New Path to the Waterfall*, offers clear proof, in "Wine," that such a position is untenable. This poem retells the story of Alexander the Great's drunken murder of his friend, Cletus. The poet's emphasis is on Alexander's alcoholism; tearful parentheses underscore Carver's identification with Alexander. When the warrior makes his maudlin vow of abstinence, Carver interjects, "I've heard such promises and the lamentations that go with them." I cannot doubt the genuineness of his self-loathing, here and elsewhere in these pages, but the emotion does not make the poetry memorable.

It is difficult to talk about *Waterfall*. I had planned to try to read the book as if it were by someone I'd never heard of; I wanted to leave the poet's biography and, above all, the Carver mythology—his sprees and grand flights and self-tootings—out of it. But that plan proves impossible because Carver evinces such touching pride in his own legend, and because an introductory memoir by Tess Gallagher pushes it upon us. "It could be," she says of this book, "that Ray . . . has done as much to challenge the idea of what poetry can be as he did to reinvigorate the short story."

My personal impression has been that Carver dessicated the short story and that his effort to trivialize the form has been as irrelevant as it was unsuccessful. I do not see him as the "American Chekhov," and I wish the name Chekhov had remained forever hidden from both Carver and Gallagher. There are lots of excerpts from the Russian here, "shaped . . . into lines" by Gallagher, and she actually begins a paragraph by saying, "Once we'd discovered the poet in Chekhov . . ."

Anyone who has read Chekhov with the least sympathy knows how distasteful this notion would be to him; his favorite hatred was of such artsy-fartsy pretentiousness, and one of his aims in writing was to get as far as possible from the "poetic." It is intriguing to think what Chekhov would make of all the breast-beating in *Waterfall*, and with what a bemused level gaze he would look upon the ending of "The Kitchen." In this autobiographical poem the speaker goes fishing, masturbates, loses his fishing gear, and returns home in a panic only to embarrass his father by finding him in the kitchen in a compromising situation with a strange woman:

> We all waited and wondered
> at the stuttered syllables, the words made to cling
> as anguish that poured from my raw young mouth.

Such gross sentimentality can be found almost anywhere here. "The Offending Eel," a poem about Carver's relationship with an ex-wife, even lapses into Victorian diction:

> But though many things
> had happened in his life, and none more or less
> strange than this last-ditch offer of great profit
> on her airplane, he'd known for a long time
> they would die in separate lives and far from each other,
> despite oaths exchanged when they were young.

Except for "Another Mystery" (despite its clumsy versification) and a beautiful tough-tender lyric called "No Need," the poems here are pretty bad. In fact, it is difficult to think of these productions as poems; they stand in relation to poetry rather as iron ore does to Giacometti sculpture.

Yet there is an important way in which all my carping is unimportant. *A New Path to the Waterfall* is a powerful, though depressing, document. If we read it as a novel in journal form—as the introduction and the interpolated material invite us to do—we find it sad and resigned, yearning toward, and almost achieving, serenity. It is darkly ironic too, in a manner more like Leskov than Chekhov, this drama of two middle-aged writers facing death, steadfast in the conviction that literary immortality awaits one or the other if not both. And the story will only darken a shade sadder if this touching belief turns out to be true.

The only trouble with Raymond Carver's poems is that he was not a poet—or that he had not time to master the art the vocation requires. His materials are genuine and his reactions full-hearted. Even the most dropsical of his pages are superior to anything in *Groom Falconer*, whose brag sheet lists thirteen other collections by Norman Dubie.

There is not much to say of *Groom Falconer* except that it is mellifluous and boring. Most of the poetry is narrative, little fantasies hard to train attention upon because the device of deliberate non sequitur is used so often that it becomes utterly predictable. Here are the final stanzas of "Northwind Escarpment":

> While we slept the tide crept in
> And the blistered troughs that are rowboats
> Banged against one another . . .
>
> By sunrise we had all died in the war. What's more
> We always knew it was possible.

Nothing wrong with these lines except that they don't engage with anything. Irresponsibly experimenting, I find that they work perfectly well as a closure for "Poem," "The Wine Bowl," "An American Scene," and "Amen." Well, not perfectly—but satisfactorily. At a public reading, no one would know the difference. My point is that Dubie's surreal manner has become knee-jerk mannerism. In "Accident," for example, we have what could be a straightforward narrative about a farmer who witnessed (or was involved in) a railway accident caused by his daughter in her stalled truck. As he lay looking in confusion, "Two men in overalls with a lantern / Stepped into the field." The poet then avers, "They were from Mars." It takes a while to figure out that they were not really from Mars; they just looked strange to the farmer in his excited state of mind. It is not probable that this farmer has spent a lot of time thinking about visiting Martians, but perhaps if he ever did think about that subject, then maybe these railroad employees would remind him of what such creatures might look like.

Maybe. But the necessity to conjecture in this way is extremely tiring.

Dubie's whimsical approach to every subject, even serious ones—as in "Trakl" and "The Desert Deportation of 1915"—destroys any credence I might feel disposed to lend him. It is pleasant to read a line like "The ruptured underbelly of a black horse flew overhead," but after a dozen or so of these they all sound alike. This is no more than crooning, the sort of semiconscious murmur one makes with his mind while engaged in the composition of actual poetry. Dubie has confused the mumble with the poem. In "New Age at Airport Mesa" we meet a woman named Ruth who has been making cucumber sandwiches for the dead:

> She had a vision that third week
> Of a naked Navajo giantess eating a peach.
> It was so real that the juice of the peach
> Ran down her chin and breasts striking the dust

Like a rain of nails. Ruth was delighted with her vision
Until she realized it was meaningless.

This final line describes too closely the way I feel about *Groom Falconer.*
But if the meaningless has its drawbacks as well as its blandishments,
the quest for the meaningful is fraught with its own peculiar difficulties,
even its dangers. Wyatt Prunty has taken this kind of danger as one of the
major themes of *Balance as Belief.* Yet his recognition of the danger has
not saved him from it.

Prunty has declared his intention to try to restore emotional density
and intellectual complexity to contemporary verse. This would be a laud-
able ambition if it were not an ambition, but instead an ingrained and inevitable mode of apprehension. A schedule to be complex guarantees
obscurity, even bafflement. A few lines from "Rio" will serve as an example of willful complication:

> Some stories have no end but tell us out
> Into an opening where, turning, we
> Begin repeatedly, listening
> As our telling takes away and gives
> Us all we ever had, missed, believed.
> Having and not having is how we go,
> Like hope beyond reason . . .

The paired opposites are fun to point out ("out/Into"; "Begin repeatedly"; "takes away and gives"; "had, missed"; "Having and not having"), and I am willing to take on faith that if I teased out all the
implications of these pairs I would wind up with a poetic paradox of ingenious clarity. But the lines don't invite me to exercise my attention in
this way, as lines by Donne and Herbert and Crashaw usually do. There
is no overarching image to control the abstractions—no compass, no
pulley, no altar or angel wings—and the forced false relationship between the verb forms *to have* and *to go* (here meaning, *to be*) makes the
final comparison, "hope beyond reason," ineffective.

Prunty has a solid talent, I believe, and he loves and respects poetry.
He only wants to mother it to death, and the more a passage tries on
complexity the more tedious it is likely to be, the more fussbudgety. At

times he finds a way, usually with an image, to reconcile the lyric impulse with the intellectual apprehending, and we get a passage like this lovely opening to "The Name":

> With an easiness we almost learn . . .
> Like the isolated shadow of a palm
> Or variegated light by which a fern
> Casts the lattice of its green calm—
> Two workers lift in place a new fountain
> For the courtyard in the starched hotel
> Where, retired, my parents visited and remained.

This poem holds up beautifully all through, until the stanza beginning "Crisp habits raise / Their own squared world," where Prunty indulges his sweet tooth for abstract lecturing. Rarely is he content to let his narrative and his images speak for themselves; just when the poem has seemed to find a quietly dramatic close, here comes a tacked-on sermon. In "With Others" it begins, "Men lose their wills to something more than will"; in "The Covined Bird," the line "He said that we were given back to him" is the signal; in "The Wild Horses" the explanation starts "To him, the horses are beautiful and sad." When I make this kind of mistake in composing it is usually because I've failed to develop the drama or premise and situation fully and am trying to make up the lacuna with posturing, or because I've underestimated the intelligence of my audience and feel I need to point out what hot stuff my poem really is. Prunty, though, may have fallen victim to the Donald Hall Syndrome, the notion that from Big Thinks spring Mighty Poems. It's obvious he is convinced that Big Thinks make Majestic Closures.

In "The Actuarial Wife" a woman makes clear her feelings about her husband's cigarette smoking:

> She clarifies their options for retirement:
> "Darling, if one of us dies,
> I'm going to live in Paris."

Everything is there that a contemporary metaphysical poem needs—wit, incisiveness, irony, humor, cleanliness, brevity, paradox, characterization, conviction, and tenderness. When we contrast this sentence with what, in "The Lake House," is supposed to be the actual spoken prayer of a worried woman we see the fulsome temptation that leads Wyatt Prunty astray:

> "If only for a moment,
> Let my thinking take the place
> Of their two absences so that
> I see them here again, the water
> Buoying their energetic waves
> As, banking, they ski beyond this lake
> Into one bright, continuous curve
> Back home, where they dwell again in me."

If Prunty may seem too fussy at times, Dennis Schmitz, in *Eden,* goes to the other extreme. He is slapdash. But it is hard to fault him for this quality because it is hard to imagine that he could write in any other way. His recklessness gives the successful poems in this flashing little volume such nervous energy that they sometimes become almost breathless. When the poems fail, as they fairly often do, they plummet with a lugubrious thump. A case in point is "U.S. Considers War with Libya," in which the speaker drifts about in a rowboat on a pond and lapses into reverie. After pondering such things as the paramecium and Keats, he collides with this thought:

> For example: no matter how often the president looks
> into the mirror & sees Khadafy,
>
> he isn't Li Po drowning
> as he tries to embrace his own reflection.

Cruel lines, these. For eight years Mr. Reagan sat in the Oval Office, thinking, "I am Li Po drowning. . . ." And now to be so coldly disillusioned! It's enough to drive a man to bomb Libya.

Yet preceding this patch of utter silliness is a pungent, highly associative, and touching lyric called "Bird-Watching." I am unable to describe the way this poem works, the images and separate landscapes being so quickly and brilliantly conjoined, but its effect is powerful. It is a mordant insight into the immanence of history, and the controlling image, binoculars, is perfect, as is the placement, temporal and spatial, of the speaker. The poem is too long to quote here and no passage gives any real hint of the whole, but perhaps one image will suggest its particular flavor: "a dead heron peppered with grit, / marshgrass poking / out the bird's buggy eyeholes."

Schmitz's strong suit is dazzle: fleet rhythms, suppressed transitions, sudden associative leaps, unexpected repetitions, nimble variations upon themes that have been only implied. Heady and exciting stuff, I think, when I keep up. When I can't keep up, as in "The Grand Egress" and "Blue," I don't think—as I might do with other poets—that my intelligence has faltered. I think instead that Schmitz's lines have slipped out of control, and the fact that I think so is a measure of the trust I put in the poet. In his most dexterous sleight-of-hand moves his poems are so clear that his mistakes are obvious. That is a healthy sign and points toward happy promise.

Between the minutely scrupulous and the hell-for-leather lies a middle way, and in *Blues If You Want* William Matthews has found it. The title of the book and of many of the poems are song titles, jazz standards mostly, and the volume is a homage to jazz. I think, though, that it can be enjoyed also by readers who don't care for the music. Still, it helps to have shared some of the experiences of the poet:

> I love the smoky libidinal murmur
> of a jazz crowd, and the smoke coiling
> and lithely uncoiling like a choir
> of vaporous cats. I like to slouch back
> with that I'll-be-here-a-while tilt
> and sip a little Scotch and listen,
> keeping time and remembering the changes,
> and now and then light up a cigarette.

The laid-back feeling in "Smoke Gets in Your Eyes" is characteristic of the whole of *Blues;* a lazy smile permeates the volume. If this book were food I'd characterize it as comfort food because there is something warm and friendly and inclusive about the act of homage; a reader feels privileged to attend the celebration. I have been lectured sufficiently, thank you, about my habit of comparing effects from different art forms, and I'm halfway convinced that such analogies are only sloppy thinking. Even so, I'm going to describe the tone of *Blues* in two words: "Ben Webster."

But of course these pages are poetry and not music. The poetic tradition they derive from is honorably ancient, and it is interesting to see how comfortably the Horatian style adapts to the subject matter of jazz. Matthews remembers his first impressions of the music—"I knew the way music can fill a room, / even with loneliness, which is of course a kind / of company." He also includes two fine casual narrative poems, "Every Tub" and "Straight Life," told from the point of view of musicians. But he doesn't commit the Kerouac-Ginsberg mistake of filling up a page with masturbative jabber and pretending that it makes a sound like Lester Young.

In short, *Blues If You Want* is not an adolescent book, even though it undertakes a plan characteristic of adolescent poetry, that of praising an adored music. Matthew's confidence keeps him from puerile errors and his humor lightens the dark seriousness that underlies all works of homage. The temptation he faces is that of self-indulgence. "Fox Ridge State Park, Illinois, October" has a flaccid puzzling closure and not much visible substance; "Couple, 70, Hasn't Aged in 35 Years" is too simpleminded; "Homer's Seeing-Eye Dog" reads almost as a flippant pendant to Leon Rooke's novel *Shakespeare's Dog* ("Wine-dark pee" indeed!). But "Nabokov's Blues" (a bit too discursive here and there), "39,000 Feet," "The Scalpel," "It Don't Mean a Thing If It Ain't Got That Swing," and a good dozen others show William Matthews's beautiful capacities for appreciation and his warm and genial means of expression. Here is a poem to end with, "107th and Amsterdam," about an incident that doesn't even furnish out an anecdote, yet shows the stance and pitch of the poet, his easy sprezzatura. Urban but unspoiled, sophisticated but not exhibitionist, discriminating but democratic, and knowing and relaxed. In short—delightful.

A phalanx of cabs surges uptown in tune
to the staggered lights and two young black
men spurt across the dark avenue (two a.m.)

ahead of them: *We're here, motherfuckers,*
don't mess up. Three of five cabs honk: *We're here*
too, older and clawing for a living, don't

fuck up. The cabs rush uptown and the lights
go green ahead like a good explanation.
Everyone knows this ballet. Nobody falls or brakes.

Tonight I talked for hours and never said
one thing so close to the truculent heart of speech
as those horn blats, that dash across Amsterdam,

not to persuade nor to be understood but
a kind of signature, a scrawl on the air:
We're here, room for all of us if we be alert. (45)

Family Matters

*F*uture generations will surely look back upon the poets of our decades in puzzlement. "Those were the years when mankind first ventured off the planet," they will say. "The time when the chemical and genetic foundations of the human being were beginning to be known. Matter was revealing its smaller and finer energies, as well as its largest structures, more clearly with every week that passed. But the poets wrote about themselves, about their childhoods and amatory interests. And often about their families. They paddled in still lagoons while the great streams of political and cultural history plunged in distant cataracts."

We must hope that the future will be kinder to us than we fear it shall be, and more sympathetic to our means of expression than we have reason to think. For it is neither egoism nor modesty that impels the contemporary poet to write about self and family; instead, we are witnessing a desperate resort to synecdoche in the belief that the less inclusive terms of autobiography can imply a pattern of larger historical and societal terms. Writing about family is a way for the poet to approach history, politics, culture, psychology, economics, and so forth with intense and personally engaged language. The poet has a real stake in the past that gave rise to his or her sensibility, for out of that past is shaped an encounter with present time and a vision of time to come.

Poems about family, then, are often presented in dual time schemes: portrayal of the present is illuminated by comparison with the past; parent and child become halves of a single trope; and the necessary continuity between generations helps to register change in time, as well as stability of identity. A good example of the dual scheme is found in Donald Junkins's sturdy and comforting volume, *Playing for Keeps*. In the poem "Swan's Island, Late Summer" the speaker is observing his grown daughter at her tasks as a professional baker. He watches her "dumping," "patting," "knifing," and "plumping // it in eight pans for the oven." Her cheerful industriousness distracts him from his perusal of Theodore Roethke, and he begins to remember his mother "stacking the rising loaves on the radiator / under towels, my father holding a baked // loaf in his hand, smelling it warm, / kissing the topbrown crust." Only this last detail is unpredictable, but it is the one that counts; it is entirely realistic, this kissing of the fresh warm bread, and the sacramental implications of the act are unforced. While the poet idles, trying to decide whether to tell his daughter he loves her, she departs to deliver her goods—but not all of them: "On the table is a loaf for us."

Junkins's best poems succeed in the most obvious ways, and that is what makes them so attractive. The materials are ordinary, even commonplace; the tone is quiet (reading is probably the activity most often mentioned); the expression is casual. (Sometimes it is a little too casual; as in the trite transition to flashback in "Swan's Island, Late Summer": "My eyes blur.") There is a confidence in these poems that past and present are conformable, that the losses and sorrows the poet depicts are those natural and inevitable with the passing of time, that history has not been pulverized by the explosions of contemporary social disaster.

One of Junkins's titles is explicit about the dual time scheme. "Running with My Son in Germany, Remembering My Father" gathers memories, present impressions, and fears about the future into an elegant though loose-jointed rhapsody. The sight of a sunflower reminds the poet of a political campaign gimcrack, "my father's plaything in the bedroom, / his Republican Party, Alfred Landon sprouting // petals all dressed up in a burst of flower / yellow." And as they run in Bavaria, his son vouchsafes a confidence: "Last week he told me that once running // alone he thought about dying / and stopped." It is not pleasant for a parent to be reminded that his son too must die, but this poem is happy. The simple act of striding forward is a communion of the generations.

> We are taking
> turns. We are passing beehives,
> yellow boxes in a field of saplings. The rain
> softens our path running, running
> toward the sun.

Donald Junkins has a talent for celebrating the continuities of life. He is able to find in the lives of his children his own childhood and, looking from the vantage of that recaptured past, to find in the figure of his father the figure of himself in present time. In order to do so he has kept his images few and simple in all his poems and has trusted their communal values: the quiet house, the dreamer's book, the murmurous warm kitchen, the still lake, and the twilit court for pitching horseshoes. There are other kinds of poems too—neatly done travel poems and a long ambivalent reminiscence of Robert Lowell—but the dominant impression *Playing for Keeps* leaves is of an America wholesome and sane and at ease, unshaken in its center even by the manic present hour. It may be that Junkins has focused his view a little too softly, that there is a touch too much of Thomas Wolfe in his pages. Yet his sentimentality is not spurious; he believes that he sees what he has seen. His sfumato rendering is the effect of his distance in time from his subject.

A closer focus is likely to produce a more distinctive and less sentimental picture. *Days Going / Days Coming Back* collects Eleanor Ross Taylor's poems from three previous volumes and adds a sheaf of new ones. Her wry voice has not changed with time, nor has her skew vision dimmed. She has always had a knack for discovering the least obvious ironies in situations, the ones that other poets would probably overlook.

"Epitaph" recalls a bit of family history, as the poet remembers where an ancestor lies in a neglected graveyard. This grandmother (or perhaps great-aunt) lived in one of those houses in the country where indoors and outdoors were not always distinguishable: "Her house was screenless; doors stood wide; / Leaves drifted unwatched down the hall; / Hens left warm eggs indoors." The woman herself was always busy in the fields and would rush to her kitchen at mealtimes and fling together a repast. Sometimes she was unobservant in her haste, as when she picked up the coffee pot from where the baby had been playing with it on the floor, filled it with water through the spout, and put it on the stove to make coffee:

> —Kate, this brew's not fit to drink.
> —What? . . .
>   Oh Lord.
> —Don't cry, Kate
>   —But I can't help it.
> I never cried for shirtwaists
> Or China cups
> Or crocheted pillow shams. I've not.
> But oh to have it said of me
> She boiled the gosling in the coffee pot . . .
>   Poor gosling!

What odd humor! Kate foresees that no matter what she does, no matter whether she spends the rest of her life as saint or profligate, no matter what words are engraved upon her tombstone, she will be known till eternity as the woman who boiled the gosling in the coffee pot. Along with this funny-sad realization, she can't help sympathizing with the bird, and in so doing composes her own epitaph: "Poor gosling!"

A pair of poems about her grandmother show Taylor's skill at producing her quick chiaroscuro effects. In one lilting lyric, "My Grandmother's Virginhood, 1870," the woman's future suitor accompanies her and her sister home from a social function:

> Walked us both home from the dance
> Wearing new black homespun pants.
> When we got up to the door
> Catched us both around the waist
> And—kissed us! Lor!
> What's he getting—kisses! from us for?
>   Little David McSwain!

This stanza and the one preceding are just about perfect in their balancing of lyric form and colloquial voice. The woman's enjoyment and confusion are unmistakable; it's easy to see that each of those exclamation points indicates a blush. There's nothing in the least strained about the diction, and the lines offer a danceable rhythm.

But in the companion poem, "Motherhood, 1880," the same rhythm is used convincingly to articulate sorrow, weariness, and apprehension. The mourning dove, with its "Oh-oh love" call, is a bitter sound to this woman after a decade of living with the husband who kissed both sisters:

> When Dave got up and struck a light
> We'd neither of us slept all night.
> We kept the fire and watched by May,
> Sick for fear she might
> Go off like little Tom . . . They say
> "Don't fret . . . another on the way. . . ."
> They know I favor this least child.
>
> No use to cry. But while
> I made a fire in the kitchen stove
> I heard a pesky mourning dove.
> Lor! What's he calling "O-love" for?

Impossible to imagine another context that would justify "pesky" to describe a mourning dove.

But for Taylor the family past can become mysterious too, losing the sharp angularity of detail that we find in such poems as "Family Bible" and "Buck Duke and Mama" and "Cousin Ida." In "The Ghost" her character portrayal is reminiscent of Faulkner's treatment of those strange, time-lost, self-sufficient old men whose relationship to the family has become almost ancillary. The poet remembers her "paterfamilias" as silent and distant, "ramrod straight" and with "tattered eyes." He bound the family to an era of history that no longer exists, and when it was blotted out the character of the family changed too. His was the time of forest and stream, hunting and fishing, and, as far as her contemporary family is concerned, a time that was nearly primeval. She records a vision of him going out with his "rubbed shotgun":

He moves on past the barn, the exiled sycamore,
and towards the running river.

A hound ears-up and
passions after.

They disappear.

The slow, dreamlike, almost cinematic fadeout here is carefully under-
scored by the sudden attentive movement of the dog—who enjoys the
two most striking verbs I have found in poetry in many a moon.

Unless the material contains some shocking element—physical abuse,
say, or sexual—it is difficult to get urgency into lines about past family
relationships. But one quality is constant in almost all of them and can
lend drama to reminiscences that otherwise may seem almost banal: guilt.
In *Forgiveness*, Dennis Sampson investigates relationships in the light of
this emotion, which is a queasy one to color properly in poetry; a poem
imbued with guilt can become, with the slightest awkward phrase, embarrassing or precious or self-pitying or frustrating or instantly tiresome.
Sampson's "Father," for instance, deftly avoids these direct pitfalls. He recalls a harmless prank he played as a child that caused his father to
swear—the only time the son ever heard him do so. The prank was
nothing dangerous in the least, but the incident remains troublesome in
the speaker's memory, and he wants to discover a way to come to terms
with it:

If time exists at all it exists in the mind
of an angel so degraded she could bathe for days
without being clean, without being cauterized. I'd like to find
my father again and say that simple name
that signifies obedience to someone wiser.
"Father," I would say, not to apologize,
"do you remember the time . . ." and he would nod,
remembering every trick I pulled as a child.

Sampson's observation about the nature of guilt—that it can adhere to incidents where it had no clear cause—is just, and his image of the degraded angel is darkly memorable. Because the poem is able to retain a

quiet force, I am willing to overlook the exaggeration of "cauterized" and the fact that the poet could not make visually clear his prank.

Many of Sampson's poems tell a three-part story of anger, guilt, and forgiveness. In the sonnetlike sequence called "The Door That Only Opens on Its Own," the story engages different family members in turn—uncle, sister, and mother. But it is the figure of the father that most often supports this narrative structure. In "Getting Fired" the father angrily berated his son for being dismissed from a construction job because of his youthful ignorance. Now the son is himself experiencing "the pain we name fatherhood" and has learned to forgive his father's impatience. The final poem in *Forgiveness* tells the same story about another incident and in different terms. In "Addendum" the son and father have visited the dying grandfather and then, driving home, the father speeded across the bridge "above the Bad River" and collided with a yield sign. Because their emotions are strained, father and son have a furious falling out. The speaker of the poem—the son—then tries to comprehend the changes in relationship that have taken place since the accident occurred:

It was hard to forgive ourselves for this.
In memory, I move in a dream
bordered by sunflowers and roses,
the beautiful sway and flow,
my father on one side and my mother on the other.
What did we know
racing down a path that is lost to us now?
And then a calm comes over us, wind cooling our faces.

Look how easily we have forgiven them all.

Dennis Sampson's poems make strong claims with their courageous choices of subject matter and their willingness to talk candidly about uneasy feelings. Sampson is hardly a faultless technician—his visuals are sometimes murky and his rhythms clumsy—and although I don't believe his poems will become better if they lose their rough edges, they might become clearer in intention.

One of the most touching acts of filial piety is the effort to imagine the lives one's parents led before the poet was born, or when he or she was too young to understand many situations. Robert Wrigley's *Moon in a Mason Jar* is a beautiful book, its articulation gentle but firm and clear. His three-part "Aubade for Mothers," complex and quite moving, is spoken in the persona of a young mother. In the second part of the poem, she sits up late alone after the daylong "elation" of a family reunion and listens to the sounds of the sleepers in the house. When she hears her mother-in-law she reflects that the sound is strange, "a mother's breath / coming from one I knew as a child!" She is not comforted by the gentle noises of the family about her, feels more exposed than ever before, and her voice is apprehensive as she looks toward the future:

> Her sleep sound is a soft wet rasp,
> her daughter's just the same. Her son
> rumbles like me: it will always be spring
> in his life, short storms, wild greenings.
> I listen to her breathing, my friend's,
> and I am lulled. I should be
> asleep too. But I can't sleep now.
> I am a mother myself, there is tomorrow,
> and now the night comes down with its rag.

When Wrigley puts himself in the place of another, he often finds the circumstances perilous. The situations of women seem especially dangerous, and in "The Leaning House" he imagines his grandmother living in a home sharply tilted and wracked with wintry weather. Visitors are troubled by the steep yaw of the place, but the grandmother is accustomed to it and looks after the needs of her family with cheerful, accustomed gracefulness:

> For the woman who lives here
> the world is an uneven place, her home
> as flat as a frozen lake. She walks
> these halls and creaking rooms
> with a balance blossomed in habit, leaning
> between us one hot dish after another,

eyeing all our plates and smiling.
We eat, and keep holding on.

The canted house is a simple trope for old age, but it lends strong tension to every line. Wrigley is very good at shading his poems with apprehension, with intimations of mortality, and when he brings this emotion to the forefront, as he does here, the effect is powerful. "The Leaning House" reminds me a bit of expressionist paintings by Munch or Schmidt-Rotluff; the activity the poem depicts is an ordinary one, but the strained geometry of its setting gives it an unsettling urgency. Everyone in the poem is fearful except the one most in danger.

"Star Dust" is Wrigley's most interesting attempt to find a context that will include the earlier lives of his parents in present time. The poet sits up late listening to recordings of the music his parents listened to, "Dorsey and Sinatra on the phonograph." The old songs cause him to fall into a melancholy reverie, and he imagines the courtship of his parents, "huddled on the old Ford's hood, wrapped / in a woolen blanket," watching the lake at night and listening to the car radio. Then, in a turn reminiscent of Yeats's thought about mothers and their aged offspring in "Among School Children," Wrigley contrasts his present predicament— his forlorn attempt to recapture a past he never could have known—with the feelings his parents must have experienced during their first days together:

> Tonight is what they could not know, when
> he would ache with his nothing, grow still
> below the weight of what is empty, all that any song will
> do. Like the star beaming outward past its death,
> the buses and the rain he loses track of,
> the music comes and goes, and he remembers again.

The mood is subdued, the tone resigned, and Wrigley's recognition that his own poetry can do no more than "grow still / below the weight of what is empty" is genuinely sad, not merely glum. His respect for the rites his parents believed in saves the poem from self-pity, a fault that always endangers this kind of attempt.

In "Yard Work," a poem about his father's burying a dog that was killed during the speaker's childhood, Wrigley finally does not escape sentimentality, and there are lines of other poems in which he comes close to it. But he is an extremely good poet, genuine in feeling and straightforward in presentation. His simplicity is never simple-minded, and—best of all—he is not clever. In fact, we sometimes see that he works a mite too hard *not* to be clever and so misses some opportunities for humor. Yet a poet is not obliged to display every desirable quality in every book he produces; in *Moon in a Mason Jar,* where the major theme is awareness of mortality, humor may be suppressed with profit.

But when a lighter tone can be managed it is an asset, and a comparison of Wrigley's "Heart Attack" with "Basketball" from Ronald Wallace's *The Makings of Happiness* is instructive. In Wrigley's poem a father is playing the game of throwing his "small, blond son" into the air and catching him. But during the game the father is struck down by a heart attack:

> He is on his knees, as his son stands,
> supporting him, the look on the child's face
> something the man has seen before:
> not fear, not joy, not even misunderstanding,
> but the quick knowledge sons
>
> must come to, at some age
> when everything else is put aside—
> the knowledge of death, the stench
> of mortality—that fraction of an instant
> even a child can know, when
> his father does not mean to leave, but goes.

The telescoping of time in the poem—the father helpless all in an instant and the child hurled toward maturity—is so expertly done that it is nearly unnoticeable. Yet it is another usage of the dual time scheme, father and son beginning to exchange roles. But only for a moment: the father dies, feeling that he is deserting his son, and the son, though barely on the verge of understanding what is happening, already begins to forgive. Here is a delicate but powerful emotional nexus, closely imagined.

Wrigley has been studying the family with a recipience the intensity of which is almost Rilkean. Ronald Wallace's book shows him to be less intense than Wrigley, but equally graceful. His method is not as deliberate, but his use of collapsed time in "Basketball" is as effective as Wrigley's in "Heart Attack." The speaker of the poem is playing basketball with his daughter in their backyard; the child is only six years old, "and the backboard sky / might just as well be / 93 million miles away."

> *Hurry up,* I shout.
> *We don't have all day.*
> And we don't.
> The next time I look
> she's sixteen, the years
> arcing up and falling
> with a curt swish,
> her laughter spinning off
> her fingertips, as
> the future, all elbows and hips,
> sets its practiced pick.

Here there are perhaps too many metaphors about planetary orbits and basketball moves too tightly jammed together, but the lines still make an impact. The cliché has worn so thin that it is transparent *("We don't have all day")*, but Wallace has found an unexpected strength in it. Fathers and mothers, comprehending so clearly the lightning passage of time with their children, are likely to feel the hyperbole as literal truth: "The next time I look / she's sixteen. . . ."

The mild clutter in the quoted lines is unusual, for one of Wallace's strongest and most constant qualities is lucidity. Sometimes this poet is even a little too lucid; a poem like "Speeding," which telescopes time in exactly the same way that "Basketball" does, is just a tad too easy. It makes its point, produces its impression, then fades away.

But when Wallace is on the mark, he writes with a relaxed clarity that persuades more by charm than by declaration. "Off the Record" entertains the same ambition as Robert Wrigley's "Star Dust," to capture in imagination some part of his father's life before the poet could be aware of it. Wallace finds in the attic one of his father's old college textbooks with a note in the margin: *"Hooray / for Thanksgiving vacation!"* The poet feels a sympathetic surge of exuberance and ponders the fact that even before he was born he was part of his father, "a secret code uncompleted, a piece / of DNA, some ancient star-stuff." Then he finds a photograph of his father holding him at age three on his shoulders, and the poet begins to speculate about the nature of time and memory:

> Maybe imagination is just
> a form of memory after all, locked
> deep in the double helix of eternity.
> Or maybe the past is but one more
> phantasmagoric invention we use
> to fool ourselves into someone else's shoes.

These are interesting notions, to say the least. The idea that our parents are but parts of ourselves that we are trying to remember, or that time is only a fantasy device of the mind—are these liberating or constricting speculations? Wallace sees himself as a sort of palimpsest, so that beneath the graffiti of his personal daily concerns are the lineaments of his father's personality, and these are what he desires to recover in their essential purity:

> It is not my voice I want to hear
> on memory's fading page, on imagination's disk.
> It is my father's in the background
> prompting me, doing his best
> to stay off the record, his hushed
> instructions vanishing in static.

Hamlet had the same ambition, of course, but was overwhelmed by his troubled circumstances. Wallace is well acquainted with the tragic aspects of life ("It is as if every death / is the first death," he tells us in "Apple Cider"), but he has determined to fashion this present volume into a happy one. He takes its title from a remark by an artist-farmer named

Nick Engelbert: "If a man can't be happy on a little farm in Wisconsin, he hasn't the makings of happiness in his soul." In order to give *The Makings of Happiness* its pleasant, and pleasurable, outlook, Wallace has made a decision to accept freely and willingly almost every painful situation in his experience. In the hands of most contemporary poets, "Bible Stories"—with its account of the crippled father at mealtimes with "that heavy book" wheezing out "the morals of the Lord" to his "hopeless," rebellious son—would be a bitter poem. But Wallace sees his later return to his "chastened, healed, forgiven / father's house" as triumphant. "Apple Cider" speaks of the murder of a grandmother and shows us "My father / red with bedsores; our daughter / swollen bright beyond us." But Wallace insists on celebration, and in "The Fat of the Land" he presents a picture of a family reunion as a convocation of sweaty, happy, overweight people all gathered "in the heavy heat of Indiana." The picture might have been painted by Brueghel, Rubens, and Botero working in collaboration:

> We sit at card tables, examining
> our pudgy hands, piling in
> hot fudge and double chocolate
> brownies, strawberry shortcake and cream,
> as the lard-ball children
> sluice from room to room.
> O the loveliness of so much loved flesh,
> the litany of split seams and puffed sleeves,
> sack dresses and Sansabelt slacks,
> dimpled knees and knuckles, the jiggle
> of triple chins. O the gladness
> that only a family understands,
> our fat smiles dancing
> as we play our cards right.

The scene is so sleek with avoirdupois that even the apostrophic O's look fatter than usual on the page.

The family is a source of much agony in American poetry, as it is in American life, partly because most of us take our filial responsibilities very seriously indeed, fretting too much about the welfare of our parents and grandparents, and fretting too much about slights and hurts we have inevitably received and inflicted over the years. But Ronald Wallace understands that since our parents most particularly desired for us to be happy, then it is our duty to try to be so. If we look a little silly in the attempt, as in "The Fat of the Land," that is all to the good, for we shall begin to look grave soon enough:

> We're huge and whole on this simmering night,
> battened against the small skinny
> futures that must befall all of us,
> the thin gray days and noncaloric dark.

American poets are a tribe of dutiful children, it seems, bent on honoring their fathers and mothers and siblings and offspring. Their poems can show us, moreover, that duties are not necessarily painful and that genuine good poems can result from a sense of duty, as well as from love. Each of the poets I have spoken of here possesses a high excellence as individual as the family that produced the poet.

Every Poet in His Humor

A dreary thing happened to contemporary poetry on its way to the American forum. It tried to grow up, to dress in long pants and coat and tie, to comb its hair, and to sullen into dark irony. All too successful in these ambitions, it no longer skipped to the rhymes of Theodore Roethke, stopped attending the rent parties thrown by archy and mehitabel and their rowdy friends, and decided that the bumptious waggeries of e. e. cummings should be treated with Clearasil. Poetic humor didn't die out, of course; it didn't even degenerate entirely into the senatorial mode of discourse. But it became less open, less friendly, and less common, its purposes classified as secondary.

Most contemporary poets employ humor in their collections more or less as Dabney Stuart does in his searching new volume, *Narcissus Dreaming:* the lighter poems are disposed here and there for purposes of balance, shading, contrast, and counterpoint. For instance, Stuart positions a satire, "Franz Kafka Applies for a Literary Fellowship," immediately preceding a happy but intense poem called "Gospel Singer," which portrays a singer who is at one moment of performance "closer to God than ever / before." He is overmastered by the exaltation of this experience that is at once religious and artistic. "Everything / rides on his bringing / his mouth down to the mike, / almost into it. It is more / than intimate." Being so caught up, he is set apart from his audience, has become a different sort of creature, until the song ends, and

> he straightens,
> disfiguring himself back
> to normal, smiling
> sheepishly, as if
> there'd never been any good
> news to bear
> into the world,
> to hang there singing.

We read the poem with keen enjoyment, a little envious perhaps of Stuart's unmuted admiration, thinking, "I wish I'd been there to hear *that.*" Yet "Gospel Singer," juxtaposed as it is, comments upon the Kafka poem, and what before had seemed only an affectionately humorous portrait of that writer begins to sound a deeper tone. "If awarded this grant," Kafka writes in his Guggenheim application, "I will burn the money / to write by. The light / will cast the shadow of my pen on the wall / behind my head. I will call / the work, tentatively, *The Foundation.*" It doesn't require much political savvy to comprehend that those coteries of mutually massaging sycophants who dole out foundation grants lack the insight—and maybe the courage—to give one to a writer like Franz Kafka, a fact the Austrian is complacently aware of:

> My happiness does not depend
> on the success of this application.
> Therefore, it is incomplete.

The portraits are a pair. "Franz Kafka" delivers a clear sentiment: if the true artist will stick fast to his task, the gates of the foundations shall not prevail against him. "Gospel Singer" then offers a model that the artist can strive to emulate, a condition of selfless concentration that is sufficient reward in itself.

My point is soon made: humor in poetry is successful only if it is serious in purpose. The poet who desires merely to make smartass remarks, to show off his wit and the finish of his verse, is fated not only to maunder trivially but also to be known as a supremely unfunny writer. Humor without real point—without hard purpose, if you will—must be found boorish or boring or both, as in television sitcoms.

Narcissus Dreaming contains more poems of lighter cast than any of Stuart's previous volumes. "The Blurb Writer" and "Moving Pictures" begin as obvious satires but then transform, darkening to acquire ominous shadows; "The Man in the Black Bear" is an allegory that works partly because it doesn't present itself portentously; "The Cabbage in History" is a dramatic monologue about the nature of human history spoken by the vegetable. Stuart uses humor not only as a means of giving his collection grace and ease but also to lend it a debonair mordancy.

A study in contrasts is Reed Whittemore's *The Past, the Future, the Present,* a new and selected collection published by the University of Arkansas Press in a sturdy and attractive format. Unfortunately, the book is more attractive as a physical object than as poetry. Almost all the poems here are intended as humorous, but few of them are because an apparent laziness in Whittemore's thought and expression invites sloppy banality. "The Mother's Breast and the Father's House" announces itself as consisting in "two lectures," but the speaker is a dull lecturer:

> Lecture One
> Here we are on this planet
> > (folks)
> Life is too long
> It needs sleep to fill in
> And sex and money and birthdays
> And most of all faith.

Whittemore always makes too easy a job of it. His poem "Today," for example, is a diatribe against your Fred Chappell sort of critic—one addicted to brassy pontification—and its opening line, though flabby, is promising: "Today is one of those days when I wish I knew everything, like the critics." But after that the poem repeats itself and becomes self-pitying ("If I came from New York I could say anything") and at last merely querulous:

> I come from Minnesota.
> I must get a great big book with all the critics in it
> And eat it. One gets so stupid and hungry in Minnesota.

He must be a pampered poet who can find no direr charges to bring against critics than this poem voices.

Many of Whittemore's poems are about literature and the literary life, and some of them are debilitated by condescension, a quality that poisons humor. Contempt for their subjects can give some poems (Pope's *Dunciad* comes instantly to mind) a brilliant savagery of wit. But condescension is a smarmy attitude that produces here sophomoric exercises like "Hester Prynne," "Lady Ashley," and "Moll Flanders." "Tess" opens with these lines:

> Tess of Blackmore Vale was whatcha might call
> Bitched from the start. Hardy had his way,
> Digging early and late the pitfall
> Where she tumbled on her tumbling day.

Every now and then, however, a sudden and interesting flash of disgust animates a passage. In "What Was It Like?" the speaker replies to his own question, "And what was death like?" He tells us, "Death was all that crap in somebody's living room / On a Saturday night with plates in the laps."

Whittemore is a little too flippant to be hilarious. His ironies can be easy and obvious ("Philanthropist"), his technical skills uncertain ("The Boy from Iowa"), his subjects too banal ("The Desk") for the lines to acquire point. Sometimes, as in "The Fall of the House of Usher," the lines are as flat as Dick Tracy's feet:

> It was a big boxy wreck of a house
> Owned by a classmate of mine named Rod Usher,
> Who lived in the thing with his twin sister.
> He was a louse and she was a souse.

Another difficulty with humor is the necessity for variety and surprise. In fact, what is required is variety *of* surprise. James Tate has been writing surprising poems for many years, and *Distance from Loved Ones* is much the same as his preceding nine volumes. By now his patented wackiness is predictable in its larger shape if not in detail, so an accustomed reader of Tate knows that he will be looking at a great many lines like these that open "Editor":

> It was a foggy day anyway,
> and my cockatoo was scorched,
> and my bikini was moping in the ruins,
> so I started reading a journal some poky guy had written
> and dropped on my doorstep disguised
> in a baboon uniform.

Tate can write this stuff by the yard, and after one reads twenty or so yards, it all begins to sound the same, like the chaff of AM radio playing somewhere in the neighborhood. This poet is always inventive but his inventions are too often of the same kind, and one wonders after a while if his whimsy has not become almost reflexive. What is needed in this volume is more shifting of tone, more phrases such as this Ring Lardner–like sentence from "Pastoral": " 'Is that you in there, Ma,' little Hank detected." Or this metaphor from "Ebb," so surprising that it is actually revelatory and not just provincial surrealist mutter: "We are completely exposed, like a rabbi facing a stork." Or this perceptive description of "The Expert": "At times he seems lost / in his own personal references, / to be adrift in a lonely pleasure craft."

There are some nifty poems in *Distance from Loved Ones:* "I Am a Finn," and its companion "I Am Still a Finn," "Saturdays Are for Bathing Betsy," and maybe "We Go a-Quilting" with its fine closure—but there is nothing to match, for instance, the genial humor of "Good-Time Jesus" in Tate's earlier *Riven Doggeries.* Too many poems here sound like James Tate sounding like James Tate. If one could read these poems one at a time, a single poem a week, they would not so blearily cancel one another out.

The same kind of problem injures Albert Goldbarth's more ambitious collection, *Popular Culture.* Like Tate, Goldbarth fashioned a certain style quite early in his career, though he feels free to vary it more strongly than Tate usually does. The poems in this collection are alike in taking a large political or philosophic concern and tying it to autobiography by means of the iconography of popular culture. We meet figures like Donald

Duck, Spy Smasher, The Claw, and Little Orphan Annie, and we are asked to ponder their relationships to the Holocaust, the Second World War, the desire for God, racial conflict, and world history.

If Goldbarth's plan seems simply to yoke violently and arbitrarily a number of heterogenous subjects, we should aver that *Popular Culture* works better than it probably has any reason to. Goldbarth is an amusing stylist and a sharp observer. "Collecting: *an essay*" contains a wonderful portrait of the poet's father; it is too long to quote here, but it is touching. In "The World Trade Center" we find a long list of women whom society has shamed in a sexually obscure but nonetheless genuine way, and the catalogue is both funny and moving:

Miss-First-Wet-Kiss-With-Its-Glory-and-Shame, Miss
Lexicon of Woe, Miss Poetry-Firing-Over-the-Skin, Miss Confusion,
Miss Needlepoint Maxims, Miss Funeral Shovel, Miss Semenburst,
Miss Everything, Miss Spider-Of-Blood-In-Its-Bodywide-Web.
We hate you. We're telling you now: we're ashamed,
Miss Amalgamated Canning Concerns, Miss Taxidermy, Miss
Soybean Dealers.

It is hard to imagine any other poet giving this roll call of advertising models anything other than a sarcastic fleer, but Goldbarth has managed to freshen our sense of adolescent masturbatory confusion, to make us understand that there is a trepid humanity behind the toothpaste smiles and gleaming thighs.

Still, an undertaking like *Popular Culture* is a highly artificial, extremely self-conscious one, and Goldbarth has decided to underscore these qualities instead of submerging them. Perhaps he was mistaken in his decision, for it has led him into some long, self-indulgent passages that are more irritating than engaging. The following interpolation in the poem "Again" is disguised as a transition, but that ploy only reveals a lack of structural inventiveness: "And if I digress right now to the story // of Chunosuke Matsuyama who, in 1784, wrecked half-dead on a coral reef / with 43 others, scratched his story of woe and goodbye on wood and / slipped it with ritual into a bottle, then the bottle in the swift Pacific drift . . . / it doesn't mean I've forgotten that hospital bed, my father / dwindling in it, or the mission of this poem."

The exaggerated noun, "mission," appears because self-referential chattiness threatens to trivialize the themes of the poem, and Goldbarth feels a need to reassert his seriousness. But such a recognition only points up the shakiness of the concept. The poet is pleased to find authority for such cute self-consciousness in popular culture texts, quoting (for instance) an exchange between Rocky the Flying Squirrel and Bullwinkle the Moose: "What NOW, Bullwinkle?" "I dunno, Rock—*shrug*—I haven't read the script." The inclusion of the *shrug* within the quotation is almost too telling, because passages in other poems amount to no more than verbal shrugs. For example, "I know; and I'll / tell, if you'll only read part 2 of this. My poem" (from "Donald Duck in Danish"). Or "Repetition is what / this poem is about, repetition is what this poem is about" (from "Again"). Or "But—why think of it? (from "Quebehnseneuf") and from a later passage in the same poem: "—Why think of it now?"

Goldbarth seems to distrust not only the idea behind *Popular Culture,* but any notion of efficacy in communication. Speaking of Depression-era photographs, he says in "All About" that

> We've seen those photos and now it isn't enough. We've
> seen the hunger-chiseled faces of Okie farmers like those
> on Easter Island: long, stern, imperturbable. It won't do.
> In their dustbowl-dun emulsifier colors, it isn't enough.

Two stanzas later we find the poet observing himself talk to a friend "whose daughter tried to pill herself to death" and wondering, "what shitty little comfort can I give her over / lunch?" This perfunctory hand-wringing reaches its nadir in "The Gulf": "(If he told you his story / of longing for the nightshift Quick-Pick checkout girl! . . . But / really, you'd be bored.)"

The composition of *Popular Culture* rests on an extraordinary concept, this linking of the seemingly irrelevant with the tragic elements of our lives, and Albert Goldbarth possesses enough stylish talent to bring it off. But a lack of confidence has debilitated his performance; where tight-lipped humor is called for he too often resorts to cuteness and—now and again—to mere campiness. Like Bullwinkle posing as a magician, he has attempted to pull a rabbit from his hat and has produced a lion instead.

Then he has behaved like Bullwinkle, stuffing it back in and mumbling, "Oops. Maybe I'd better get a new hat."

My complaints about Goldbarth have probably been too severe. *Popular Culture* is usually entertaining, at least, and the idea behind it allows a colorful variety of subject matter and commentary. In *Why We Live with Animals,* Alvin Greenberg permits himself no such latitude. This volume consists of sixty sonnets, every last one of them concerned with the subject of keeping pets—mostly dogs. But Greenberg has made his book as interesting as *Popular Culture* throughout, and his humor is more genial and much less precious than Goldbarth's. The theme of Greenberg's volume is the necessity for human beings to be in close contact with "something / that isn't us: some other animal." The fourteenth sonnet includes a catalogue of the Greenberg dogs and a thought about the effect they have made upon the Greenberg family life:

> just think of them all!
> the ones that are with us still, sonny and lily,
> retrievers, yellow, and domino the old dalmatian,
> and rosie, wild rosie, the irish setter. and think
> of our whole history of dogs: lassie (lassie!), bernard
> the saint bernard, beebe brief and black, that great
> dane schnapps, dora, dear dora, shiloh and louis and sweet
> sad sam—how all the colors and dispositions they've shared
> with us won't let the world be merely what we think.

The book is as sentimental throughout as these lines I've just quoted. But it is unabashedly sentimental: Greenberg is not shy about his love for his pets, and the result is on the whole disarming. If he tried to dissemble his feelings or to fancy them up with complicated conceits, *Why We Live with Animals* would fail miserably. It is much more difficult in our weird times to speak unreservedly about our feelings of affection than it is to talk openly about our sex lives, and the openness of Alvin Greenberg's expression is what makes it charming.

Perfection is not possible with such a design, of course—sonnet 6 is too similar to sonnet 4; the Latin tag in 58 is erroneous; 54 is too reminiscent of John Berryman ("this, friends, is not fun"); 46 is too sententious by half ("a dog's an act of belief")—but we are offered sixty poems here, and fifty of them are palatable and a good two dozen are warm and funny and bright. So far as I know, Edward Lear never wrote any sonnets, but if he had done so, one of them might have resembled, just a little, Greenberg's 49:

> prescription: dog: take one three times a day
> for a walk in the park. take four. take five
> or six. take whatever it takes to keep you alive
> and out of trouble. leash up the cat on your way
> out the door. the gerbil. the parrot. and hey!
> don't forget the tropical fish: they can save
> your life quick as the rabbit, which you can shove
> under your jacket while stowing the white mice away
> in your pockets. with the hamster under your hat
> and the duck tucked under your arm, you're all set
> for the worst the world can do, ready to go forth
> with all the protection you need. why, no one can see
> if there's even anyone there: just a mobile menagerie
> strolling the park, the very picture of health.

It is not likely that Greenberg had thought of Edward Lear in composing his poem, but there are similar qualities between them. Once upon a time, however, William Jay Smith has clearly thought of the grand Victorian humorist and produced—as T. S. Eliot had done before him—a delectable variation on one of Lear's most famous verses:

> How rewarding to know Mr. Smith,
> > Whose writings at random appear!
> Some think him a joy to be with
> > While others do not, it is clear.

And this poem, "Mr. Smith," goes on to echo one of the most important elements of Lear's nonsense verse—its vaguely threatening, slightly unnerving undertones:

> He weeps by the side of the ocean,
> > And goes back the way that he came;
> He calls out his name with emotion—
> > It returns to him always the same.

> It returns on the wind and he hears it
>   While the waves make a rustle around;
> The dark settles down, and he fears it,
>   He fears its thin crickety sound.

There—just that tinge of shadow and no more. It takes a long time for an American poet to realize that a humorist like Lear is stronger, and as a poet more important, than those so many others who pretend to deep philosophy and spiritual profundity. But Edward Lear's Chankly Bore is in many ways a more evocative place than Robert Bly's Minnesota or Robert Duncan's San Francisco or Gary Snyder's Kyoto. A strange virus of consumerism has crept into the judgment of poetry: that work is thought best which shows a bottom line rich with spiritual profit, and for this reason boring propagandists like Nikki Giovanni and Allen Ginsberg are taken seriously by the misguided. A distinction commonly made is that these poseurs write "poetry" while accomplished craftsmen like William Jay Smith only write "verse," but a finely turned insouciant verse is generally more profound than almost all other poetry except the greatest. Craft is profound in itself as an expression of human capability teasing its limits, and that poetry which is without craft—or which pretends by rationalization to a craft it does not truly achieve—is generally without poetic interest. There have been poets who could write poetry without being able to craft verse—Whitman and Traherne come to mind—but they comprise a lonesome few.

William Jay Smith is such a fine craftsman that craft is rarely the first thing one notices in his work. Like other good versemakers—X. J. Kennedy, Donald Hall, Stanley Kunitz—Smith has his view of humor well thought out. One section of his *Collected Poems* is called "The Tall Poets: Light Verse, Epigrams, Satires, and Nonsense (1950–1980)." There are twenty-one poems here, most of them quite successful. But other poems, equally light in tone and sometimes even funnier than these, are scattered in among the more serious efforts. "Death of a Jazz Musician" (which I admit is not really a case in point) is lodged between a poem about the nature of time and one about reason versus emotion, and this placement underscores the seriousness of its humor:

I dreamed that when I died a jukebox played,
And in the metal slots bright coins were laid;
   Coins on both my eyes lay cold and bright
As the boatman ferried my thin shade into the night.

   I dreamed a jukebox played. I saw the flame
   Leap from a whirling disc which bore my name,
      Felt fire like music sweep the icy ground—
And forward still the boatman moved, and made no sound.

Some may object that this is not a humorous poem, that there is nothing funny about it in the least. But most literary humor is not funny in the humdrum *ha-ha* sense; Chaucer's characterization of his Pardoner is immortally comic but hardly hilarious. The long tradition of overstuffed official elegies for dull statesmen is one historical context that "Death of a Jazz Musician" sets itself in contrast with, and the intrusion of the Greek figure of Charon into the alien mythology of American jazz is the fundamental comic strategy. Smith's poem is menacing, but it fits securely into the comic tradition.

One of the funniest poems here is "Dachshunds," in which the figure of a dog and his "elongated wife" move through various stages to a mystical-celestial apotheosis, like Belinda's lock in Pope's epyllion. "The Dachshunds seem to journey on: / And following them, I / Take up my monocle, the Moon, / And gaze into the sky," the poet reports, and then supplies a stanza that with an easy but inevitable pun shows us with what tact he has approached the subject of humor:

      Pursuing them with comic art
        Beyond a cosmic goal,
      I see the whole within the part,
        The part within the whole.

For Smith it is no stretch from "comic" to "cosmic" because he keeps continually in mind the inadequacy of human efforts—and especially the poet's inadequacy—in proportion to the tasks at hand. This knowledge, however, has not prevented him from attempting to deal with the cosmic by more direct means than humor. In poems like "Fishing for Albacore," "The Tin Can," and "Journey to the Dead Sea," he has written long-lined oracular verses that take on heavy subjects with a sometimes orotund rhetoric that is not always on the mark. A couple of versicles from "What Train Will Come?" make pretty accurate examples of Smith's later, highly elevated style:

> O violent earth: I think of the morning Darwin saw you,
> "the very emblem of all that is solid," a world
>
> That had moved overnight beneath his feet "like a crust over
> a fluid," and when he sailed into Talcahuano Bay
>
> All was strangely still.

"Strangely still" is the kind of cliché Smith would never employ in one of his witty poems, unless for purposes of irony and satire, and its presence here underlines the fact that his vatic voice is rather hollow and unconvincing—though "At Delphi" works pretty well, and "Venice in the Fog" and "Morels" are very good indeed.

Smith at his best is a classy poet, and Scribner's should have treated his *Collected Poems* better than with flimsy binding, cheesy see-through paper, and a klutzy dust-jacket design. He is, after all, the author of the classic—and *funny*—"Plain Talk," which I insert here for the benefit of those who haven't read it in a while:

> "There are people so dumb," my father said,
> "That they don't know beans from an old bedstead.
> They can't tell one thing from another,
> Ella Cinders from Whistler's mother,
> A porcupine quill from a peacock feather,
> A buffalo-flop from Florentine leather.
> Meatless shanks boiled bare and blue,
> They bob up and down like bones in a stew;
> Don't know their arse from a sassafras root,
> And couldn't pour piss from a cowhide boot
> With complete directions on the heel."
>
> That's how *he* felt—that's how I feel.

One of the most curious productions of the season is *The Death of Cock Robin*, a volume consisting of a very loose sequence of narrative poems by W. D. Snodgrass that are accompanied by paintings by Deloss Mc-Graw. The paintings—bright gouaches a bit reminiscent both of Paul Klee and of children's art—sometimes tangentially illustrate the poems but mostly do not. The poems are concerned with the death of the nursery-rhyme figure of Cock Robin, who soon takes on much shifty symbolic import. Sometimes Cock Robin is the poet Snodgrass, sometimes merely The Poet in Society, sometimes The Scapegoat; he is a trickster, a dodger, and an avatar of childlike delight, of melancholy, of tragedy. In short, he is Pierrot dressed up as Papageno. There are other figures in the sequence, too: Kafka, Dostoevsky, Mr. Evil, and W. D.—who, like Cock Robin, is sometimes Snodgrass but often not.

It won't be long until worthier scholars than I begin to elucidate the story these poems tell, and to unfold the implications, and I cheerfully resign the job to them. The narrative line, such as it is, reflects the composition of the volume: here a poem suggests a painting; yonder a painting suggests some verses. The improvisational character of the relationship is one of its best pleasures.

An example of this organizational looseness is "W. D., Don't Fear That Animal." It is a parody of Wordsworth, and only the slight mention of Cock Robin in the fourth stanza tugs the poem into the sequence. The first two stanzas are irresistible:

> My hat leaps up when I behold
>   A rhino in the sky;
> When crocodiles upon the wing
> Perch on my windowsill to sing,
> All my loose ends turn blue and cold;
>   I don't know why.

> My knuckles whiten should I hark
>   Some lonely python's cry;
> Should a migrating wedge of moose
> Honk, it can shake my molars loose—
> Or when, at heaven's gate, the shark
>   Doth pine and sigh.

The volume is a Cartier's window of prosodic forms of every sort, and most of them are handled with the ebullience and aplomb we find in these stanzas, via lines that draw much of their energy from nursery rhymes and other folk and popular sources. Shaped poems, free verse, all kinds of invented stanzas, traditional quatrains—these forms and others abound. One of the cleverest formal patterns, in "Cock Robin's Roost Protects W. D. from Mr. Evil," is so well done that Snodgrass genuinely earns the right to an atrocious pun at the end, "across Styx" for "acrostics." It goes without saying that there is metrical and rhyming ingenuity in plenty.

Snodgrass's taste—or maybe his sense of propriety—is not flawless. Some poems come apart under the strain of so much cleverness ("Assuming Fine Feathers, W. D. Takes Flight"); some go on a bit too long ("Storm Family's Anthem"); sometimes a painting didn't provide sufficient inspiration for its companion poem ("W. D. Disguised as Cock Robin and Hidden Deep in Crimson").

The best poems may be those that approach the ominous tone of nursery rhymes, like the one that ends, "Here comes a chopper to chop off your head." In "W. D. and Cock Robin Discuss the Dreaded Interrogation," the nature of the antagonist is neatly defined; it is a bureaucracy in full possession of that "cold superiority / On which authority depends: / The right to hold things in contempt." In "W. D. Sits in Kafka's Chair and Is Interrogated Concerning the Assumed Death of Cock Robin," the bureaucracy itself speaks:

> Now "W"—we'll call you "W,"
>   Okay? We like the friendly touch.
> Just a few questions that won't trouble you
>   For long; this won't hurt much.
>
> First: name, sex, race, genus,
>   Specific gravity and species;
> Hat size, color of hair and penis;
>   Texture and frequency of faeces?

The final stanza is equally matter-of-fact, equally chilling:

> A simple yes or no is all
>   We want; the truth always shines through.

Thank you. Please wait out in the hall
Until somebody comes for you.

I wondered as I read through this book if it might possibly be suitable for children. John Bunyan, Lewis Carroll, E. A. Abbott, Madeleine L'Engle, and other writers seem to have no trouble presenting complex ideas in ways attractive to children—and McGraw's paintings would interest them. I concluded, with real disappointment, that the story line is too murky and many of the references too exclusively literary for children to enjoy. Too bad. That's a missed opportunity.

But when I complain I begin to feel like the speaker of "The Ugly Little Bird," a fowl who gives us to know in cock(!)ney dialect that he was no friend of the recently deceased Cock Robin:

> There's some says those should get a medal
> As shot him down—he made a muddle
>   Of manners and strytforward meanin's.
> I just says: give me real ideals,
> True cheerful thoughts—none of your idle
>   Moonin' about and moanin'.

If *The Death of Cock Robin* is fated to be merely a book for adults, it's as good anyhow as adults deserve—and maybe better. W. D. Snodgrass and Deloss McGraw have done themselves proud. And so has the University of Delaware Press, which published this oversized (9½″ × 11″) book with a stout cloth binding, glossy paper that reproduces the color pictures very well, and an interesting afterword by William Chace. They ask $19.50 for it, while Scribner's wants $25 for the shameful production job they gave William Jay Smith. Whoever shot Cock Robin got the wrong bird.

For we don't want to discourage humorous poetry. I've been harping on the fact that poetry cannot be humorous unless it is serious, but the obverse is also true. The poetry that believes humor is infra dig, and that to be funny is to be featherweight, is not truly serious. It will crumble under the burden of a stuffy comportment; it will presume to such significance that it cannot be approached affectionately; it will wear a uniform of such sober splendor that it will finally deny its tedious human hangnails and pale, shivering, skinny human shanks. Then someday a bright-eyed child will happen along and point out that here waddles a heap of ambulatory clothing with no emperor inside. You can almost hear e. e. cummings's voice ringing out the sentence.

Brief Cases: Naked Enterprises

Contemporary American lyric poets prefer to write poems of between thirty-five and seventy-five lines in length. Poems of this size comprise the bulk of their volumes. Often there will also be a longer poem included, taking up a complete section of the book, or a sequence of closely related poems intended to be read as a whole. Short poems are scattered about, looking rather as if they were chinking up holes in plaster.

Too often a reader feels that the poet does not attach much importance to the smaller pieces, that they are present as transitions between different kinds of subject matter or new formal arrangements. We find short poems that are only mild jokes, introduced for the sake of a contrasting tone. Sometimes they appear casual and slovenly, like notebook jottings for longer poems that didn't work out. Sometimes they are too obviously passages salvaged from wordier poems that went down in ruin.

But the art of the short poem differs from that of the longer lyric, and the poet ought to fix the fact firmly in mind in order to prevent errors like Claire Bateman's "Retroactive Causation." Bateman's volume, *The Bicycle Slow Race*, is really quite good. Such poems as "Shrinking," "Not Thinking About God," "Technology," "The Nursery-Web Spider," and "Trying" are thoughtful, graceful, clear, and sometimes piercingly direct. But "Retroactive Causation" tells us about an old newspaper from a time that the speaker labels her "prehistory":

where Floyd Patterson is "ice in a glass,"
and Eisenhower is intricately wrought, as implausible
as Christ's nativity:
God riffling through the calendar,
putting his finger down on the wrong square.

After two more equally silly lines, the poem ends with a picture of the speaker's mother marrying into freedom out of the bondage to her own dominating mother.

There is nothing irredeemable about "Retroactive Causation"; it is only bland, patchy, and incoherent. The thoughts and impulses behind it might well have made a good, even a moving, poem, but the whole never came together. There is something makeshift about its presentation as a short poem, and I'm inclined to believe that it once harbored different ambitions.

Bateman, when she designs to, can write good short poems. "What Gifts They Have for Us" and "Fifth Brandenburg" are not bad verses (though perhaps the latter is trite in concept); "Reliable" is a neat piece of work, witty and observant. I like "Berries" best; its Rousseau-derived sentimentality is enlivened by its brevity, and I have read longish pastoral utopian novels that delivered less redolence than these ten lines:

Back then people died often, not bored.
You were playing by the river,
something not yet music tickling your throat,
when you saw the berries, heavy and clustered.
You climbed the hill to bring some to your grandmother.
She crushed one and rubbed it on her lips.
By sundown there was no numbness or blister.
She swallowed a fistful while everybody watched.
The next day when she woke up as always,
you all went down to the river with baskets.

No other poem I know of presents so simply and briefly the idea that the pastoral mode denies the existence of death, even in elegies like Milton's "Lycidas." The wish that makes up the story line is so deftly tendered we almost don't recognize it; the efficacy of magic is convincing because the poem so swiftly projects its mythic locale.

But poets who are attracted by mythic material and are able to treat it gracefully and with emotion usually require more space in which to work their effects. This is true of Claire Bateman, whose longer poem, "Greek Myths," is one of her best efforts. It seems a trifle unfair to complain about the short poems of poets whose better gift is for the other sort, and I should like to urge readers toward *The Bicycle Slow Race*. It's not a perfect volume, but it is a good one, a solid one.

There are readers (and editors!) for whom brevity indicates triviality. For them no four lines of Dickinson or six of Jarrell or eight of Housman will ever bear the significance of a poem that discourses for forty or fifty lines. They are intermittently convinced that the seriousness of a work's literary intention is in inverse proportion to the delight it offers. These are judges who will condemn on grounds of triviality *The Really Short Poems of A. R. Ammons* from its title page to its final line.

They go too far, even though it's true that there are a number of trivial verses in the Ammons volume, as well as incomprehensible ones, silly ones, flat ones, and some that are so dumb it strains the mind to imagine they were produced by an organic entity. "Coward" is the shortest poem—one line—and the dreadfullest:

Bravery runs in my family.

It does offer us a case study, however. In another poem, the slight humor in the pun might serve as ornament, if the poet was careful to make the line a throwaway. Or in dialogue it might serve to characterize the speaker. As an interpolation in mock-serious exposition it could add a note of gentle irony. But it only looks bald and in agony when exposed in a five-word sentence in the center of a page.

The severe brevity of the "really" short poem magnifies every detail. The little tics and halted gestures that sometimes almost unnoticeably infest other poems are blown up to giant size, their deficiencies showing up timorous and withered in the antiseptic bedsheet of so much margin. A thought the poet had taken quite seriously shrivels to insignificance when dribbled down the page, as in "Natives":

> Logos is an engine
> myth fuels,
> civilization
> a pattern,
> scalelike crust
> on a hill
> but the hill's swell
> derives from
> gravity's
> deep fluids
> centering elsewhere
> otherwise

To other poems falls the reverse destiny. A modest thought, even a subtle one, will tumesce into pretentious language in the effort to become an apothegm. "Increment" is a case in point:

> Applause is a shower
> to the watertable of
> self-regard:
> in the downpour
> the watertable's irrelevant
> but after the shower passes
> possibility takes on
> an extensive millimeter.

The clearest meaning I can puzzle out of these lines is that a person receiving praise may think better of himself at a later hour. How much better? Well, as much as "an extensive millimeter." Ammons's habit of flinging scientific terminology at tenuous psychological musings is often irritating and sometimes alarming; it is a little like watching a casual tourist wander into a medical laboratory and begin fiddling with the serums and petri dishes. In "Increment" such vocabulary is rawly inappropriate.

It is difficult to be brief and clear about complex subjects; "Turning" is muddled and "Double Exposure" I cannot get to make sense at all. "Reflective" is merely cute and "Photosynthesis" proposes a paradox but cannot formulate it cleanly. In fact, in this book Ammons makes just about all the mistakes that short poems invite.

I am not satisfied, however, that I would like all of them gone. Ammons's work is best read in big irregular chunks, taking the good and the less interesting together. He has a longing for precision but an untidy talent; a high regard for patience is rendered in a nervous impulsive style; his gift for close observation is sometimes distracted by the urge to metaphysical exhibitionism.

But at his best he is incomparable. No one else is so cheerfully quirky, so slyly sensible, so oxymoronically accurate. Most of us think in clichés, I'm afraid, but Ammons appears to think in reversed clichés; it's hard to believe he ever met a thought he didn't want to stand on its head. When he has done so, the effect may be merely clumsy. But it may also be utterly fresh and original, witty, unexpected, serious, and even profound. If this poet's intelligence is a little too restless, it surely gets a lot of limbering exercise, and there is more substance and suggestion in the seventeen words of "Settlement" than some poets can muster in as many stanzas:

> It snowed
> last night
>
> and this
> morning no
>
> track in or
>
> out shows
> on the
>
> cemetery
> road.

He even tries a few epigrams and does well with them, as in "The Upshot," which tells us that "It's hard / to live // living it / up down." That is simply nifty—especially the final line. "Lost and Found" is written in imitation of Robert Frost's late epigrams, and Ammons does his model proud:

> Apostasy is such, if you doubt on,
> You return by the road you set out on.

Since I've griped about Ammons's unsuccessful use of scientific diction in one poem, justice demands that I note that in "Transducer" and "Miss" (a poem about neutrinos) this kind of language works pretty well. Many of the jokes are actually funny; "Their Sex Life" makes its acerbic point with swift dispatch: "One failure on / Top of another."

I will surmise, though, that many readers will like best in these poems what the poet does so well in his longer work. Ammons's determination to look as closely as possible at the mechanics of nature gives his lines an authority that makes newer ecological poets sound like political parrots. Among modern poets only Robinson Jeffers and Gerard Manley Hopkins have been so devoted to this task, though Robert Morgan comes close. Perhaps there are others, too, but they do not spring vividly to mind. "Rainy Morning," at once minutely precise and romantically suggestive, produces effects reminiscent of the small watercolor sketches of Turner:

> Sometimes the ridge across
> the way transluminous
> emerges above the mist
> and squares and detached rondures
> of vapory ground with
> dairy barns and old trees
> break out afloat
> separated in high lyings

A. R. Ammons is a poet entirely unique, and when we think we've found another poet whose lines closely resemble his, it pays to take a careful look. Here, from her volume *Heroes in Disguise*, is Linda Pastan's "In This Season of Waiting":

> Under certain conditions,
> when the moon in the western sky
> seems frozen there, for instance
>
> even as the sun is rising in the east,
> so that soon two sides of the coin
> will be facing each other;

or when the snow
which is a stranger here
fills our tree with its cold flowers;

when the single
bluejay at the feeder
is so still

it could be enameled there,
then the earth becomes an emblem
for whatever we believe.

At first glance, this poem seems to read a little like one Ammons might compose. The wintry landscape, the careful spare detail, the unusual astronomical image with its surprising metaphor of a coin sliced in half through its edges, the eccentric line breaks in the fourth stanza—all these usages might belong to one or another of Ammons's poems. But then two elements become noticeable and mark the poem as a product of Linda Pastan's sensibility, a warmer one than Ammons's, and rather a softer one.

Her employment of fond and straightforward personification, "the snow / which is a stranger here" and fills the trees "with its cold flowers," is a strategy Ammons might well reject. One of the best things about Pastan's work is that she does not fear sentimentality, the quality that nature personification usually verges upon. She doesn't always succeed in keeping her balance; "Spring" (in which the personification of the season may be modeled after a Botticelli figure) is too much like those "Love is a warm puppy" exercises. But in "In This Season of Waiting" the personification adds movement and presence to the scene and draws our sympathies.

Pastan is also willing to proffer interpretation. The closure is, in fact, a suggested interpretation, advising us that these natural images are emblematic and charged with transcendental meaning. She retreats from setting down the meanings she might prefer; underscoring the implications of her title, she leaves it to the reader to address his own possibilities for belief. In doing so, she also points toward a possible reinterpretation of the personification. The "stranger" with the "cold flowers" may be something less seasonal, more final, than snow.

Ammons chats and natters, mugs and nudges, but his presence in a poem is rarely intimate. He keeps his distance, even while confessing personal secrets, and it is clear he's willing to confess them because he doesn't consider them important. His long suit is the strong image and he prefers to let it do most of the talking for him. For my money, the best lines in *The Really Short Poems* are autobiographical; yet "Coming To," in the form of a traditional conceit, is not indiscreet. The justness in the comparison and the revelatory aesthetic effect are undeniable, but there is no personal intimacy in these durable lines:

> Like a steel drum
> cast at sea
> my days,
> banged and dented
> by a found shore of
> ineradicable realities,
> sandsunk, finally, gaping,
> rustsunk in
> compass grass.

In "Unveiling" Linda Pastan also offers something like a conceit, and the contrast with Ammons's "Coming To" is illuminating—and welcome. Her task is more difficult than in "Coming To," which offers us a single image choosily detailed to correspond with a single subject, the speaker's present condition of life. "Unveiling" compares a childhood apprehension of mystery with a present state of mind, but both are defined simultaneously and are made to seem to depend upon one another. The poet has found that the earlier experience is incomplete without the later one:

> In the cemetery
> a mile away
> from where we used to live
> my aunts and mother,
> my father and uncles lie
> in two long rows,
> almost the way

> they used to sit around
> the long planked table
> at family dinners.
> And walking beside
> the graves today, down
> one straight path
> and up the next,
> I don't feel sad, exactly,
> just left out a bit,
> as if they kept
> from me the kind
> of grown-up secret
> they used to share
> back then, something
> I'm not quite ready yet
> to learn.

If I may ring a change on a reviewer's cliché, I'd like to say that Linda Pastan writes with receptive simplicity. "Unveiling" looks to consist in two straightforward prose sentences that were willing for poetry to happen to them. And so it does, in gentle small touches like the dispositions of "live" and "lie," the foreshadowing detail of "the long planked table," the half-line of the closure, and so forth. Neither the diction nor the versification calls attention to itself for fear of muffling the final effect. The subtlety of the poem's theme is at stake; the idea advanced is that the comparison of a childish state of feeling with an adult one can bring us to a mature understanding of death, and I cannot think how it could be more gracefully or guilelessly put.

Pastan's poems require some subtlety of thought and feeling to be interesting at all. Ammons's "Coming To" achieves a great deal of resonance with its single-image comparison, but when Pastan attempts the same thing her fine simplicity becomes simplemindedness. I cannot find in her "Crocuses" anything but a two-term comparison in the old-fashioned Imagist manner:

> They come
> by stealth, spreading

the rumor of spring—
near the hedge . . .
by the gate . . .
at our chilly feet . . .
mothers of saffron, fathers
of insurrection, purple
and yellow scouts
of an army still massing
just to the south.

When we say that the short poems in collections too often look like exercises, we might offer "Crocuses" as a prime example. We might also throw in "Posterity," uncharacteristic of Pastan in its use of rhyme, its resemblance to Frost's work, its distracting pun in the final line, and its unsubtle statement.

If clarity and brevity are qualities difficult to conjoin, then to combine subtlety and brevity must be nearly impossible. Pastan's longer poems tend to be her more attractive ones because they give more opportunity for her to articulate her observative meditations. "The Myth of Perfectability" is a beautiful poem, and one of its best details concerns the placement of windows in Japanese buildings. But seven lines are required to make the detail clear; the poem is better for its discursiveness. So, too, "Topiary Gardens" and "After the Funeral" and "Letters" (though the conclusion is strained) and "Bed" and "Misreading Housman" are improved by discursiveness. So, too, especially is "The Happiest Day," a poem filled with details, each of them necessary and perfect.

But Pastan can also write a masterful short poem. At first glance "Woman Sewing Beside a Window" might seem to share with "Crocuses" the fault of being a too easy and rather obvious comparison. The title is taken from a painting by Edward Vuillard and the lines draw a parallel between the subject of the poem and the painter painting his subject. The qualities praised are patience, close observation, unwavering concentration, and unsullied devotion to art. But when the poet adds an epigraph from Vuillard's writing—"Pure and simple observation is a deed . . ."—we inevitably read the poem as a description of Pastan's own methods, an ideal she strives toward, and a credo she embraces. Their best pages attest that not only Linda Pastan but also Claire Bateman and A. R. Ammons will pledge to the same credo:

> He captures light
> by painting its slow
> diminishment: the woman
> leaning over her work,
> mending the flower-dark day
> stitch by gathering stitch
> which she will finish soon,
> and fold, and put away.

Maiden Voyages and Their Pilots

There must be some truth to Baudelaire's remark or it wouldn't bite so cruelly: "An author with his first book is as vain as a schoolboy with his first dose of the clap."

But the sharpest barbs can be only half-truths. If such bon mots were always truthful, La Rochefoucauld and Voltaire would ascend to the highest ranks of philosophers. While a poet may be justifiably or unjustifiably proud of a first book-length foray into the world, he or she will also feel trepidation, fear, and sometimes outright panic. The woods are dark and deep and filled with irascible critics like yours truly, monsters who make but fast-food snacks of maiden efforts, ogres who lie in wait for the sensitive young to attract our notice so that we can pounce.

Then there is the other peril, worse than the wolfish critic or the airbrained reviewer: the possibility that the axe will never fall because the executioners considered this first book too piddling to dull good blade on. It takes temerity to submit a book of poems to a publisher; if it is accepted, the poet must gather up real courage in order to go ahead and publish. What is hardest is to endure being ignored, to stick it out and keep writing when no one is looking—not even those whose job it is to look. Many are the first-book poets who have said, "Let them say their worst—but let them say *something!*"

Then, after the fact, they have changed their minds.

I will mollify Baudelaire's bitterness with a comparison that may be Pollyannish yet is true to my own observations. Often I think of a first book as rather like a young man or woman on a first date. There is a fevered ambition to put the best foot forward, to shine, to show mastery of the latest approved style, and to risk exhibitionism in the hope of seeming highly individual. There is an almost embarrassing desire to be sincere; sincerity is the young poet's substitute for honesty, a quality that can be acquired only with experience and long meditation. If the poet does not succumb to the temptation to be ingratiating, the temptation to shock may entrap him. And of course there are the usual technical fumblings, rhythmic embarrassments, and lapses in syntax and grammar.

One trait that generally betrays a book as being a first effort is the usage of the first-person pronoun. Contemporary American poetry clings to its "I" like lichen to a sandstone boulder. Personal anecdote, personal observation, knotty personal reverie: these make up the ordinary shelf stock of the contemporary lyric. The I is part of our poetic weather; it unnoticeably immerses the tyro as completely as the nitrogen in the air. When the young poet does notice the I in poetry, the one that attracts his attention is likely to be the beguiling self-celebratory one of James Dickey or Anne Sexton, a glamorous and appealing voice to speak in and about.

There is nothing wrong with a versemaker's deciding to employ, or even to overemploy, the I. It has advantages as well as attractions. It bespeaks personal witness: "I was the man—I suffered—I was there." It enjoins companionship ("Let us go then, you and I"), even intimacy ("I might not tell everyone, but I will tell you"). It can report religious revelation ("I saw eternity the other night") as well as animal needs ("Water, water, I desire"), strange wistful yearnings ("I should have been a pair of ragged claws"), and even boisterous brags ("I'm a Yankee Doodle Dandy").

But the poet ought to realize that there are disadvantages associated with the first-person pronoun and ought also to be aware of certain habits of expression that may enter unnoticed into composition. A girl on her first date often doesn't know what to do with her hands; a poet may feel just as awkward about the I.

Patricia Claire Peters has a pretty good grasp of the pronoun, but then she is no beginning poet. Her work has appeared in journals for a long time and her first book, *When Last I Saw You,* is tardy in arriving. As the title implies, most of the poems are autobiographical, and when the episodes are straightforwardly and ingenuously related, Peters's lines can be delightful, as in the opening of "Arabian Night": "I go to Tina's after weeks of isolation, dullness, / I go to Tina's in the Village and meet Nancy, / A gamine with the shining eyes and flaring nostrils // Of a new born calf."

This poem goes on to tell of the pleasures of a night out with the girls, the discovery of a secret garden, the amiable fun of reading poems to a friend while sipping iced coffee at a sidewalk café. It all ends brightly:

> This is an Arabian night and we are women
> Spinning gossamer tales, wearing lightly life.

As long as the poem keeps to this open carefree tone, it is quietly appealing. The first line, though, has told us of the speaker's "weeks of isolation, dullness," and Peters disserves the occasion by repeating this note toward the end: "My gloom lifts and with it the weight / Of middle aged failure."

When the I of the poem judges himself or herself as a "failure" or a criminal or a cripple or a madman or an outcast, the reader is immediately put off. The I may legitimately harbor these feelings as sometimes we all must do, but only indirection dramatizes them effectively. Bald statement coming from the I smacks of self-pity, but when the same estimate about personality is ascribed to a different speaker, the awkwardness is ameliorated. "Walk in the Park" describes a perambulation that takes place after a nerve-racking day "in this poor home where you / Watch T.V. and yell at me, pet the cats and say I'm / Worth about as much as the ash on your cigarette." If the I had drawn this last description of herself—and in other poems by Peters occur self-descriptions that approach it—the result would be almost laughable.

In fact, it is when Peters manages to laugh at herself that her lines become winning. In a suite of "Sympathy Poems," a verse called "Vignette" speaks of clumsiness in ruefully funny terms. The I tells us she'd like to write a "perfect poem," but is unable. "Instead I / Clump along much as I do in / Life, I step on cats, desks and // Chairs attack me, if there's a / Wall nearby, I'll find a way to / Collide with it, at times I've // The grace of a land-bound auk."

No one is asking the I to pull punches. If an autobiographical lyric isn't honest, it is worthless, no matter how sincere its intentions. The first two poems in Peters's volume illustrate the difference between honesty and sincerity. The dedicatory poem to her daughter, "When last I saw you," is honest and, despite an inept change of tone at the end, makes a memorable impression. The next poem, "Swallows," begins well enough but ruins its ending with sincere but uncontrolled anger.

The I of a poem is one of its methods of control, and when the poet forgets that the speaking I is not and should not be the same figure as the live person writing the poem, the result can be shymaking. The uncontrolled I damages "Crabbing," "Bob Morgan in Asheville," "Confusion," and a few others. But when Peters has the pronoun well in hand, she shapes moving poems like "Natural Selection," "Venice Light," "The Middle-Aged Girls," "Mexican Rose," "Gardening," "Chinese Rice," and "There Is No One at Home But You."

An edge of raw feeling gives some of Patricia Peters's poems real power, and I recommend *When Last I Saw You* despite its occasional inelegances and sometimes because of them. There is a dangerousness about the I's uncertain control that draws one's attention—even though, when control is truly lost, the poem is much worse than one a safer poet would have set down. Now and again Peters shows an unexpected sense of humor and, humor being one of the most insouciant means of control, she might do well to employ it more often. "Sensitivity" is a cheerful but lightly touching self-portrait:

> Like a plant that clamps
> The hand that feeds it,
>
> Or like a nose that smells
> Gas, or like a lady's skin
>
> So sensitive she breaks out in
> Hives at the sight of
>
> Strawberries, my sensitive
> Approach to life drives

Me up the wall! I wish I
Was callous as an onion,

As thick as shoe leather,
I wish nothing bothered

Me but food! Oh well,
I muddle through somehow.

Like an ant daintily picking its
Way across a crowded

Sidewalk, like a Venus
Flytrap starving for fear

Of offending hairy-legged insects
Whose beauty is just too much to bear.

In most contemporary poems the I is simply a reporter of feelings
and observations about incidents enjoyed or endured; rarely is the I physically involved in any significant action the poem might record. But sometimes the I performs an important action simply by making an entrance.
A common dramatic strategy among contemporary poets writing personal lyrics is to withhold the presence of the I or to hide its dominance
or to disguise some of its qualities until near the end of the poem. William
Aarnes, in his engagingly straightforward *Learning to Dance*, employs
this technical device fairly often and usually pretty well.

"Conception" is a casebook example. The tone of the poem is warm
and fondly detailed as it describes "a Saturday night / —no, a Sunday
morning / in April 1946" when a married couple prepare to make love.
All is familial and familiar, and though there is not the least hint of pruri-
ence in his lines the poet breaks into the scene with authorial second
thoughts: "No doubt, / my account of this is mistaken, / false, needs
revising, / needs to be slipped / face down into a drawer." This intrusion seems gratuitous until we learn that the conception the title refers to
is the speaker's own: "Mother was forty-four / and Father thirty-
eight / when I was born." As a young man he never thought of his parents as lovers, the speaker tells us: "But now, / in my forties, I like to
think / that, however weary, they loved / with the eager ease / of care."

Quite apart from the ambiguities of the final noun, there are many reticent complexities in play here. It is easy enough to distinguish the I of the intrusion ("my account of this is mistaken") from the I that was born forty-odd years ago. But it is also worth noting that the I of the closure ("now, / in my forties, I like to think") is different from the I of the intrusion.

Both the intruding I and the I of the closure can be identified as speakers of the poem, but they cannot be identified with each other. The intruding I admits to healthy pudency when he contemplates his parents in the act of love. But once he identifies the scene as the moment of his own conception he changes as a person—or as a persona, at least—and begins to *like* to think of that scene. He now recognizes, because he has reached the same period of life his parents had reached, that the meaning of the scene is no longer predominantly sexual; the imagined scene now discovers the theme of enduring daily love in the face of mortality.

In distinguishing three different flavors of the I in these lines, I am not trying to be subtle. The strain—believe me—would be onerous. I am only trying to understand the dramatic function of the I in our contemporary lyric poems and finding it to be a more complex chore than I had reckoned on. But one quality of the use of the pronoun as a walk-on presence toward the end of a poem can be discovered pretty quickly. The I often represents, or brings to bear upon the subject, present time; "I" often means "now," and many times forms a duad with that adverb.

Aarnes has a nice touch in rendering scenes or parts of scenes of ordinary life. He doesn't overburden his lines with detail, nor does he leave them so starved as to lack visual interest. There is a warm enjoyment of dailiness in *Learning to Dance* that reminds me a little of small Dutch genre paintings. And when his I enters his closures the intrusion is noticeable, but rarely feels forced or looks self-important. I especially admire in this book such poems as "Authority," "Dishes," "Footing," "The Visit" (particularly good), and "To a Familiar." Another good poem, "Now That It's June," illustrates handily the identification of the I with present time. Here the I is visible from the beginning, but only as a figure in past situations, a character in the story. In the last four lines, however, the I brings present time into the poem and in doing so sets its theme in place:

If only you were clapping me awake,
insisting "It's six, it's six,"

saying you were already ready,
the eggs boiled and peeled,

the bread toasting, and "Quick,
quick" we were in the Bel Air

parking up hill from the diamond
where I'd charge grounders

and sinking line-drives, bobbling
a few, making backhanded snags,

you forcing me toward second,
toward third, till I'd lie sprawling

the ball snug or rolling away.

"Not bad!" you'd call.

If only

I were still looking up, now
backpedaling, now tiptoeing forward,

your popup now poised to fall.

Like William Aarnes, Judson Mitcham is a good poet, one of the best considered here, and if his use of the I is not one of the most important characteristics of his work, still it deserves examination as being in line with the usages of his contemporaries.

"What You Have Need Of" is a prime example. The speaker remembers being led by his brother out into a field at night, "away from the lights of houses," to be shown about the stars and the constellations "how the whole figures are not there, / and therefore, you draw your own lines, how then / you can link what's scattered into anything." The I of the first three stanzas is hardly in the poem. In the reported scene he is a child, and the speaker refers to himself only once. Then the poem makes a turn almost like a sonnet's in its distinctness, and the I is brought to the foreground:

Tonight, when sleep, failing, has fallen into old grief,
I have walked out into the back yard, hearing that voice,
and waited where the land slopes downward miles
to the town's lights, a clear lake raised to the stars,
darkness floating on the far last ripple of streetlights.

Again we find that the emphasized I brings a poem forward into present time. The introduction of present time serves to anchor the memory in a past more precisely located than in the earlier lines. The last stanza attaches the whole poem more closely to a certain kind of present situation—a dream, or perhaps a waking reverie—and "links" the "scattered" moments of the poem into a single figure, a constellation of bright instants:

There are those who defeat their dreams, who know,
when the brother of childhood stands in the doorway,
not to believe, but I am not one.

Mitcham's gift for indirection, for quiet subtlety that is always lucid, is underlined by his two negatives in his ultimate line. Though that locution may seem arch or persnickety to some, I do not see how love for an absent brother can be more warmly spoken without sagging into sentimentality.

This tone is pervasive in *Somewhere in Ecclesiastes* and is maintained partly by a careful submergence of the speaker's presence. The I speaks almost all the poems here but is for the most part an observer concerned with the feelings and situations of others. A tone of wary sweetness results, and poems like "For an Old Man Who Can't Remember His Mother's Face," "Rocking Anna to Sleep," "Nature," "Loss of Power," parts two, five, and nine of the long title poem, and the last section of "Notes for a Prayer in June" achieve a well-mannered semiformality that any contemporary poet should envy. There are a couple of poems centrally concerned with the I, but even they, taking for their subjects powers the speaker would like to have rather than those he boasts of possessing, are charmingly ego free. These are "Wonder" and "On the Otis Redding Bridge," two delightful presentations.

Another poem does celebrate a quality of style the speaker is proud of, but his pride is justified because the poem is a tribute to someone else. Again, as in so many other instances, the I is importantly advanced only in the last lines, and here too the entrance of the I brings us into present time. In this poem, though, the theme of mother admiration is brightened with humor and we are persuaded that the lady would enjoy a mock-heroic simile quite as much as we do. Before I explain the life out of it, here is "The Touch":

> You stepped out the back door, drying your hands
> on a plain white apron
> and watching me slap the new basketball down
> on the driveway's nearly flat hardpan,
> unable to control it or to stall,
> for long, its falling still.
> You held out clean, wrinkled hands for the ball,
> let it drop and caught the rise
> *with the fingertips, never with the palm,*
> allowing no sound but the ball's hollow bounce,
> crouching low, either small hand
> moving *with* the ball.
>   And years later,
> when the Newton County Rams came down,
> like the cavalry at dawn on a few Cheyenne,
> in a hot-breath man-to-man press, the best plan
> was to get the ball to me. Even now,
> I return to that late fall morning
> when you taught me what a softer touch could do,
>
> how to go where I needed to, never looking down.

I will admit that the last two lines are shameless homiletic, but I find them effective. The strong force of the poet's feelings is deftly buffered and the careful comparison illustrates the poem's subject—finesse. There are varied excellences to admire in almost all of Judson Mitcham's poems, including this one. (For instance, diphthongs that make a noise like a dribbled basketball: "allowing no sound but the ball's hollow bounce.")

If his usage of the I is a lesser excellence, still it is genuine and adds to the luster of *Somewhere in Ecclesiastes.*

David Scott Ward's employment of the walk-on I for his closures may be fairly described as devoted. The endings of the first six poems of his better-than-auspicious debut, *Crucial Beauty,* depend upon the device. But with Ward this is no thoughtless habit; he has recognized his strategy and cogitated it, and in one fine poem, "Shacks," he addresses it as his subject:

> I love abandoned places. And their buildings.
> Any sudden roadside opening where trees are waiting
> patiently to take the field again
> captures me. I want to be among the last
> to see the sun buck the work of plumb
> and level, to chance floor boards aslant
> on stacks of flat rock. I want to be the last
> to know a place's solitude. I risk the trespass sign
> and intrude. Empty rooms hold an odor
> of old quilts, damp, mildewed; the barns,
> harness leather and hay. In autumn's changed
> light that mingles the shack and its softer shadow,
> but sets the flaming oaks to starker
> colors, I seek out the lonely places.
> No cattle, wind, or birdcall. Only the scrub
> of my steps and their changed echo
> behind me sound as if another pair of feet,
> a stranger's gait has entered with me,
> and I could turn and question the farmer's widow,
> the son who stayed, ask, what did you make here,
> is this all, this shotgun shack, the curing shed,
> slowly giving up their shelter? I am alone,
> a stranger among this brief and crucial
> beauty, the tragedy of all things fallen
> from their use.

"Shacks" is not a perfect poem; I think Ward might have difficulty justifying some of his line breaks, and he says *among* where he means *amid.*

Perhaps the poem comes at us a bit too head-on, as if it were hiding a measure of defensiveness. But it articulates clearly what Ward clearly feels is necessary for him to say and, when set in context with other poems, stands as a manifesto. "Shacks" begins with generalizations about the speaker's feeling for certain kinds of settings; then it moves almost unnoticeably to specific locations; then the poem ends with a description of the nature of the I: a "stranger" amid "crucial / beauty," an observer of the "tragedy" of disused objects.

Ward's description of the I will apply to a great many other poems besides his own, but his I is different not only in being more self-conscious but also in finding in certain qualities of its own nature a poetic responsibility. It is not by accident or bad luck that Ward's poetic I has become a stranger; this poet sees it as a duty to become one. Only as a stranger can he bring to bear the special powers that make his observations poignant.

Romantic poets traditionally imagined the poem's I to be more sensitive than ordinary personalities and therefore set apart from the thick-skinned herd. There is as much pride as pain in Shelley's cry: "I fall upon the thorns of life! I bleed!" Some revenance of this attitude haunts much of contemporary poetry, but poets like David Scott Ward and Judson Mitcham have recovered for the I a more classical role.

Let us attempt to outline one typical kind of contemporary lyric. With a few phrases the poet locates the speaker in or near a setting new to him or her (or a dramatic scene that can be observed, or an object whose presence can be experienced). The greater part of the poem is given over to a careful and largely dispassionate description of this setting/action/object. The poem concludes when the I is reintroduced and allowed to utter impressions and ideas about what has taken place. This outline of the role of the I in a poem reveals a format we are all familiar with: the art history lecture. The speaker introduces him- or herself briefly, shows selected slides, and concludes by telling us what it all means.

This particular brand of contemporary poem has rediscovered the concept of the poem as a speaking picture, the *pictura loquans* of the ancient Greek and Roman poets and critics. Horace was especially happy with this notion and begins one of his best-known works with a drawn-out joke about it. There is, of course, a difference between the I of a twentieth-century poem and the I of one of Horace's odes—the Romantics have seen to that. A modern poet can no more shed every vestige of the Byronic-Pushkinian-Rilkean persona than he can divest himself of his shadow (though Brecht and Eliot gave it the old college try). Still, the contemporary I is more likely to be an explainer than a sufferer.

I regret that "Island" is too long to quote in full; it is the best example of Ward's use of the explainer format. It begins with an unexceptionable generalization that introduces a setting with neat celerity:

> In some places we are always strangers,
> and this was one: a concrete ruin
> of an abandoned tavern,
> covered with snaking kudzu, in the heart
> of the woods, its black door cut
> in walls of tangled shadows.

The speaker then describes at some length this ruined tavern that contains "on one black wall" a mural of an idyllic South Sea island by a "barroom artist" who "surely knew a beer hall / is a sad refuge, how desperate / the heart can be, how unwieldy with yearning." He then tries to imagine the life of this alcoholic folk artist, thinking of him as a deeply unhappy man, as unhappy as the whore who used to inhabit the upstairs room. Both imaginary figures must have endured a "struggle / with life's bitter longing, / its nameless despair and shame, almost / impossible."

As the poem ends, the I recollects himself to present time and muses upon the possibilities for ruin that lurk inside all lives, even his own well brought up and "innocent" existence:

> Now every time I sit at a bar, my mind
> a banked fire, I see behind the mirrored, inscrutable
> face before me, shadows of palms
> and grass, and faces in glimpses that break
> like light on boundless water.

It would be easy to misread these final lines, to make them seem to say no more than "There but for the grace of God go I." But the long middle of the poem forestalls banality with its affectionate description of the wall painting reflected by a mirror on the opposite wall, this doubled landscape imprisoning the speaker inside the abandoned dream of a vanished loser.

"Island" is a strong poem and sits well beside other good ones: "My Father and I Carry His Mother," "Interloper," "In the Old Casino at Bangor Cave," "Distance," and "The Old Convalescent Home, Blount Springs, Alabama." There are poems in *Crucial Beauty* that don't work—two poems about the biblical King David and "The Choosing," which seems unfinished, and "Airborne," which almost repeats a better poem called "My Brothers Make a Lantern." Sometimes this young poet has problems with syntax and diction (as in "Island," where *pitifully* is used for *pitiably*), but David Scott Ward has made a thoughtful, genuine start, and his best is undoubtedly yet to come.

I'm not sure that the same can be said for Cathy Smith Bowers; *The Love That Ended Yesterday in Texas* is such a fine book that its author need not fret about further improvement. Not that she's perfect: "Hanging the Screens" seems confused, "Saviours" is strained, and one poem is almost as cute as its twenty-seven-word title. In fact, Bowers can never be a perfect poet; she sets herself tasks so difficult that sometimes she is bound to fail.

Even her fineness has a dark side; her subject matter is rarely appealing for its own sake. The first forty pages here contain poems about illness, death, dire trauma, catastrophe, old age, and disfigurement. It is a measure of Bowers's talent that she makes us willing, even eager, to read about these topics; still, it is something of a relief to come upon a poem that celebrates, and tries to emulate, the simplicity of a child's religious faith, "I Love How My Niece Loves Jesus."

Bowers has an adroit hand with anecdote, skillfully turning the stories in "Wanting Them Back" and "The Party" into allegories. "October" shows what she can do with an old-fashioned conceit, and "The Love" takes this technique one step further. Her diction is ever the plainest, simple and sauceless, and her effects are rarely striking. She has forsworn rhinestone and sequins, but her lines are the more comely for her modesty—and more moving too. Here is a poem about how the children of alcoholics become addicted to family chaos. "Bone" speaks about as plainly—and forcefully—as a poem can:

Our house was a needle's eye
you shoved a camel through.
You gave us each a bone.
Arm finger toe and ankle
to be tucked in childhood's baggage
and lugged around from day to day
as if we always waited
to board some invisible train.
When you finally died
we were surprised
at the benignancy of doors,
passivity of pots and pans,
the incipient incipience.
The quiet you left
hunkered in corners
like sacks of tongueless kittens.
For a while we kept our distance,
trying hard to love the silence
then one by one
we gathered with our sticks
and began to poke.

"Bone" takes *we* for its speaking pronoun, and Bowers is in fact less an I-fancier than many other poets. But for all her welcome originality she too sometimes employs the walk-on, I-reaction format. "Losses," though not one of her best poems, serves as a good example. In this poem the I is introduced in an ancillary role, letting her dog out of his pen in the morning. The poem first describes fully and accurately the actions of the retriever as it "circles and circles, sniffing out / the perfect spot," then lopes into the woods "as he was trained." The dog taking care of his business reminds the speaker of an infant in Indonesia she had once seen, "stooped like a little frog, emptying / his bowels onto the sand." Now the I breaks into the poem with a reaction that serves as the ending:

> Was it then I knew
> I would never have children? Could not bear
> at so close a range those leaks

and solvents. Would get instead a dog
I could train to go off into the woods
carrying deep into shadow the body's chronic losses.

The explaining I is put to her mettle in this last sentence, and I believe she strains unduly to squeeze a dramatic conclusion out of her comparison of unlike scenes.

Here lies another pitfall. Even if a poet's I doesn't lapse into carping self-pity or ugly braggadocio, the concluding explanatory lines are susceptible to know-it-all pomposity or exhibitions of mere ingenuity. We are sometimes accosted with an attitude less like that of a well-intentioned lecturer than of a facile stage magician: "I'll bet I've got you fooled; you dopes think there's no rabbit in the hat." Bowers escapes this peril for the most part; "Losses" is exceptional in having an unsteady closure. Most of the poems in *The Love That Ended Yesterday in Texas* are tightly stitched, with closures assured and satisfying. "Thunder" shows how a final emphasis on the speaker can suddenly reveal the true subject of a poem and reveal at the same time the true nature of a relationship. The subject seems at first to be the petty angers and nettlesome discomforts of physical separation, but the concluding image of the speaker changes it into a portrait of vital love:

> My husband calls
> from his month-long trip to California
> still nursing the anger
> he left me holding like a small child
> in the dwindling window of the airport
> and hears from my side of the continent
> the crack of thunder.
> And yes, yes
> that is what he misses most
> about South Carolina.
>
> Not the dust rising
> in red puffs above the corn.
> Not the lakes of carp and catfish

turning deep
in their tentative dreams of flight.

But the way
when the land is long given up for dead
and farmers have disinherited the sky
for good this time
it breaks sudden and big as forgiveness.

They don't have that here, he says
as if he were speaking
of grits or Dixie Beer
or a woman
who would stand in a storm
holding the receiver to the sky.

It's impossible for me to imagine a better picture of a loving and faith-ful wife than this one of the speaker braving the risks of a storm in order to relay some glory of the world. Come to think, it's also a pretty good description of Cathy Smith Bowers as a poet.

Perhaps a great many contemporary poets embrace such a picture of themselves, or others very like it. It has a lofty self-assuring aspect and is useful in bringing drama to ordinary situations. A less forceful image of the I would produce less dramatic poems, but perhaps other qualities might be gained that would compensate. Thoughtfulness, for example, and broad perspective and historical awareness—these three qualities are conspicuous in Martha M. Vertreace's *Under a Cat's-Eye Moon* almost to the same degree that her I is restrained. Vertreace's book contains fewer autobiographical poems than any other of the volumes discussed here; quieter tones and more-considered views prevail. This writer is smitten with the postimpressionist painters and includes lots of poems about Gauguin, Van Gogh, Chagall, and others. Emphasizing how large a part of her personal life these painters and their works have become, she mixes the different kinds of poems together: an art study stands next to an autobiographical episode that companions a character portrait of a relative.

Vertreace is not yet a polished poet. There is some ragged clumsiness in almost every poem. But *Under a Cat's-Eye Moon* is undeniably the work of a dedicated poet whose strengths—only partially discovered as yet—may well outlast those of poets much more widely vaunted than she.

In "Starting from Scratch," an autobiographical essay included in *The Confidence Woman*, Eve Shelnutt's 1991 collection of essays by women writers, Vertreace has addressed explicitly the use of I in her poetry—and has been able to observe her audience's reaction: "Sometimes, at readings, members of the audience will ask personal questions about some event or situation which appears in my poetry. . . . When I explain that I portray a composite of several people—real and invented—or that an encounter which I collapse into a few stanzas took years to actualize, or that the 'I' of the poem does not necessarily identify black or female or Martha Vertreace, a shade of betrayal crosses their faces as if I had transgressed a moral law."

There are indeed readers who think of such fiction making as artistic, if not moral, transgression; Stanley Plumly has declared himself one of them and has defended his position in a longish essay. But the proof is in the poetry, I believe. Though Charles Bukowski's daft confessional I may be in some sophomoric sense more naked than Vertreace's composite speaker, his poems are not more authentic, and his I is certainly not more interesting.

In "Time Is a River Without Banks," for example, Vertreace follows the common practice of holding back the entrance of the I until the end and turning the last lines toward personal statement. But the I is not really personal; she is able to extend the implicative functions of the pronoun until it almost serves the same purpose as *we* or *you*. She is able to establish an intimacy between speaker and reader closer than the confessional I can achieve:

> A fish flies through night clouds,
> moonlit wings freed of the river's
> edge. Its finny arm bows the violin
>
> which freezes time within the golden
> pendulum of the grandfather clock.
> My brother once knocked our wind-up clock

off the highboy; its cracked face stayed
circling hands into a fractured smile. He
picked up wheels and gears piece by piece.

By the river bank, lovers seem unaware
that music crystallizes their mutual
promises, he, touching her breast forever.

They never heard the clock chime drown
the violin. Another Chagall trick,
this changeling fish, perhaps a herring

whose flesh fed him, which shut its gills
to lucerne dreams of the Luga, turning
moonrise into scales, and scales to wings.

Did you supply oars to my ironwood ship
before my transatlantic voyage?
A carved mermaid lashed to a bowsprit

breaking in storm winds as spume rises
dry as dust devils, my rainbow scales
cut my skin under rope knots.

I invent a secret which saves you,
the ending of a poem which saves me,
which I guard until I escape, as the ship

flounders belly up. When it rights itself,
I'll be tillerman and I'll grow wings.

"Time Is a River Without Banks" is not a successful poem—its ambitions overmaster it—but it shows what advantages can accrue to the composite I. In the context of the whole volume this poem serves as a fugato passage, pulling together many of Vertreace's separate themes and images. Time is a dominant concern in this book, and images of sundials, astronomical orbits, watches, and clocks (usually broken or dismantled) are found throughout. In this poem too appear Vertreace's love of modern painting and her involvements with family and childhood. If the poet's reveries are often messily cluttered, images jumbled, meditations inchoate, impulses multidirectional, that may be because she has imagined the book as a single work divided into separate poems rather than as a collection of separate poems that are stacked together like toy blocks to make a volume.

Historical poems like "Apples," "Vincent in Flames," "Study from an Antique Cast, 1886," and "Radium" sit beside personal episodes like "Ash Wednesday," "Muse," "Homegoing," and "What Matters." The effect is whole, but not harmonious. I think that what Vertreace aims at with *Under a Cat's-Eye Moon* is a construction very similar to the Chagall painting she describes and practices variations upon in "Time Is a River Without Banks." Images from postimpressionist and surrealist art serve her well by giving her leitmotifs that help to colligate poems in groups and by lending her techniques for rendering light and space so as to suffuse lines with subtle but almost palpable atmosphere. In "Maize" we see how "The sickle moon hangs his shadow between stooks," and we witness an effect of light that Monet might have striven for:

> Where dust falls, green rises like the blush
> which rises when you hold me.

Under a Cat's-Eye Moon is not one of the very best poetry books published recently. But it is a good book, and one that its author should be staunchly proud of. If I give it more credit for effort and ambition than for accomplishment, I believe that to be a first book's rightful due.

Among the books talked of here, none matches the surprising debut triumph that Patricia Storace made with *Heredity* or Belle Waring with *Refuge* or Robert Wrigley with *Moon in a Mason Jar*. On the other hand, none is as ragged and hollow as my own first poetry volume. These are all solid beginnings, the products of well-stocked minds and serious temperaments, and their authors are to be congratulated. Good beginnings do not always signal stellar careers, of course. If each of these poets has important things still to learn, all of their books show an eagerness to discover, to assimilate, and to make experience comprehensible. A proper knowledge of the use of the first-person singular pronoun will be a useful tool. I admire the last lines of Martha Vertreace's "Entering the

Dream" because they show so wonderfully how history and the present-time speaking voice can be brought together in a single dramatic gesture:

> I think that I, like van Gogh, stand in the shadow
> of a child misborn—I think
> of pressing your hand to my face for a thousand years.

Five New Southern Women Poets

My best guess is that if you ask someone knowledgeable to list a few prominent living Southern poets, you will hear of James Dickey, A. R. Ammons, Robert Morgan, Dave Smith, Charles Wright, A. B. Spellman, Andrew Hudgins . . . well, quite a few luminaries can be identified. You might hear of Ellen Bryant Voigt and perhaps of Kelly Cherry, but I have my doubts. I think you would not hear of Heather Ross Miller or Betty Adcock—and though Maya Angelou might be mentioned, she would not count in the opinion of most other poets, her best fame resting on steadier foundations than her verse. Female Southern poets get short shrift.

I can't say why this is so. The feminists will offer their predictable elucidation, the conservative canonists will offer theirs, yet neither explanation will seem conclusive. It is as hard to think that there is a prejudice against poetry by Southern women as it is to believe that Adcock's achievement falls short of, say, James Whitehead's. It may be that the tradition of the deep-drinking, recklessly womanizing, varmint-slaughtering, good-ole-boy Southern Poet makes such testosterone racket that the sofer voices are drowned out. Yet the quiet lines of Donald Justice command wide respect, as do the plain-speaking stanzas of Henry Taylor.

Nor can the deficit of reputation be imputed to subject matter. True, the women often write about subjects we might, however unfairly, anticipate—romantic and filial and parental love, family matters, childhood, religion—but then so do many of the male poets. This list of topics would cover most of the work of James Applewhite and Dave Smith, as well as that of T. R. Hummer and Gibbons Ruark. We might add history to the list, since that is a favored topic of the menfolk, but here too the women are strong: Kathryn Stripling Byer is as perceptive a searcher as Andrew Hudgins, but her approach is more oblique, centered upon personality rather than event.

In fact, this seems to be true in a general sense. The women often attack their subjects from inside or from surprising angles, while the men are likely to bull at them head-on. It is hard to imagine a Southern woman writing a poem like Dickey's "Cherrylog Road" or David Bottoms's "Shooting Rats at the Bibb County Dump," in which experience is delivered so explicitly it seems only highly stylized (though undeniably powerful) reportage. In *Friends and Assassins* (1993), Heather Ross Miller's "Cloudless Sulfur, Swallowtail, Great Spangled Fritillary" deals with material no less striking than that of Dickey or Bottoms, but it plunges so immediately into its drama that much of the situation has to be deduced not only from the few details that are given but from the emotions that are portrayed. If I may be allowed a large, perhaps inaccurate, but (I hope) dimly suggestive analogy: the differences in presentation between the two genders of Southern poets are a little like the differences between D. H. Lawrence and Virginia Woolf. It is easy to say which of those figures made the greater stir in their contemporary world, but not easy to claim he was the better writer.

So it is in the spirit of discovery that I undertake to look at five volumes of poetry by Southern women. All of these books are deserving and all are finely individual, despite certain similarities of tone and duplications of subject matter. But defining the individualities is a difficult task because the poets are so indirect in method and so tactful in sensibility; it is less a matter of distinguishing the trumpet from the violin than of distinguishing among members of the soulful woodwind family—English horn, bassoon, oboe d'amore.

Perhaps the most easily accessible—the most welcoming, one might say—of these volumes is Dannye Romine Powell's *At Every Wedding Someone Stays Home*. Powell's situations—even the imaginary ones—are familiar, her tone confident as well as confidential, her lines mostly short and seemingly transparent. Her lyrics offer few difficulties of comprehension from stanza to stanza but often surprise the reader when interpreted as wholes, for Powell's subtlety develops not from her plain (and sometimes bland) diction but from the obliquity of statement the whole poem makes.

An obvious case in point would be her opening poem, "Memory":

> I know where you sit:
> in the back rows
> of old theatres,
> the kind with stenciled stars
> in the navy-blue ceiling.
> The films you watch
> are spliced, scratched,
> the actors dead or forgotten.
> On days like this—
> cold, the sky overloaded—
> you could be someone's uncle,
> huddled in your overcoat,
> eating popcorn, feet propped
> on the seat ahead.

Here the key to understanding is the pronoun "you," often employed nowadays to lend immediacy and personality to otherwise unattached observations. Usually this "you" is no more than a displaced "I," but in "Memory" it substitutes for an old-fashioned trope, personification, and the quality here personified is loneliness. Powell neatly sidesteps the creaky embarrassment currently attached to traditional personification by making her poem address the personification directly the way "you" poems often address real people; she manages to hold at arm's length the unavoidable sentimentality of the subject.

Yet "Memory" is an unusual poem for Powell, not because its means are simple but because the situation is pruned of its personal context. This poet, like many other Southern women poets, prefers to place her readers in the swarming middle of incidents; she uses long information-filled titles that give the poems running starts: "You Are Sitting Across from Me at the Kitchen Table in Full Sun," "Let's Say We Haven't Seen Each Other Since Ninth Grade and We Meet as Adults at a Welcome Center in Southside Virginia," "Sorrow, Looking Like Abraham Lincoln, Keeps Knocking on My Back Door." This practice might appear unhandy, but it works.

In one poem she tells the story of a corpse being dressed for burial, then laid in "a cast-iron casket / deep in Louisiana soil" where it is found a century afterward by a plowman who reburies it, frightened by his discovery. Later still, the casket is found again and shipped to Washington where it is opened by an anthropologist. The poem ends suddenly, at the moment the casket is breached:

> Finally, it comes to this:
> Skull, teeth, ribs, a brown chunk of liver,
> silk and broadcloth collapsing damply against bone.

The poem would be confusing or even pointless without its title, but once we know it the pieces fall into place to form an allegory: "Hope, Which for Years Kept Resurfacing, Now Crumbles."

Powell's longest title—and for all I know a candidate in this category for the *Guinness Book of World Records*—is "The Day You Died I Thought It Would Be as Hard as Having to Haul All My Furniture into the Backyard Then Sweep up in Less Than an Hour." But it is not just a cute gimmick; it is the device that allows her to hold her poem to two stanzas in length. Even the dedication—"For my father"—helps to set the stage, so that the poem proper can begin by picking up at the title and setting readers down in the center of the emotional state: "But it was only like dusting." Then the allegory of setting a house in order is pursued: the task keeps becoming more complicated, more onerous, until the speaker realizes that it can never be completed; the house will never be truly clean, the sorrow for the death of her father will never finally disappear: "I'm beginning to see I could be sweeping / this one room for months. Sweeping / this one room. This one room. Empty and dumb."

In a later poem Powell resurrects still another dated trope, the pathetic fallacy, and makes it newly expressive. The speaker of "On What Would Have Been Our Twenty-Fifth Anniversary" remembers one persistent activity of a former marriage, the refurbishing of dilapidated or inferior furniture with coats of paint. In one town she painted the baby carriage yellow, in another rented house she "splashed / flat apricot / on the refrigerator," then later turned to "the outdoors: / fences, shutters, porches." The poem ends with a surprisingly effective turn on the all-Nature-weeps figure:

> The day you said you were leaving
> I could hear paint peeling
> all over the state.

The dismaying sense of a past left unreachably behind is all the more poignant because of its wound of betrayal and its muffled undertone of anger. What is lost is more than the destroyed innocence of early love; a whole landscape is sealed away in time, unchangeable, irrecoverable.

This theme of the loss of a past life inextricably tied to the loss or disappearance of place is common to all five of these poets. It occurs at least a half dozen times in Alice Rose George's *Ceiling of the World*. George's treatment of this particular kind of loss begins with a traumatic event—the burning of the family home—that like a tolled knell sends successive echoes through many of the other poems, including some that have nothing to do with that original dread occasion. "The Cutting" opens with a pungent image that fixes the recollection: "It's Sunday afternoon all over again. / The ash I keep taking from my teeth reappears / and the tears of a child settle in the creases of aging skin." In the conclusion of the poem the speaker locates the start of all her meaningful experience in this one memory:

> Without walls
> we are shocked out of connection and meaning.
> How stupid a house is, how unemotional wood is
> but without
> It
> how can we hold together what was within?
> Years later, it is still the first Sunday afternoon

the voice rang through the air "our house has burned."
Stunned breathless.
That was the first diamond cutting.

It wouldn't be difficult to find fault with "The Cutting," to observe that the sentiment verges on mawkishness, that the versification is lame, that the final metaphor is distracting because it has not been prepared for. As a poem it is much less effective than her "Lost Play" and "The Remains," which deal with the same subject. But because it is the most explicit treatment, it readies the ground for poems like "Prelude," "Landscape," "Cut Magnolia," and "Papa," to which it does not at first seem related.

The middle stanze of "The Cutting" asks a haunted question: "Where was Daddy? Sick. Nearly dead, I'd been told." The absence of the father during this crucial episode magnifies the distance from him that the speaker feels. In "Papa," an elegy I would describe as being half-querulous, he is imagined as a Pharaoh who died millennia ago: "I see the Egyptians are building / a pyramid on top of your house / and the crows are beginning / to sing in the eaves." Unlike Dannye Romine Powell, George does not pursue consistent strategies; she quickly reminds us of her anachronism: "It is you, Papa, in a white suit, / who smoothes the sandy blankets / over my sleep so I can grow up / to wonder who you were." Then in the final lines she merges the two widely separate eras in a peculiar yet moving meld:

> I see, I see,
> and I saw the day one sperm
> and one egg united: a hot,
> a relentless sun, the Egyptians
> were building a pyramid,
> cotton white from the wash
> unraveled into the sky
> like a jet plane exhausted
> into blue memory.
> I, the daughter,
> call on your death, Papa.

Why did you die?
I thought you, of all people,
would live forever.

Attempting to establish the speaker as a witness, George includes an image of her own conception ("the day one sperm / and one egg united") in the vision of the dead but oppressively persisting father. This notion is too intrusive to succeed, a failed leap in a poem already perilous with risks.

Other poems marred by puzzling excesses would include "Wild Card," "Banker," "My Man," and "Expatriate." Some of the best poems in the worthy *Ceiling of the World* are the calm travel poems. I admire particularly "Italian Vista," which begins with a resigned personal confession about this foreign place—"Between it and me is a great distance"—that broadens into a striking presentation of the expatriate state of mind. Sitting on a hill in Italy, she notes the geological changes that have taken place in the valley below. But other details give her to know that the essential identity of the place remains; the place and its people are stable, only she herself is not:

And so it goes,
generation upon generation, I have none
to pass on to, I am like the stones
in brittle separation, just my human eyes
looking, looking out from another sea of life
in the afternoon sun, shaded under the tree.

Not many of the poems in Marnie Prange's *Dangerous Neighborhoods* are about travel, yet the home left behind is a subdued theme of this prickly book. The first line of the poem "Trying to Get Home" confesses, "It isn't easy." In fact, nothing is easy in Prange's work, partly because she allows herself no fuzzy-warm nostalgia. In "Childhood," the parents party through weekends from which the husband does not recover. The mother, a "paragon of resolve," rouses on Mondays to feed the children breakfast, but it is a "table set for unhappiness." Hoping to avert an angry scene between their elders, the children try to get their father on his feet:

Emissaries from the foreign country of our fear,
one by one we'd tiptoe into the spermy halflight
of their room. *Dad-dy,* we'd whine. And beg him
to get up before Mommy came. He'd grunt, roll over,
fall back asleep until Mommy did come
—a fury in black ponytail and red lipstick,
tearing back the covers, ripping the pillow
from his head. Under the banner of housework
she'd start in on the rugs. We'd flee for the bus,
while behind us the roar of the vacuum
roused the living dead.

But if there's no easy nostalgia here, neither is there anger or self-pity. Prange simply reports the facts and allows phrases like "the roar of the vacuum" to make their point as they propel the story forward.

"Tripping the Light Fantastic" offers every opportunity for sentimentality, since it describes the speaker's dancing with her grandfather, but Prange concentrates on the harder edge of love. The grandfather was kind and generous to his grandchildren, but the poet remarks wistfully that "my grandfather never touched me." It takes a long time ("I had to grow up / and go away") for the poet to understand that his keeping a physical space between them was a purposeful part of his teaching:

> Years later,
> I understood his lesson—his distance
> a preparation for the dialogue of gestures
> that would be my heritage with men.
> Read the signs, he taught me,
> no matter how small and inscrutable.

Still, there was one acceptable moment of physical closeness—a dance around the Christmas tree to a "new Tina Turner tape"—and the speaker recalls it happily:

> I leaned against the strength I trusted
> in my grandfather's arm and he bent me back

against the suppleness he trusted in my spine—
low, lower still, until my hair swept the floor
and I threw back my arm for balance.

"Tripping the Light Fantastic" is a poem about reconciliation, the
granddaughter coming to understand and accept the wisdom of the
grandfather. There are other poems here with a similar theme—"Her
Father's Daughter," "Her Dream of Clay Pigeons," "The Burning
Bush," "Wild Apples," "With What Is Left"; each of them presents an
uncomfortable situation or disturbing truth with which the speaker comes
to terms at the end of the poem. But none of the reconciliations is easy,
each requiring some measure of determination.

"One on Whom Nothing Is Lost" offers the most problematic example. Down-and-out men on the street annoy the speaker ("Hey girl, hey
girl, they said, / hey, girl on the sidewalk"), but she loses neither her
sympathy for them nor her composure. She chooses to believe the one of
them who had told her she was going to heaven when she gave him a
handout. Finally, though, her compassion is sorely tested:

> The last wino I talked to didn't want
> any money. Seated on the library steps,
> he wanted to know, he said,
> if I thought my mouth big enough
> to go around his dick.

She retains her bravery and sense of humor and pretends to consider his
question seriously; "I found the call numbers for geometry, / for sex ed-
ucation, for the bible / and the seven deadly sins." When she goes outside again the wino has departed, but she hears someone making chirping
sounds at her in the mocking manner peculiar to angry street people.
Then Prange locates the source of the calling, and the poem ends with a
moment of comprehension that characterizes the strongest qualities of
Dangerous Neighborhoods:

> Then it was only the black-capped sparrow
> lounging in a tree. One more bottled spirit
> making his music from the inside out.

Lynn Powell's *Old & New Testaments* offers poems as hard-angled as those of Marnie Prange, but there is little feeling of reconciliation. Powell prefers the open-ended poem in which discomfiting situations are not resolved and thorny questions go answerless. Her deeply felt religion seems to flood into every niche of her life, but more to perplex than to console. When in "Notoriety" her daughter asks the poet, *"Mommy, / what's the baddest thing that can happen to somebody?"* she does not reply. During the course of the book, however, one comes to believe that the answer might be: *To be Jesus, or the mother of Jesus.* That thought surely stands behind her sonnet "After Bonsignori":

> He's damp from his bath and mad as hell,
> so I nurse him naked as a baby Jesus.
> His mouth, quick and expert, eases
> my tense breast. Kicks loosen the towel
> till it falls aside and reveals the voluptuous
> child, boy-orchid and tiny nipples alert.
> My hand feels the work of his eager heart.
> Now I know what could crush
> my life.
>   The earth moves us into frank noon
> while at Castelvecchio the light grows mild.
> A sound of heels and the door pulling shut.
> Each Mary alone now with her only child.
> Warmed just by a meager shirt,
> one's already sleeping on a bed of stone.

The pressure of religion upon childhood is Lynn Powell's most constant theme, informing not only "Nativity" and "After Bonsignori" but also "Raising Jesus," "Creed," "The Calling," "Sword Drill," and others. Sometimes this influence is seen as a regrettable necessity, sometimes as a source of hope.

"Judgments" is not hopeful. In this poem the speaker's daughter is busy crayoning the "Picture-the-Bible Coloring Book sent / from Great-Grandma." While the radio reports news of the Gulf War and President Bush's gratitude to God for the Iraqi dead, the little girl is distressed to discover what the biblical phrase "burnt offerings" means. Logic dictates that she use red to color the slaughtered animals in her coloring book, but her natural compassion chooses a different hue:

> My child frowns at the opened book, intent
> on the sacrifice. Then slowly, with lavender,
> she cools the covenant,
> salves the unsuspecting lamb.

Probably most people make peace with the hardest terms of their religion by turning a lavender-tinted gaze upon them, but the little girl's aversion stems from motives less self-serving than those of adults.

"The Calling" displays many of Powell's concerns and strategies. It recounts a childhood experience, summer Bible camp, and the speaker's decision to become a missionary to Rhodesia, a promise she makes during an especially emotional revival service: "Down the makeshift aisle I walked with the other weeping girls / and stood before the little bit of congregation left / singing in their metal chairs." Later that night, as she bathes before going to bed, she discovers a luna moth in the shower stall. She tries to frighten it away but it refuses to move, letting the speaker come so close to it that her breathing strokes "the fur on its animal back." This moth emblemizes the dire promise the young girl has made, and it represents more than that too. But the other implications of this image remain obscure. The situation is left unresolved, and the closure of "The Calling" typifies some of the memorable complexities of *Old & New Testaments*, a collection that reveals a religion valued not for its comfort but because it is comfortless:

> One by one the showers cranked dry.
> The bathhouse door slammed a final time.
> I pulled my clothes back over my sweat, drew
> the curtain shut, and walked into a dark
> pricked by the lightning bugs' inscrutable morse.

Jane Gentry's title poem opens *A Garden in Kentucky* with two stanzas that contrast a new landscape with the old one where home is located, though the dislocation here is not geographical but temporal. The old values and the new exist side by side, yet very far apart:

Under the fluorescent sun
inside the Kroger, it is always
southern California. Hard avocados
rot as they ripen from the center out.
Tomatoes granulate inside their hides.
But by the parking lot, a six-tree orchard
frames a cottage where winter has set in.

Pork fat seasons these rooms.
The wood range spits and hisses,
limbers the oilcloth on the table
where an old man and an old woman
draw the quarter-moons of their nails,
shadowed still with dirt,
across the legend of seed catalogues.

Dannye Romine Powell and Alice Rose George also employed the double landscape—the past contained within present time or imagistically yoked to it—and so did Lynn Powell and Marnie Prange, though to lesser extent. Jane Gentry explores the notion more thoroughly and openly than any of the others. Sometimes her work is unabashedly nostalgic, and it is interesting to compare her "Moving" with Danny Romine Powell's "On What Would Have Been Our Twenty-Fifth Anniversary." The latter mixes feelings of sadness and wry humor, loss and relief, into a bittersweet compote; the former speaks simply of the regret we feel at life-changes, as the speaker sweeps from the house she is deserting "broken crayons, brown / apple cores, nail parings." The life her family led here will stay on as a ghostly presence: "With all we own / gone, puzzled / like a jigsaw in the van, / the empty rooms hold / what we can't clear out / and leave here."

At least ten other poems in Gentry's collection meld past and present in a single landscape. One of the most plangent uses of this trope occurs in the last stanza of "Hungry Fire," a long work about the death by accidental houseburning of a reclusive homosexual farmer. The poem spends more time on past family relationships and historical background than on the present-time narrative but then brings everything into focus with the image of a blue-and-white china plate salvaged from "the white ash of the kitchen." A muted allusion to W. B. Yeats's "Lapis Lazuli" bol-

sters the importance of the plate as a symbol not of loss but of "miraculous duration":

> For in that plate's
> round continence, three small blue men among blue
> trees, flowers, houses, cross a blue bridge
> toward the sea, toward distant mountains, a comfort.
> Deep in its scene, far beneath its glaze,
> on the other side of the world in fact, stands
> a white house. Its windows catch the morning
> sun among green trees where guineas will clatter
> themselves to sleep in the long peaceful fire of sunset.

Of the books discussed here Gentry's is perhaps the most likable. I
don't mean that it is the most profound, the most thoroughly worked, or
even the easiest to read. It is, however, the one least fretted with contra-
dictions, least perplexed by mazes of anxiety. I certainly would not declare
it the best, but there is a calm assurance about it that makes even puzzling
poems like "Flood" and overdone ones like "Your Vacation" unobjectionable. Like Dannye Romine Powell, Jane Gentry has purposefully
chosen simplicity as her manner and has achieved shining success with it.

In the last lines of "The Whale," Gentry makes explicit the theme of
past-contained-in-present-time and shows why this theme is important to
her, why she has made it the tacit central theme of *A Garden in Kentucky*.
She tells us that while she is going through the most ordinary routines,
peeling potatoes or switching radio channels, "grief / may without warning break my face, / my everyday skin." Then she gives the reason:

> Because there was
> a summer day when the clouds overhead
> like magic slates rewrote themselves in silence,
> because the falling chatter of the chimney swifts
> at twilight sank tighter and tighter into circles
> of darkness, I know that the world does speak,
> but in all its tongues each word means good-bye.

If there were women poets who commanded as much respect in their
metier as Eudora Welty, Mary Hood, Anne Tyler, Alice Walker, Lee

Smith, Elizabeth Spencer, and Ellen Douglas do in theirs, it would be a good thing for Southern poetry. I have a distinct foreboding the tough-guy stance and the moralized anecdote that have so broadly characterized the Southern male poetry of this present generation are losing freshness and interest. Perhaps the time has come for a subtler poetry that thrives upon the kind of psychological nuance we find in Eve Shelnutt, Betty Adcock, Kathryn Stripling Byer, Martha Vertreace, and others. Though such an approach has not been lacking in some males—Rodney Jones, Gerald Barrax, and Judson Mitcham come immediately to mind—it has not been the dominant note of the ensemble. But if Southern poetry ever learns to sing to the moon instead of howling at it, we will have to thank the alto and soprano ranks, the softer but not necessarily sweeter voices.

An Idiom of Uncertainty:
Southern Poetry Now

What does it mean to be a Southern writer?

It means that interviewers ask you that question more times than you would have thought possible.

What does it mean to be a Southern poet?

That's the question they do not ask, the one that used to have a round-about, imprecise, but fairly satisfying answer. A Southern poet was some-one who ransacked his experience, or searched in familiar history, for stories or specific images that implied a world of significance he could count on his readers—his Southern readers, especially—to share. He was expected to be something of a philosopher; his metaphysics helped to lend his narrative a certain high literary tone. Such was the way of John Crowe Ransom, Allen Tate, Robert Penn Warren, and a fair number of others. If he struck an anti-intellectual pose, as did James Dickey and his friends in their I-kilt-me-a-bar-and-chawed-off-his-hide poems, then it was recognized that Romantic Primitivism was the philosophy he es-poused. The story and the image constituted an old-time religion, and if it was good enough for Billy John the father, it was good enough for Jim Bob the son.

But that cozy camaraderie has begun to drift from the fireside. The cool twilight shadow of self-consciousness begins to steal over Southern poetry, dessicating echoes to whispers, contorting tropes into reflexive shapes. There is more complication in the fabric of the thought; whether there is more complexity is debatable.

James Applewhite's *Lessons in Soaring* is a case in point. Applewhite in his earlier volumes has been a careful delineator of the local, the pungent, the quintessentially Southern. As lovingly as any artist named Wyeth, Applewhite has presented us the immediate: the tobacco leaf, the brackish river, the savor of heat and pine woods, the smell of the barbecue pit.

He still does so, but now one can hear an undertone of distrust in the lines. "I depict the pegged, / Heart pine, Civil-War-era farm-house: / This clipper ship structure afloat on the vernacular / Fields." True enough. The tall house and the family that inhabits it, with their beautiful customs and their slow unexamined pieties, have made up much of this poet's subject matter for a long time. The poem concludes, however, with a demurral:

> But no more than a ship in a bottle
> Encloses the sea do these light lines embody
> The dark swells below these graves.

Two companion poems, "Good as Dad" and "Back Then," are actually heartfelt critical attacks on Southern folk attitudes; the latter denounces sexism, the former is an excruciating portrait of the kind of redneck who is neither quaint nor appealing.

The title of one longish meditation, "The Failure of Southern Representation," is symptomatic. The South's representation of itself is vitiated by sentimentality and vain distortion of history. "The columned, white plantation / Invents itself on front porches now wholly vanished, / Inherited from fictitious aunts, fabulous uncles." But that is not the whole of it. The harder task for representation is to portray the paradoxical nature of the place in a comprehensible way. The South is still cognizant of its history, still "furious with its phantoms." But contemporary time, "commercial assault," comes to it relentless. The romantic past is still with us—Applewhite points toward "the stelae in Confederate cemeteries"—but it has fallen silent. Now all is given over to the interests of business enterprise, "eighteen-wheelers / At docks in Atlanta, the diesel thug thug, / The tin clang of dimes buying polyester scarves."

No one escapes, not even the poet. In "Sweet Poison" he too yields to the blandishment of economic comfort: "I turn toward home, wanting a beer, / Glad my wife and I can afford / A new sofa. Money is delicious, / I sigh, like flesh."

Lessons in Soaring is a winning volume, substantiated by Applewhite's wonted seriousness of purpose. But surely its history is faulty. There was never a time when the South was uncommercial; the unhappy bases of its old economy—slavery, cotton, and tobacco—were what set its interests apart from those of the other states. For all his determination to confront the new, Applewhite still subscribes to the Agrarian fairy tale about antebellum culture. It forms the ground of his critical stance when he looks at the South about him now.

Robert Morgan seems at first inspection to have retained his faith in the power of the image to imply a multifoliate shared history. Even Southern readers for whom Appalachian culture is a touch exotic have responded to Morgan's poems about smokehouses and slop jars, glossolalia and corn cribs. *Sigodlin,* his eighth fine book of poems, continues his accustomed usages with poems called "Grandma's Bureau," "Writing Spider," "Moving the Bees," "Baptizing Trough," "Broomsedge," and so forth. Morgan also continues in his habit of writing poems about scientific phenomena, so that we find "Inertia," "Radiation Pressure," "Shadow Matter," and "Jet Trails." He has always balanced these two sorts of subject matter in his books; scientific observation has been a way for the poet to link the homeliest rural objects and activities to universal constants.

"Purple Asters" nicely illustrates Morgan's method. The poem takes as its subject those wildflowers that bring a purple cast to the fields in "late summer / and early fall" when we notice "the first purple / puffs on thistles" and see "the joe-pyes / lean like giraffes above the undergrowth." Then the poet employs a learned comparison that gives his image both a scrupulous visual precision and a dimension of historic import that broadens his context to the widest extent:

> Down by the branch, grass
> darkens the same color Charlemagne had
> his Irish scholars dye their pages for

> jeweled lettering to play on like cities
> in the desert sky.

The aura of history and legend the trope produces is warmly suited to the sense of late-season mellowness the poet intends.

"Deer Stands" uses a similar strategy to similar purposes. The poem begins by simply describing some kinds of these casual constructions. "Some are no more than a slat nailed / across the forks of an ash tree," Morgan observes, but "others / are reached by rough boards for rungs up / the trunk to the platform." In these ramshackle lodgments hunters wait for deer to browse in the clearings below, where they can get clean shots at them with their .30-30 rifles. Easy pietism will find deer hunting a bloodthirsty business, but close concentration upon his image brings Morgan to revaluate the nature of the activity; he sees the deer stand as

> a perch tiny as the porches
> the ancient ascetics sat on
> for years above the desert's and
> their own temptations, looking down
> on the world as the visions
> and love's most vivid and ghostly
> exultations wandered near them.

Someone is bound to object that the deer hunters they know have little in common with the ancient saintly hermits, but Morgan's appreciation of the similar qualities of desire and asceticism between the two vocations is a subtle one and points up the remarkably democratic view of poetry he holds. Every object is equally open for equal treatment in his art, the minute as well as the grand, the homely and the gross as well as the glorious and the conventionally beautiful.

As scientific data become more tenuous and theoretical, however, they become harder to assimilate into local context. "Shadow Matter" describes the possible antiuniverse that mirrors our own in a "dark brother- and sisterhood," though it does little more than describe, and "Dung Frolic" treats its subject in the same way. Both are good poems, but they lack the implicative power of "Moving the Bees," "Drop the Handkerchief," and "Ninety-Six Line." This last poem claims as its subject the dividedness the poet feels as a native of the old Appalachian wilderness and as a highly educated citizen of the late twentieth century. He has placed, he says,

> one foot in the English
> country, one in the high dark
> hunting ranges, and felt a chill
> when stepping across to either
> imaginary dominion.

Even Robert Morgan might predict, though probably with real regret, that as time goes on, as both regional history and scientific theory become mistier and less certain of their old truisms, his task will become more difficult. One poem here, "Rearview Mirror," is a brief meditation upon the nature of time, and it voices some of the poet's natural dismay:

> This little pool in the air is
> not a spring but sink into which
> trees and highway, bank and fields are
> sipped away to minuteness. All
> split on the present then merge in
> stretched perspective, radiant in
> reverse, the wide world guttering
> back to one lit point, as our way
> weeps away to the horizon
> in this eye where the past flies ahead.

Politics too has come to darken our dear old red-clay-and-cornpone commonplaces, but for the past couple of decades Southern poets have largely ignored contemporary politics. Even in the clamorous 1960s they wrote scant protest poetry. Perhaps they felt defensive. The main tenor of Southern politics was harshly illiberal during those years, and it became difficult to attack reactionary attitudes without seeming to attack the South. And as long as the South was under attack from other parts of the country for her political views, most of her poets would stand by her. But now that some other areas—Boston, for instance, and Los Angeles and New York and Philadelphia—have revealed their own shams and shames in racial issues, politics has become fair game for Southern poets.

Some had spoken politically all along—Lee Howard and Jim Wayne Miller, William Harmon and James Whitehead—but their political views were usually secondary to other issues. Recently poets like Rodney Jones and C. K. Williams and T. R. Hummer have begun to allow politics to color their lines. The result in the case of Hummer's *The 18,000-Ton Olympic Dream* is an access of power, but of darkened power, a force less clear than that produced by the narratives and lyrics of his earlier volumes like *The Angelic Orders* and *Passion of the Right-Angled Man*. The conclusion of "The March Personifications" will show what kind of force I refer to:

> The old patriarchal world, the old lie of the derelict self
> Degenerate here, and the stranger in the residue
> Fumbles the brown bag from under his arm,
> Slips out the bottle, breaks the seal, and takes
> One small hit of cheap whiskey, to let its chemical bite
> Of faintly tinted back alley peatsmoke take him farther down
> Toward the shattered edge of the rain, the place he came from.

Hummer's title poem is about an oil tanker named *Olympic Dream* that sank in the Mediterranean in 1987 at the same time the Irangate scandal became public. The poet was residing in Cornwall at that time, and the incident as he followed it on television drew him into questions about his national and personal identity. He found himself "vaguely ashamed" of his native country and his manner of speech: "my voice / An indelible brand no amount of goodwill / Or cautious politics can hide: American." But even though his poem is a protest poem, Hummer doesn't feel sure of his ground; worse than being politically incorrect is to be smugly self-righteous:

In the stop-time of this illusion
Of dramatic guilt, this pitiful
And suspicious effort
                    to be political, liberal,
I could say *My friends wake up*
And the rented car, American,
Takes us west to Land's End,
Ourselves again, healed and whole.

He despairs of achieving this happy resolution because he doubts the basis of his judgment: "The truth is, I / Don't seem quite right myself."

"Bluegrass Wasteland" is a forty-two-page poem which tells the story of a love affair in Mt. Vernon, Ohio, "a place of various edges." This subject would seem to be safe—in the United States, at least—from political intrusion. But not for Hummer. He often breaks into his narrative to talk to himself about his purposes and methods, and he has decided that not even the most personal incident has real meaning until it discovers its relationship to historical context. When he chooses a single image (a memorial statue to the Union dead in the town square) to supply a gravitic center for his speculations and narrative incidents, the poet is irked by his self-consciousness: "This is the voice / Of desperation, looking for a method / To speak of these things without alienation, without scorn."

He observes at night that other lovers carrying on affairs in their "love-cars" circle the statue and that it serves as a rendezvous point even as it staunchly preserves a fine reactionary integrity:

Rhetoric thrown against the unyielding cold
Surface of statue-pedestal, circumventing every word
Of cynicism, irony, criticism, scorn, doubt,

Denying the existence of illusion, denying error and sin,
Obliterating the private life except as it gives itself up
Pro patria: voice and countervoice

Collide, cancel out, resurrect themselves,
Renew each other, wrestle toward death, desire each other
While the center of town trembles its silent detonation.

The passage is overwritten because the statue is overread; Hummer has asked his image to carry too much contemporary baggage. He must rely too heavily on the image of the statue because his story line is inadequate for the significance it must bear. T. S. Eliot might say that "Bluegrass Wasteland" lacked an "objective correlative," and Hummer admits as much himself: "There is no true or adequate story," he says.

Aristotle and I believe that the poet is mistaken, that the narrative vehicle he needs to support his almost ponderous meanings is out there somewhere in America awaiting him, but he has failed to light upon it. Even so, his conviction that our present time supplies no such story is heartfelt and helps to give *The 18,000-Ton* Olympic Dream much of its surly power. T. R. Hummer is one of our very best.

If the desertion of accepted certainties from science, history, and philosophy has begun to undermine the poets' sense of Southernness, an even more powerful force for disintegration would be the lack of assurance about one's identity within the family. Cleopatra Mathis, the earnest and talented author of *The Center for Cold Weather,* explores this situation with some thoroughness. It has been a characteristic of the poetry of Southern women to examine, often in intense and rather thorny fashion, the relationship between the speaker and her family. Volumes by Eleanor Ross Taylor, Betty Adcock, Ann Deagon, and Heather Ross Miller offer vivid illustrations. Of course, the family is a staple subject for Southern narrative, but the female poet has found a sharper, pricklier way of handling it than the male poet, and she is edgier even than her sister in fiction.

The dilemmas of her identity come at Mathis from different directions. In regard to her dead brother she is a grieving sibling, and to her parents she renders full filial devotion. She feels rather distant from her Greek heritage, but still she celebrates it and enlarges upon its importance. She feels perhaps more clearly her displacement as a Southerner from Louisiana to New Hampshire.

"Grace: Two Versions" exhibits the contrast between South and North. Vermont in September of 1986 represents "safety," with "Animal, vegetable, everything proven / around me in this clatter, the manifest / color in motion." The animals that emblemize Vermont are "a family of raccoons, fat / clowns in the business of climbing porch posts." But the portrayal of Louisiana in 1954 begins with a warning. "Stick to the waterways, they said." And the representative animal is no clowning raccoon.

> I was seven,
>> shaky with the cursive S
>> I practiced in swamp, silence, nest—
>> meaning snake. I moved, open-mouthed, sliding
>> indirectly through the tangle
>> to the stumpy clearing of solid ground;
>> cutting my teeth on worry, the eventual
>> suck and spit, the rehearsal at supper
>> of what to do if and Jesus saves.

The childhood memory of the Southern swamp is more vivid than her present situation. And even when she looks at her infant daughter she experiences a "spooky / bilocal vision," seeing in the baby's face "others / in places where I was not." She sees there the features of her dead brother and cannot dismiss this revenant of her Southern past:

> Be sensible you say,
>> eager to call any trick of sight
>>> double vision, or afterimage, the guest of sight
>> riding the rooms we live in, as a prism
>>> manages to touch and roam.
>> I tell myself, be sensible.

But how is she going to be sensible? She is still a Southerner, still oppressed by the Southerner's inheritance of the memoried past and the South's overwhelming natural landscape. In "August Arrival" she experiences once again the return of her brother: "And all the past lies down for the ordinary / and triumphant scene on this one morning," she says, and concludes the poem with the sort of bold expression of faith that Southerners resort to with little hesitation.

> And we rise, unburdened, all of us who believe
> you are alive, not dead at twenty-six in D'Arbonne, Louisiana.

Cleopatra Mathis is not exactly easy to read because her determination to face all her emotions at once is an ambitious one. Yet the ambition gives her work a hard honesty and a durable steadiness of presentation.

The difficulties Mathis presents are much less formidable than those of Bin Ramke's *The Erotic Light of Gardens*. Ramke is one of our most challenging contemporary poets, and he may well be one of our most rewarding. He would seem to have a horror of uttering a cliché or of saying anything that might smell of the obvious. It is a real shock to find now and then a trite phrase (in "Tarzan and the Slave Girl," for example, he refers to "the sound of one hand clapping"); these infrequent lapses show that he has smartly succeeded in keeping his presentation oblique, his allusions sophisticated, his language highly suggestive.

Southern poetry has offered us few practitioners of the sort we might compare to Laura Riding or Charles Tomlinson, poets for whom poetry is a method of investigation more than a dramatization of foreknown attitudes. In trying to fix Bin Ramke somewhere in the literary landscape, one has to imagine his reading Allen Tate's "Ode to the Confederate Dead" with admiration but little sympathy, and reading James Dickey's "The Sheep-Child" in cold disbelief. Ramke's skepticism is so thorough that it begins by distrusting the irony that is its tonal mainstay.

He is given to sententiae which he will revise in order to expose their fallaciousness. "What the Servants Thought" begins by saying, "It takes time and it takes distance / to tell the truth or lie"; "Figure in Landscape" avers that "art is the mere manipulation of memory, after all"; "Harvard Classics 16, *The Thousand and One Nights*" opens with what will seem a flat preachment: "The lives of former generations are a lesson to posterity."

But the three poems in which these statements appear transmute and even refute them as the lines develop. In fact, each of the statements serves to introduce an unfolding of thought wherein the statement itself is doubted and mocked. The lives of former generations might offer some sort of lesson—but only "if the telling of tales could save lives and virginity / and teach that nobility lies in complexity." In Ramke's poem, storytelling is merely aggrandizing itself, claiming a heuristic nobility that it may not possess. In the second part of the poem the speaker compares Shahrazad's web of stories with youthful daydreams of warrior glory debased by the untruths of politics, and Ramke ends his strange comparison with a fleering repetition of his opening sentence.

> I played soldier among the trees
> killing quite adroitly quaint masses
> of enemy—plenty to choose in the fifties,
> Germans, Japanese, Koreans, the faint
> remaining trace of Indians.
> The lives of former generations
> are a lesson to posterity.

Most poets would probably be content to end here, the point rawly made. But Ramke—characteristically—pushes the thought further, telling us that little boys' pretend-wars are a form of pastoral because removed in time and distance; they are like "sheep grazing / beneath the cedars of a far hill, / a simple oriental pleasure like Lebanon."

The word "Lebanon," however, no longer holds the same pastoral associations as in an old phrase like "cedars of Lebanon," and its contemporary associations of violence and ruin alert the speaker to its anomalous qualities; perhaps "I slept through it all," he says, referring to "the night / without end," and "perhaps lived better than I knew or loved."

The poem then returns to the career of Shahrazad, remembering that her storytelling was unavailing, that the king killed "out of fear / of repetition, his sultry modern mania / for the original, for verse without reverse." And that should be the end of it, the web of narrative-within-narrative torn brutally, arbitrary force victorious over imagination. Yet it is not. The storytelling that was ineffectual for Shahrazad is in the course of later history triumphant:

> There followed a thousand further versions.
> There followed the consideration of histories
> of preceding ages, and the contemplation
> of the woman's flesh, the veil and flimsy fabric,
> that he might be constrained
> spread out as he was on this earth like a bed.

"Harvard Classics 16" is a suggestive, fertile, provocative, and sometimes perplexing poem. These qualities make it typical in Ramke's work.

Some of his poems—"On Hunger as Hardest of Passions," *"Compulsion* as the Critical Element in a Defined Perversion," *"Es Könnte Auch Anders Sein"*—have remained utterly opaque to me. Others—"One View of the Wide, Wide World," "The Future of Supplication," "Calculating Paradise," "Elegy as Origin"—disclose their beauties and some part of their import with patient reading.

But never does one feel cheated. The difficulties here are not artificial, not manufactured to make the poems or the poet look clever. Ramke exhibits his work in an apparent spirit of cool disinterest, a manner we might associate with poets of the New York school, but he engages with his subjects in a thorough intellection; he does not skirt round them with teasing mannerisms.

When he chooses to write a more straightforward poem, he is as potent as any of his less indirect colleagues. At first glance, "The Private Tour: Circle 7, Round 3" seems a surprising piece to find in this collection. It is a reminiscence of a boy's visit to a hydroelectric plant with his father and tells of the boy's admiration and his later adult affection, grateful and wistful. The poem makes a strong impression, partly because it is more personally revealing than most of the other work in *The Erotic Light of Gardens.*

What boy doesn't, once, admire his father?
There was nothing to be known he didn't know,
that day, about water. I entered behind him
great electrical caverns where cascades like
the tropics fell cleanly to cool air
for operating rooms; I crawled with him through
boilers down, bulging with rust and power.

He taught me to titrate, and to pronounce
fine-grained words, and to think full phrases
like parts-per-million, like Erlenmeyer flask.

When a man dies he divides the world precisely
as any chemist can. Having ridden the beast
he tells his child, I will ride between you
and the tail, lest you be poisoned by it.

Clear, open, gracefully phrased, warmly felt. The poem would seem to be uncomplicated by Bin Ramke's characteristic dark ironies until we recall that Dante reserved Circle 7, Round 3 of his inferno for the violent against God. Then, once again, the mordant tone of self-consciousness asserts itself, and "The Private Tour" firmly takes its place in the purposely infirm idiom of contemporary Southern poetry.

First Night Come Round Again

End as they may, classes in Creative Writing: Poetry, which is numbered in the university catalogue as English 527, begin in desperate fear. It is hard to say who is the more terror-stricken, the students or the instructor. An unengaged observer might guess that the instructor is afflicted with the feebler nerves. He has arrived twenty minutes before the start of this first class of the semester and has already made three visits to the water fountain down the hall. Each time he has returned to his customary seat he has seemed gloomier, more uncertain that human existence bears comprehensible purpose.

He had to come early to Barton Lounge—a seedy faculty meeting hall that serves as the writing classroom—in order to establish that the couch seat under the hanging lamp, the only area here with good light, is indeed his customary seat. If a student occupied it by mistake, there would be no diplomatic way to claim it and the instructor would be reading manuscripts in eyestraining half-dark for four months.

The disadvantages of early arrival make themselves apparent. The students come in one by one; they spot him in his well-lit seat and disconsolate mood; they identify him as their instructor—but now what? He doesn't yet know their names or anything else about them. There is no opportunity for conversation, neither chitchat nor earnest discussion of the philosophy of literary composition. Those students who are already acquainted with one another may murmur banalities, but there is no ease.

All the students must try simultaneously to acknowledge the fact of the instructor's presence and to pretend that it is of no consequence. But they are taking minute stock; he feels their secret glances on him like the crawling of invisible centipedes.

And he *hears* their questions, the ones they will never ask him, the ones they are scared to put to themselves. The atmosphere of doubt in the room is as thick and suffocating as smoke from a tar-pit fire. What am I doing here? the students wonder. How did I ever undertake such a fool venture? If I really want to write, why am I not on a tramp steamer, plowing the wild South Seas, squinting at the seabirds mewing as they wheel? Isn't it perfectly true that—as my parents, teachers, friends, acquaintances, and passing strangers have informed me—*creative writing cannot be taught?*

Perhaps they would like to be reassured. Perhaps they would like for the instructor to snap out of his dour trance at this instant and exclaim: "Don't worry. Be happy. There are only a very few tricks involved in the writing of poetry and after I show you those, the path is open before you. Nothing can stand in your way."

He is not able to say these sentences because he is assailed by the same doubts as the students: What am I doing here? Where are my lemon-scented South Seas with palms and sarongs? How much time for my own writing will I be able to shoehorn into this semester? But he does not ask the question about whether creative writing can be taught or not. He does not have to; everyone he has ever met since he began teaching this class twenty-five years ago has asked it of him.

It is impossible to express the virulence of his hatred for this question. Those who ask it either understand its implications or they don't. If they don't, then they are so obtuse they must fall below any limit of social comprehension that qualifies them as human. If they do, then they are casually malicious.

But can anyone really teach creative writing?

Meaning: You, sir, are a fraud and a parasite; you set yourself up to teach the unteachable, to say the unsayable; you lure gullible young fools into your clutches, fill their heads with nonsense, delude them with lurid fancies and vain dreams, waste the most precious hours of their young lives, win their confidence and even their affection with false promises, receive a living wage for your perniciousness, avoid like the coward you are the responsibility of taking a respectable Ph.D. degree, fleer at the Department's dress code, behave outrageously at parties, become much too familiar with your students, absent yourself from campus in order to score literary junkets, and affront your colleagues with local public readings of your own obscure scribblings.

Tell us this, Mr. Creative Writing Teacher, how do you go about instructing someone to be a genius? Do you discuss the Secrets of the Human Soul at greater or shorter length than the Care and Feeding of Revelation? If I come into your class and take observant notes and turn in my stories on schedule, will I land a title on the best-seller list and win the Nobel Prize? If not, then where the hell do you get off?

The instructor has long ago formulated short answers to these queries that are really accusations in barely polite clothing. "I don't teach creative writing so much as creative reading," he says. "We spend our time on structural and stylistic analysis." When he tires of the long reply he may aver, "You cannot teach students how to write, but you can teach them how not to write." Or when he trusts that there is a modicum of good will on the part of the questioner, he may essay an epigram: "Creative writing cannot be taught. But it can be learned."

Sometimes, though, his patience has been so thoroughly mauled that he must bite his tongue. He too could ask leading questions. He might ask the physician if all his patients enjoy long and healthy lives because of his care and escape death at the last. He might inquire of the minister if every member of his congregation is guaranteed a refulgent throne in heaven. He might request that the farmer disclose how he manages to get the right mixture of rain and shine for his crops and germinates every seed.

To the graduate professor of literary studies he might say, "Is it really possible to teach scholarship? How do you ensure that your students will never make errant literary judgments or ascribe anonymous manuscripts to the wrong authors or fall for ridiculous Shakespearean hoaxes? Which of them have you cultivated so carefully that he or she must become an Edward Gibbon, a Barbara McClintock, a Michael Ventris, a Helen Gardner? Are you not, sir or madam, an arrant fraud, misleading the impressionable younger or almost desperate older students into believing that by memorizing current reference procedures, gaining some acquaintance with computer networks, and acquiring a few broken phrases of German they are in some fashion contributing to the sum of human knowledge? What have you vouchsafed your prize candidate by granting him a Doctorate in Philosophy for his dissertation on Gender Confusion and Displacement in the Minor Dramatic Works of Neil Simon?"

It may be true that creative writing cannot be taught and that the whole notion of the enterprise is phony, but it is demonstrably less fraudulent in intention and in result than the other fantasies our universities promulgate. Because to begin with, I, as a teacher of writing, promise only failure. That is my one guaranteed product. I deny the concept of literary success; I maintain that if someone's happiness is dependent upon literary good fortune then that person's life is diseased.

As for a teaching job, I can promise only that in the unlikely event a writing student is able to land one, he will receive a lower salary than his colleagues with traditional degrees and his prospects for advancement will be dimmer and that once a week without fail—rain or shine, hurricane or halcyon, fire or flood—one or another of his colleagues will accost him in the hall to inform him that creative writing cannot be taught. They will wink and smirk; they will let him know they see through his little game.

Hard thoughts these—and yet they are not the considerations that have made our instructor sit here now so glum and apprehensive. He knows that this question about the feasibility of teaching the subject is not the one that most deeply troubles the students. Nor are the most obvious ones the most distressing: "What are you going to do for me? When will I be rich and famous?" The questions at the bottom of the cold gray dread that possesses everyone present are these: "Are there matters at stake, hazards and pitfalls, I don't know about? If I choose writing as a way of life, can I ever be happy? Will I be transformed, changed utterly from what I am now into a creature I cannot recognize? What is the worst, the absolute worst, that can happen as a result of my choice?"

The worst thing that can happen is that the student will give up writing and become one of those who wander the halls of English departments, muttering in a trance-state the sacred formula: Creative-writing-cannot-be-taught, creative-writing-cannot-be-taught, creative-writing-cannot . . . But this catastrophe shall not take place because the persons who seriously put themselves, for even a short period of time, through the disciplines of trying to compose worthwhile fiction, drama, or poetry understand that the question has no practical meaning.

It doesn't matter in the least whether the craft can be taught or not; as long as it can be learned, as long as its essentials can be acquired by close and sympathetic reading or by imitation of established authors or by dogged observation and unremitting application or by any means whatsoever, it makes no difference whether writing can be taught by wise sages to eager students or picked up like a social disease on a congressman's fact-finding mission. The only important thing is the page that is produced; if it is true and beautiful the means of its production are almost entirely irrelevant. That fact is the first and last thing to keep in mind—and it is the one rarely understood by those who do not write.

Most academic students do not go on to become purely professional scholars. They become teachers and they then discover that this profession offers so much challenge and so little reward that to double hardship by adding on the second profession of scholarship proves very difficult indeed. In order to garner salary raises and achieve promotion, they find it necessary to undertake a modicum of research, but this research does not present itself as their first responsibility, nor does it take first place in their affections.

The case is much the same with those who have taken degrees in creative writing; the trials of composition and the relentless assault of rejection stop off their literary careers before they begin. If they teach in colleges, this is the point where they usually start to take up regular academic careers, going through the Ph.D. ordeal, publishing a few papers, struggling up the shaky ladder that someone is always trying to pull out from under them. A degree in creative writing is no hindrance to teaching or scholarship. In fact, since the kind of close analysis that workshops emphasize is what undergraduates are expected to learn, many discover it to be a durable asset.

Some few creative writing graduates are able to fulfill their double dream; they find a job teaching and have some little success in writing. *The Gruesome Horsecollar Review* accepts a couple of sonnets; then *The Agni Review* publishes the lengthy sequence "A Night of Pure Sauerkraut," and finally *The Sewanee Review* or *Poetry* or *The Kenyon Review* accepts three brief lyrics on the birth of the poet's second daughter. He makes certain that the chairman of his department is aware of these glad tidings and he keeps plugging away, pinching pennies but not coeds, keeping a dutiful straight face during committee meetings, and turning in student evaluation reports that give him praise so unqualified it amounts almost to adulation—just the same kind of evaluation reports all his colleagues turn in. At last the great day arrives. He receives notice from the University of Southeastern New Mexico Press that his manuscript has been accepted for publication; *The Thousand Sheep of Hector Berlioz* will be listed in the forthcoming autumn catalogue.

Now, he thinks, I have played the game by the rules and won. This book will open up the track; some sweet day I may be a full professor. But when he apprises his department head of this delightful intelligence he learns that he has *not* played the game by the rules—because they have changed the rules. The Faculty Credentials Committee has met and decided that more will be required of the creative writing staff; the equation now in place is that two published novels or three published volumes of poetry equal one Ph.D. dissertation. (The dissertation does not have to be published. Or publishable.)

Still, he has his book. He feels it is a solid achievement. If hard work makes poetry live, this volume must be splendid, for he has sweated out every iota, giblet, and semicolon. So has his wife. So has his one friend in the English department, the only other teacher here who reads modern poetry. The book appears and he and his wife go out for a dinner they cannot afford. Next day his friend comes over and they drink more beer than they can afford. He gives copies of *The Thousand Sheep* to six others in the department. Why not? They have traded greetings in the hallway; their smiles have seemed genuinely polite. He receives in reply two cards that promise the senders will read his book soon, really quite soon, just as soon as they can get some paperwork out of the way. The other card is a formal one that says in embossed gold lettering on the outside, "In Deepest Sympathy"; inside there is no message, not even a signature.

These developments do not much dampen the spirits of our struggling bard. He is no naïf, and everything has turned out pretty much as he expected. Poets are not supposed to have bright professional careers. One of his old friends, a poet he respects, once remarked that the poet occupies in the university the same niche that a jester filled in a medieval court. His tasks are to fleer and flyte and frolic, to dodge hurled hambones and empty wine jugs. The modern poet in academia is advised to defend his office the way rock bands defend their platforms in raunchy bars: tootling their music inside chickenwire barricades.

Most of the class has assembled now, sitting in chairs ranged along the walls of the room, leaving in the center the open space the instructor knows will often, in the weeks to come, fill up with uneasy silence as with a wind-whipped snowdrift. He begins to size up his students furtively, trying to look as if he is not looking at them.

On his far left, by the closed door, sits a pale, slight girl with mouse-blond hair and delicate features. Her eyes are closed, her hands clasped in her lap; she presents an appearance highly spiritual, almost pre-Raphaelite. He pegs her as a devotee of Sylvia Plath and hopes she will not identify herself with that figure too closely. The results of such an experiment can be tragic.

On her left sits a slight, bearded young man with an orange canvas book-bag at his feet. He wears steel-rimmed glasses and his black hair is a mass of tight curls. He glances jerkily from one to another of his class-mates, careful to avoid seeing the instructor. It is as if he does not want his worst suspicions to be confirmed. He is the earnest northern student, the star of his undergraduate writing classes at Brown or Brandeis. He just missed getting fellowships to Stanford and Iowa and is wondering if he hasn't made an irreparable mistake in coming to this obscure, sleepy Southern university.

Next to him is a striking African American girl with a patient demeanor and calm hands, neatly and tastefully dressed. But "tastefully" in this context means unfashionably, and in truth she is the only person in the room, including the instructor, who doesn't share in some degree the routine grubbiness of students. She is confident, she knows what she wants and believes she knows how to go about getting it. But the instructor can foresee one of the first lessons she must learn: that writing is not a ticket into the Establishment. Poetry is, beginning to end, a supremely *unrespectable* vocation.

And the young man in the cowboy hat, the Adidas, dungarees, and Beavis and Butt-head T-shirt. He slouches in the chair, his legs stretched out so that latecomers have to step over. His air is a studied casual superciliousness, easy to read. He will be comparing the work of his class-mates to that of such *titans* (his actual word) as Allen Ginsberg and Lawrence Ferlinghetti. He will become impatient with such terms as *ca-dence, closure,* and *transition* and insist that the most important element in writing is something he calls *it,* or *the thing.* "You have to hit *the thing* and move on," he will say, "nail *it* and move on." He will write explicit sex lyrics that the women here will object to on grounds of technical impos-sibility. Near the end of the first semester he will leave town and head vaguely west.

In the righthand corner perches a woman who looks to be in her early fifties. She has dressed for the occasion but seems not entirely comfort-able in blue jeans and a green plaid shirt. A notebook is already open upon her knee and she is already writing something in it with a felt-tip pen. In the large canvas handbag by her feet there will be three other pens, a safety measure. She is the only student in this class who can un-derstand that art is punishingly long and life unmercifully brief, but this means that she will rush at her poems, trying to pack everything she knows and feels into too few lines. The instructor understands her; in fact, he loves her and decides that he must cause her to laugh. If only he can get her to laugh, her work may relax and unknot into gracefulness.

The young man next to her is a bit overweight but still in fighting trim and has the humorous seedy air of a high school football coach. His costume is the most traditional of writing class costumes, a black leather jacket with a tiger and a girl in a pink bikini painted on it by his sister. He is a professional Good Old Boy; the sound of his poems will inevitably remind his readers of Willie Nelson; he will make animal noises of dis-gust whenever the instructor mentions Anthony Hecht.

Beside him sits a girl with lovely copper hair cut into bangs in front but falling straight over her shoulders in back. Her dark soulful eyes are steady on the book she is reading, and the instructor is disappointed that he cannot make out the title. She is shy but determined to acquire critical convictions and to stand by them. She is so serious about writing that she regrets just a little her youth and is considering the notion of commenc-ing a love affair simply in order to gain some experience of life. Some of the males here will be boisterous, one or two may be bullies—but this quiet girl will show more courage than any of the men because one of the most difficult elements of courage is endurance. She will be able to go on writing in the face of rejection, failure, and sorrow.

And so on down the line . . .

It is like a Dickens novel in which the characters first present themselves as rather outlandish Types, but then enlist our benevolence more strongly as we are more exposed to them. The instructor knows that he must understand that the greater part of all this posing is ironic. The poses of young writers belong to a species of practical joke; they are trying to elicit reaction from a world they believe is unironic, bourgeois, and shockable. In a few weeks much of this garish veneer will wear away; the more facile an irony is, the more onerous to maintain over a period of time. They will notice this fact about themselves, but will require more time to find it true of their writing also. By semester end, they shall barely remember their first impressions of one another; the dramatic unfolding of personality as it takes place in a writing class expunges accidents of physical appearance and calculated manner. Except for the inevitable sexual impulses, they shall begin to see each other in terms of ideas; it is a giddying stage of discovery. But it too passes, though it never passes entirely. Sweet traces shall remain. The students shall have formed loyalties that will not be apparent to them until—sometimes—decades have passed.

Reflecting fondly but warily upon his new students and the prospect of a fresh semester, the instructor realizes how accustomed he must have become to young writers, to their various physical appearances, their mannerisms of speech and dress, their drinking habits, in order to make out this sort of descriptive catalogue. These students attend other classes too; they take courses in Linguistics, Medieval Literature, Eighteenth Century Studies, and so forth. The academic instructors used to tease the writing teacher. "Your budding geniuses are a weird-looking crew," they tell him. "As soon as I walk into my first class I can pick out the MFA people."

Later they circulate anecdotes about the lack of academic discipline on the part of these pupils:

"Your Mr. Albertson asked if he could turn in a dramatic monologue about Swift rather than a term paper."

"What did you tell him?"

"I informed him that in the real world graduate students write term papers."

The MFA students acquire unsavory reputations in other areas too. It is said that they drink to excess, pursue Lawrentian—even Milleresque—sex lives, are as lazy as delta rivers, and show alarming symptoms of emotional instability. Haven't there been breakdowns, incarcerations, death threats, and suicide attempts by the members of *your* bewildered flock?

The instructor acknowledges the truth of these observations—and refrains from remarking that all these same incidents have also taken place among the regular M.A. and Ph.D. program candidates, as well as among faculty members. Instead, he makes a collegial offer: "Tell you what, Dr. Beauzeau, since the writing students are such a nuisance, why don't I advise them not to take your classes in Advanced Environmental Hermeneutics? That way you won't have to put up with them." He receives a jolly thrill in watching the unhappy expression that passes over his friend's face as he replies, "Oh, no need to do that. I'm here to teach, you know. Can't discriminate." For they both know that the MFA students are generally the best of the lot. By and large, they are the more intelligent, the more widely read, the more industrious. And it is in them that any teacher can discern a genuine love of literature.

Not that they are perfect students, by any means. Their reading is overbalanced in the direction of the moderns; they display irritated impatience when discussions touch upon books they have not read or, worse, have never heard of. They have also picked up from their academic courses the dismal habit of employing political correctness as an aesthetic standard and have become fond of claiming that their classmates' poems show unconscious biases toward various ethnic groups, economic classes, and genders. The instructor used to take pains to point out to them that their one abiding prejudice, their almost unanimous blind spot, was toward history. Like Huck Finn, they put no stock in dead people. Only a few sensationally tragic or pathetic corpses interest them: Dylan Thomas, Sylvia Plath, Anne Sexton, John Berryman. And Jim Morrison. Somehow or other Jim Morrison has entered the pantheon of modern literary figures. To the instructor this is rather like finding a plaque of Red Skelton in the Baseball Hall of Fame.

This particular reaction is one that sets him apart from his students. A few of the cheekier call him "Teach," underscoring the fact that the division between student and instructor in the writing program is never so wide as in the academic courses. In those the professor's years of intensive reading and investigation, his attendance at learned conferences, and his own ceaseless or casual researches into his subject matter invest him with authority. But the writing instructor stands on shakier ground. When he tells a student that a particular scene in a short story seems to lack relevance or purpose, he can only give his best cogent reasons for his opinion. An argumentative student may find reasons just as cogent—and to her thinking more compelling—why the same scene is a brilliant success. The impasse that results from this disagreement can usually be broken, but more times than not the instructor is satisfied to let the impasse stand. Writing is not often a rote art like bodybuilding or bus driving. Perhaps for some readers this confused scene will have meaning and interest; his task has been only to point out that in it all four characters talk exactly alike. The final artistic decision must be the student's own.

There is always this ticklish matter of how far to go in discussing a student's work. One is supposed to be helpful without interfering, the instructor believes. The heavy hand is oppressive, the careless shrug chilling. What he wishes for is a Magic Smile; he would like to be able to read a manuscript, smile upon it beatifically, and have Disney-like moonbeams of palpable influence change its missteps in sequence, smooth out its stylistic perplexities, and provide theme for pages where none can be discerned. But as Disney has failed to provide this gift to our schoolteacher, he must rely on class discussion and personal conferences.

Personal conferences are preferred for discussions of style. When a writing class discusses prose style or poetic diction it will often bog down in trivial personal association:

"I just can't stand the word *macaroon*. My stepfather was always calling me a *macaroon*. I hated that son of a bitch."

"When you use the word *moreover* in this line what exactly do you mean by it?"

"*Splurge?* Why did you put that word in? It reminds me of pulling my boot out of swamp mud."

Often young writers are at that stage when they first become acutely aware of the complexities of association that words and phrases call forth.

Words are so important to them that they take for granted that most of their subjective associations must be important too. They have learned that language has the power to suggest and they are likely to suppose that the more it suggests the greater its power. Experience will prove that language also gains power by limiting its suggestiveness in the interests of clarity—but they don't have a great deal of experience. The instructor is supposed to supply counsel from his own.

And this fact also is largely misconstrued by students and colleagues alike. What fits a teacher for instructing in creative writing is not his imputed successes. He has earned a few by now: *The Thousand Sheep of Hector Berlioz* was followed by a pretty well-received book of satiric verse called *Say What?*, then came the novel *Blue Risotto,* and the book of stories *Bermuda Delights.* His long narrative poem, *Killing Cockroaches at the Lovesick Motel,* is now in press. He has become an associate professor and the way looks fairly clear—as clear as it can look in the murky landscape of academia—to promotion to full. He has done passing well in the eyes of the administration and his department chairman; if anybody could be qualified to teach creative writing, this man is. For, look you, he hath spread his name and gained some credit on't.

But what really qualifies a teacher of writing are not his little triumphs but his failures. For if he has not made the same bonehead mistakes his students make, if he has not dropped into the same spiked pitfalls and wallowed nearly to drowning in the identical quicksand, then he has no advice. He is able to tell someone that his story lacks steady narrative pace because more than one editor has told him the same thing about some of his work; he can advise a novice dramatist that she needs a second-act curtain because he had to struggle so long to find a clinching line; he can suggest that the nervous wet-eyed girl's poem actually begins with her third stanza because he has learned—slowly and painfully—to look at all his own poems with this strategy in mind. When he says (with the properly tentative inflection), "Well, if this piece were mine, I might think of lengthening it out in the middle just a bit," what he means is: "I tried foreshortening an ending in this manner one time and it made the story halfbaked and addled. I had to learn to develop the middles of stories and to stop being so entranced with openings and closures, the glamorous parts."

But when he tries to tell his students that he has made the same errors they make, they sometimes do not believe him. They cannot see how anyone ever started so far distant from success as they are starting now. They lack, in short, confidence. To criticize—however benevolently, however courteously, however encouragingly—the writing of a young person who lacks confidence requires the diplomacy of a Senate-hearing witness, the charitable disposition of a Mother Teresa, and the bland ease of manner of a TV game-show host.

(Anyhow, that's the composite tone this particular instructor attempts to strike. Other writing teachers much better known than he display quite different strategies. Some are terrifying ogres; some are egregious clowns; some behave as if they were senior editors at *Esquire* or *The Kenyon Review;* some teach more about karate than about plot mechanics; some pursue love affairs with students of any sexual persuasion; some go over manuscripts with microscopic intensity while others fake the whole thing, rarely reading a line of student work; some insist that student work deal with certain kinds of subject matter; some insist that traditional narrative is dead and that students must compose metaliterature; some require that students read widely in European and Asian literatures; some do not allow students to read contemporary literature at all; some try to guard their charges from their own "influence," while others desire them to write just the way they themselves do. . . .

(Well, as Kipling should have said, there are a million different ways of constructing tribal lays, and every single one of them is wrong.)

But even the best efforts at diplomacy don't always work. Some students are natural Weepers. If they are told that their pages might improve with fewer adverbs, they burst into tears; if they hear that one of their poems is better than anything Auden, Marianne Moore and the instructor himself ever wrote, the floodgates open again. The instructor wants to cry out: "Look, it doesn't matter what I say—whether I condemn your dialogue or praise it, whether I treat you scurvily or award you gold stars. For a writer, criticism of his or her work always comes down to one of two words: an editor's Yes or an editor's No. And the judgment of that editor may be better than mine or it may not; what is certain is that it will be more hasty than mine, and more final."

He might go on to add that never again in this young person's writing career, whether it ceases with his graduate school experience or whether she goes on to fame and fortune in the quality lit trade, will his or her work be subject to such close and mostly friendly scrutiny. The audience one encounters in a writing workshop is necessarily small but it is the most attentive and generally the best-intentioned one that exists.

But this is another article of unqualified disbelief. Do you mean to tell me (the student would like to ask) that when a new issue of *Poetry* or *The New Yorker* appears, people don't rush to inspect the poems, to admire and memorize them, to try to figure out why the editor accepted these special lines instead of the ones we luckless others submitted? —Well, they don't (the instructor would reply). The *New Yorker* poems are mostly scanned, hurriedly or listlessly, by patients in medical waiting rooms after they have savored all the cartoons and advertisements and have tasted all the nonfiction. As for *Poetry*, it is read almost entirely by poets, a few professors, and by students to whom it is assigned in composition classes. Is it true, then (the student might ask), that more people write poetry than read it?—Yes. And that's the way it should be. Literate citizens should be expressing their thoughts and feelings on paper; their emotional lives are so furiously busy that they really don't have time for the secondhand emotions of others, no matter how genuine those feelings are or how adroitly they are presented. If the competition for publication is daunting, think how disheartening is the competition for attention that published writers suffer. It's a wonder that poetry and fiction are read at all—by anyone. Yet this situation is healthier for a writer than one in which people did little else but peruse short stories and lyric poems. As long as readers engage with the complexities of their lives in an unforgivingly factual world, they must deal with literature only sporadically and haphazardly—and this situation makes them valid critics. If they dealt only with literature in their lives (as writers sometimes imagine they would like for people to do), they could never appreciate fine work nor distinguish bad. The present situation for writers is not perfect; in fact, it is pretty bleak. But there are numerous realities that are preferable to imagined utopias.

These considerations are likely to send students into black depressions, to make them question their purposes:

"If what you say is true, then how is it possible for me to get my work published and to become known as a writer?"

"That is not possible," the instructor might reply. "Forget about it."

"It must be possible. What about Candace Flynt and Rodney Jones and

Kathryn Stripling Byer and Tim Sandlin and all the other young writers who made successes?"

"They are anomalies. Don't think about them. If you think about them you'll go crazy."

"Then, if there's no chance for me, not even the sickliest glimmer of opportunity, why am I doing this?"

Here the instructor falls silent.

He knows the answer, though, and could say that the one reason to write fiction or poetry is because you cannot help doing so. You must try to write the very best you can without thought of publication, without the least hope for any readers. Once upon a time it was possible for a young writer to look to the career of F. Scott Fitzgerald as a possible model; now it is better to think in terms of Emily Dickinson.

Is it time to begin class?

The instructor goes out into the hall for another gulp of water and returns to call the roll. He informs his charges that this is a graduate-level class, English 527, in the composition of poetry. He explains that there is no assigned textbook because, of course, they will be writing the textbook that they all shall study. There is no assigned amount of pages to be composed; it is taken for granted that they intend to write. Why else would they be here? But since many feel uncomfortable with such unwonted freedom, perhaps they should aim at the equivalent of a dozen fully completed poems during the course of the semester.

Then he tells them his name, and this is the moment of the evening he has been dreading, one of the moments he dreads most in the teaching year. For it is equally embarrassing if the students know who he is or if they do not. One can never be famous enough or obscure enough to teach a writing class.

Let the instructor be as celebrated as Ezra Pound or Robinson Jeffers, a certain number of the students already reject what they imagine to be his "vision," his way of thinking about writing, his way of looking at experience, his way of choosing experience to write about. If he or she is very famous indeed, they will resent just a little that they must stand, even now at the outset, so deeply in that fabulous shadow. The more famous the teacher, the sharper the temptation to beg easy favors—rec-

ommendations, introductions, invitations, and so forth—and then to become angry for asking. There is almost no way for the famous writer to
put students at ease; and of course there are some renowned writer-
teachers who do not desire to do so, preferring the advantages of superior position.

It is just as awkward if the teacher is unknown, or only faintly known,
as a writer. He will not readily admit it, but the student feels aggrieved
that he is not studying with a person of more consequence in the literary
world. A student is prone to think in old-fashioned terms like *literary
world, prestigious publisher, major author,* and so on. He imagines in foggy
brightness an opulent and gleaming bar somewhere in plushest Manhat-
tan; there Wallace Stevens and Edna St. Vincent Millay are having a drink
together, and they are not talking about the two slim books his instructor published so long ago. What can it mean to go out into the world and
proclaim, "I studied creative writing with Chappell," if the person on the
receiving end of the proclamation inquires, "Who the hell is Chappell?"

Though he will not do so, the instructor could tell his new friends here
that their charming passé notions of literary eminence no longer apply.
Thomas Wolfe and Ernest Hemingway share the oblivious dust with
Byron and Trollope. Not many American citizens could confidently identify the names of John Updike, Mark Strand, Wright Morris, or Richard
Wilbur. Accost a random sampling of people in an airport and ask them
to name a famous living American author. Some few of those who don't
say "Longfellow" or "Rod Serling" might mention Norman Mailer, but
you will search a long time before finding anyone who has read a book
by Mailer all the way through. An impressive number are carrying paperback copies of novels like *Do Me Again,* but if you ask one of these
readers for his opinion of its author, Sheldon Steele, he will give you a
baffled stare and mutter, "Steal Who?"

So that if the aspiring writer does achieve the fame she longs for, she
shall have impressed only a small but shrewd band of readers whose
tastes are broadly democratic. In this writing class, for example, one is
likely to find as many devotees of Djuna Barnes or Susan Howe as of
George Garrett or William Stafford.

The instructor does not tell his students these facts because he knows
that however cheerful and just he reckons them, the students will find
them disheartening. Notoriety remains general, however brief in dura-

tion—there were a few weeks in which Jack Abbott, the murderer Norman Mailer got released from prison to murder again, was the most widely known American author. But genuine literary fame, like scientific and philosophic renown, has become specialized. Even a writer anxious for fame settles to the fact that it is only a limited number of people he wants to be known to, though he wants to be known to them for a long time.

Better not to distress the students' quaint notion of fame, though, because it is a concomitant of their necessary and touching faith that good works shall be rewarded. The students still believe not only in literary fame but in the idea that recognition can be achieved if one learns to write honestly, brilliantly, and with a certain individual flair. The instructor might tell them that this is a good way to win acclaim but also an equally good way to achieve neglect. Let them go inquire of his colleagues who teach American literature their views about the poetry of William Meredith, Dabney Stuart, and Daniel Hoffman if they wish to observe how sterling quality fares in its encounter with casual indifference. Perhaps they may see too how the university all unwittingly furthers some of the worst instincts of the commercial publishing houses and how deeply academic career interests may be vested in a few established writers like Seamus Heaney and John Ashbery. Then the students may be able to take note that literary enterprise is not *free* enterprise in the finest liberal sense of that adjective; the promotion of one deserving reputation is always at the expense of some other reputation.

But if the students do find out these matters, it is still more important for them to learn not to be bitter about them. This is simply the way the situation is, and the kind of injustice that obtains in the literary ranks is motelike as compared with the larger and more urgent injustices of society. These latter concerns must be the subjects students address in their writing in some fashion, however oblique, and self-indulgent whining about the vagaries of reputation amounts to enfeebling distraction.

Sigmund Freud, who claimed to understand a great many things, also claimed to understand why writers write. They write, he said, for fame, for money, and to attract the love of beautiful women. That is a formulation so thoroughly Viennese as to be useless. Does a grown man perform any action whatsoever for reasons other than these? Well, if anyone does—if a scientist, for example, may be allowed disinterested curiosity as a motive—then Freud has not adequately described the motives of the contemporary writer, for there are easier and less gloomy ways of acquiring fame and fortune than by writing; and the favors of beautiful women have become much less scarce than those of influential literary agents.

What the instructor *will* say to his class, as soon as possible, is that the only authentic recompense for decent literary work is the work itself. Not the finished product, which is inevitably and always a disappointment, but the process of creating that product. The delicate and furious search from noun to noun, from comma to comma. The virtuous agony, the saintly tedium. When the force of literary discipline has taken solid hold of the writer's personality, even rejection and ugly critical notice are not mere disappointments but also serve to brace up resolve, have the effect of fixing the writer's attention more directly on her ultimate goals. On one large side of its nature, writing is a monastic exercise, and the hair shirt an indispensable element of its stringency.

Some of this arcana he will not yet reveal, fearing that his young friends may find it much too overbearing. As yet he will not tell them that a time is coming for them when they will welcome rewriting, even to the fourth and fifth versions, with more joy than setting down the first draft. They will certainly not believe that, and he had better not stretch their credulity too soon.

He does tell them how the class operates on its mechanical side. They are to write poems and photocopy them for their classmates, to read attentively the work of the others, and to be prepared to discuss it cogently, honestly, and diplomatically. No points accrue to brutality, none to pusillanimity. Any parade of erudition about literature, art, music, science, and political ethics is a waste of time. The Golden Rule applies: Be as useful to the poem as you would have it be to its readers.

He advises them that he will not promulgate a consistent theory of poetry. The rule in Barton Lounge is that every poem generates its own aesthetic laws and theories and is to be judged entirely on its own terms. It is the student's task to discern, by attentive regard, what those terms are. This takes practice but is less difficult than it seems once specious standards are jettisoned. The poems here are not to be compared to poems in print; a metaphysical poem will not be set beside "A Valediction Forbidding Mourning," an exercise in ironic wit will not be humiliated by the example of John Crowe Ransom.

Because no matter how much poetry they know they can never know enough. They have read Chaucer, perhaps, but probably not Petrarch. Almost certainly not Deschamps, Verhaeren, James Russell Lowell, Shenstone, or Stuart Merrill. In order to have adequate bases for comparison as a practicing poet, you have to know all poetry. And it is too easy for discussion to bog down in disputes about the comparative merits of Adrienne Rich and James Dickey. Let us then stick closely to the material that you have written.

Which means that unless you write and turn in material we shall have nothing to talk about in class. But the class will still meet, even if we must sit for three hours in silent meditation ... No, don't giggle; I'm perfectly serious.

But that's no problem. It is easy to see that you are all highly productive geniuses of the first water.

Of course, they are not all geniuses of blinding brilliance, and just as well for them too. The literary scene as she is currently observed in the United States is ill equipped to handle genius. Reading through a few literary trade journals and hearing some of the gloomier comments of his agent, the instructor has been startled to realize just how little room is left in the larger publishing house lists for the best innovative new work. It has come home to him that some of the work he most admires, books he learned to love and envy when he was learning to write, would now have to depend upon the smaller and more uncertain presses to see the light of day. *Mrs. Dalloway, Remembrance of Things Past, The Beloved Returns*— if works like these were submitted to the big trade houses with unknown names posted as their authors, junior editors would reject them summarily and no agent would be interested. In fact, he vaguely remembers that someone tried such an experiment not so long ago—and with predictable results.

But these sad facts need not be the instructor's essential concerns. He is not, after all, an agent or editor or publisher; the economic hardships of publishing he will outline for his students, but he is not obliged even to condemn them with much warmth. His task is not to see that young writers get published, but that they discover and utilize their best talents, that they have some grounding in the basics of literary expression, that they can tell a mixed metaphor from a forced simile at one hundred yards. After that—like everyone else—they're on their own.

Some of them will never publish a line anywhere. Others will publish a little, then lose interest. A few will publish a sufficient amount of quality work to land sound editorial or teaching jobs. Some will publish fine books and win prizes. A few will become ghost writers for politicians, join advertising firms, transform into hermit poets singing in the actual wilderness. One he knows of became a member of the Secret Service. Another invented a machine to make marijuana smoke more potent, and his gadget was written up admiringly in a Sunday supplement of *The Boston Globe*.

And, anyway, why would a sane person desire literary fame, or fame of any sort? The instructor's experience with media exposure is small indeed, but it has been enough to cause some awkward moments:

—An aggrieved woman, a stranger, telephoned to ask why modern books are all such morally degraded trash. She has not read the instructor's books, of course, but since he writes them he must be part of the conspiracy to tear down the Christian family and the foundations of America. His reply, that he found contemporary literature to be morally degraded at about the same degree as the contemporary Baptist church, did not mollify her.

—One of his department colleagues, meeting him in the hall, told him with a serious and troubled air, "If I see your picture in the paper one more time I'll puke."

—One of his undergraduate students dropped out of school, ran away from home, and became a successful department store manager in a northeastern metropolis. Her family blamed the instructor for what they considered the young lady's "failure." "You filled her head with poetry," her father said to him.

—In a manila envelope in his university postbox he found a paperback copy of one of his novels, torn to shreds.

—After suffering an unfavorable review in a local newspaper, he received seven copies in the mail. One of them decorated with yellow highlighter ink the severest passages. None of the envelopes carried a return address.

—The father of an undergraduate called his home one evening to tell of his own literary leanings. "I used to write some poems," he said, "but not this modern kind. I believe in the good old simple words like *love* and *truth* and *businessman.*"

—Etc.

—Etc.

—Etc.

He decides at last he has but a single thing he wants to tell this new English 527. He had remained undecided, until this very moment, about whether he would begin to teach this evening or cancel the class and go home and never return. But he wants to tell them that the poem is the only thing that counts:

"The poem is what you want to deliver, to render in the clearest possible terms. The poem is so much more intelligent than the person who writes it down that your job is always to treat it with deferential respect. Do not impose yourself upon it; do not clothe it in language strained, outlandish, or cute; do not force it to say things it doesn't want to say or make it pretend to feel things it doesn't really feel. Do not become an obstacle to its articulation. You are not the master of your material; poetry has no masters, only a company of skillful, devoted, and unobtrusive servants."

He cannot say these sentences tonight, and by the time he does get around to saying them, the students already know. If he does his job well, the instructor shall have made his occupation seem redundant.

But most of these matters, these wise and trivial disappointments, belong to the future. Now the students want to begin, and, despite his anticipation of the oncoming bone-deep weariness, the instructor wants to begin too.

He excuses himself to make a final trip to the fountain, where he drinks for a long time and, dipping his hand into the cold arc, splashes his face. He returns to the room and sits again under the best lamp. He detaches a sheet from the sheaf of copies, mutters a prayer, and then intones that ponderous, necessary, ineluctable, anguished first word of the poem, the word that heralds the onset of the furious tempest: "The."

Taking Sides:
Six Poetry Anthologies

Every poetry anthology probably shows political bias, even if its politics is only literary. For instance, the political purposes of such a volume as the extremely interesting *Chinese American Poetry: An Anthology*, edited by L. Ling-chi and Henry Yiheng Zhao (University of Washington Press, 1992), are immediately apparent. Less apparent are the biases of *The Wesleyan Tradition: Four Decades of American Poetry*, edited by Michael Collier (Wesleyan University Press, 1992), yet still they obtain in a collection that purports only to represent the achievements of one of America's oldest poetry publishing programs. William Harmon, who published three books with Wesleyan, is allowed but three poems, while Donald Justice's two books get him seven. This selection is surely just a matter of editor Collier's taste, but the result is political, since one poet is set over another. Even the most earnest attempt at fairness may come out looking wonderfully odd: *The Norton Anthology of Modern Poetry*, Second Edition (edited by Richard Ellmann and Robert O'Clair; Norton, 1988) is notorious not only for textual errors and misprints but for its deliberate omission of younger white male poets. Whatever its effects in social programs, the minority quota system is lugubrious when applied to poetry anthologies.

Perplexities remain even when the politics of selection are open and avowed and schematic, as in a theme anthology like Carolyn Forché's *Against Forgetting: Twentieth-Century Poetry of Witness*. The first problem will naturally be in trying to define "poetry of witness." Forché spends twenty-eight pages of an interesting introduction in her attempt, but she fails to settle on a logically satisfactory definition because of the enormousness of the subject and the necessary abstractness of her terms. The idea for the collection began, she tells us, as "a thirteen-year effort to understand the impress of extremity upon the poetic imagination." After that, her focus narrowed and broadened at the same time; she decided to include poems about language—poems, she says, that "bear the trace of extremity within them." This decision allowed her to include a great deal of work we would not usually classify as political, but it also made necessary some way to circumscribe her selection: "I decided to limit the poets in the anthology to those for whom the social had been irrevocably invaded by the political in ways that were sanctioned neither by law nor by the fictions of the social contract. The writers I have chosen are those for whom the normative promises of the nation-state have failed."

Such statements might sufficiently describe her reasoning if in the next paragraph she did not declare (using an almost sophistical readjustment of terms) that the social and the political are not really opposed to each other: "For decades, American literary criticism has sought to oppose 'man' and 'society,' the individual against the communal, alterity against universality. Perhaps we can learn from the practice of the poets in this anthology that these are not oppositions based on mutual exclusion but are rather dialectical complementaries that invoke and pass through each other." If these latter two sentences are accurate, then the "political" can never invade the "social" because both are but necessary parts of a single entity. Where, then, can injustice come from? Well, only from bad persons in authority, it seems, as in the "unwarranted pain inflicted on some humans by others, of illegitimate domination."

I fear that many of us will find this "evil empire" explanation rather too simple-minded, but the final test of a poetry anthology is in its selections rather than its announced rationale. Its poems should define and illustrate the intended rationale, whether or not it can be outlined with logical consistency. *Against Forgetting* includes almost all the poets who come immediately to mind when we think of political duress: Anna Akhmatova, Garcia Lorca, Nazim Hikmet, Yannis Ritsos, Paul Celan, Bertolt Brecht, et al. Some inclusions are surprising—H.D., Anthony

Hecht, Saint-John Perse—and so are some omissions. It is good to have the whole of Louis Simpson's neglected "The Runner," a poem blemished but not badly damaged by its clichés ("Santelli's death had made them strangely silent" and "They spoke; their words were carried on the wind"); but where are the war poems of William Meredith, Karl Shapiro, Richard Eberhart, and Lincoln Kirstein? Randall Jarrell's "Death of the Ball Turret Gunner" is overanthologized, but it is the definitive statement of a persona "for whom the normative promises of the nation-state have failed."

After reading a few hundred pages of *Against Forgetting*, one might begin to wonder if Meredith, Jarrell, and some others were omitted because their work was too graceful, too aesthetically satisfying, to be considered sufficiently anguished as outcry. Forché paraphrases Theodor Adorno, who wrote about Hitler's Germany that its art "rested on the social inequities and objectifying tendencies that made Fascism not only possible but inevitable." But what about the art fashioned in protest of "official" culture—the poetry that employs demotic rather than aristocratic expression, the diction of factory and wheatfield rather than of senate chamber and classroom? It, too, may be invalid after Auschwitz, claims Forché. The language of the everyday "may not present an adequate language for *witness* in situations where the quotidian has been appropriated by oppressive powers. The colonization of language by the state renders that language inaccessible to a poetry that wants to register its protest against such depredations."

Such logic, if carried through, seems to mean that no poetry can be legitimate because all art is criminal since it all serves, even despite itself, the status quo. According to Brecht's "To Those Born Later," neutrality in art is no longer possible:

> What kind of times are they, when
> A talk about trees is almost a crime
> Because it implies silence about so many horrors?

And this question of the possibility of poetry in a century of horrors occurs again and again. The Guatemalan poet Otto Rene Castillo calls down shame on the "apolitical intellectuals" of his "sweet country"; Nicanor Parra feels that he must invent an "antipoetry" because "It makes

me sleepy to read my poems / Even though they were written in blood."
Yannis Ritsos, imprisoned after the coup of the generals in Greece in
1967, bitterly records in "Not Even Mythology" that the props and fur-
nishings of one of the richest of Western cultures no longer support or
comfort:

> And later, when the lamps were lit,
> we went inside and again returned to Mythology, searching
> for some deeper correlation, some distant, general allegory
> to soothe the narrowness of the personal void. We found nothing.
> The pomegranate seeds and Persephone seemed cheap to us
> in view of the night approaching heavily and the total absence.

But if Ritsos's despair is echoed by Robert Desnos, Dan Pagis,
Tadeusz Borowski, Gertrud Kolmar, and many if not most of the other
poets represented here, his wry paradox is noted, too, and also employed
by others. Ritsos expresses his loss of hope by means of a classical allusion—springtime of spirit shall never return to the earth, the myth of
Persephone has become a falsity—at the same time that his poem decries the use of classical allusion. His attitude toward mythology is bitter, but his reference to it implies, if not a faith in its efficacy, then at least
a recognition of its inevitable presence in our modes of thinking and
feeling.

Hope's expression is so heavily contorted and fragmented that ingenuity is often hard put to find it, but there *is* hope in many of the darkest
poems Forché has included. One of Tadeusz Rosewicz's speculations in
"Questions About Poetry Since Auschwitz" is "Whether it rose up as a
small brown bird / out of the smoke of cremation ovens." Then he
avows the answer is one "that only lyric poets know / who steadfastly
call / for wild bird protection / in a world soon to be whole again." The
conclusion of Brecht's searingly ironic "From a German War Primer"
also emits a gleam of hope:

> General, man is very useful.
> He can fly and he can kill.
> But he has one defect:
> He can think.

Is there not something exorbitantly sentimental in the question of whether poetry composition is legitimate after Auschwitz? Why do we not ask if eating is legitimate after the Holocaust, or farming, fishing, talking, making love, and building bridges? Poetry is a function of the human organism as inherent as observation and digestion, and only when one defines poetry as something like "effective and politically correct humanitarian speech" can its pursuit and enjoyment be classified as illegitimate or irrelevant. Statements like Adorno's are melodramatic, and where we find melodrama in criticism we find sentimentality.

Let us suppose for a moment that all poets, even all human beings, subscribed to this program of choking off poetry. In "Voices" Primo Levi describes the condition this way: "The place we're going to is silent / Or deaf. It's the limbo of the lonely and the deaf." Does this deafness, this silence, cripple, hinder, weaken, or retard totalitarian cruelty in any way whatsoever? In fact, does not silence instead aid the progress of state-sponsored misery? To me it seems that if poetry had ceased after Auschwitz the Nazis would have triumphed in a manner very close to the one they planned: they would have changed the nature of the human organism—because as long as this organism is capable of life it will produce poetry, out of something like the same instinct whereby birds build nests. And it may be that all our poetry taken together will show about the same amount of political intelligence as a bird's nest, an amount never negligible even if insufficient to found national policies upon.

Forché's dire standards of judgment must result at last in poets being ranked by the "genuineness" of their "witness." The best poets will be those who have suffered most from oppression. At the very top will be found people who, like Robert Desnos and Otto Rene Castillo and Roque Dalton, lost their lives; then will come those who were imprisoned, and the amount of time served shall determine their respective excellence. And so forth . . .

I am not, of course, ridiculing the terrible and terrifying sufferings that so many of these poets have endured, but only pointing out that trying to measure the amount and quality of "witness" a poem offers is a dangerous and unhappy business. A good protest poem should be first of all a good poem, but *Against Forgetting* includes dozens that are—well, forgettable. For instance, Ondra Lysohorsky's "Ballad of Jan Palach, Student and Heretic" seems little more than a string of platitudes:

One man alone understood the eternal heretic:

the student whom yesterday no one knew
and whom the whole world knows today.

And he acted at once. And for ever.
Seeking the truth. A heretic. A hero.

Yehuda Amichai's "God Has Pity on Kindergarten Children" strikes me
as fatuous, especially in its first stanza: "God has pity on children in
kindergartens, / He pities school children—less. / But adults he pities
not at all." I shall never understand why kindergarten children burned,
maimed, and blinded in bombings are to be considered more fortunate
than adults who suffer wounding and torture. But perhaps I am missing
something important about the poem.

Reading through this anthology, I often had the feeling that I needed
more facts about particular poems, even though the editor has made a
noble effort to supply information. The book is divided into fifteen sections, ranging from "The Armenian Genocide (1909–1918)" to "Revo-
lutions and the Struggle for Democracy in China (1911–1991)," and each
is prefaced by a brief but informative essay in historical background as
well as by a headnote supplying a bit of biography for the individual
poets. There is also an extensive bibliography, although no publication or
composition dates are given for the separate poems, and these are sorely
missed. Ordinarily I'm no fan of heavy footnotes in poetry books, but this
is one volume where they would have been justified.

Even so, *Against Forgetting* is valuable. Its weaknesses as a poetry anthology are inherent in its purposes. Yes, too many of the poems repeat
themes, sentiments, and rhetoric; yes, flatness of language characterizes
too many of the translations; and yes, a seemingly unavoidable aura of
self-righteousness plagues the whole enterprise. Certain poems that used
to be declaimed with pious regularity at war-protest gatherings—e. e.
cummings's "(i sing of Olaf glad and big)" and Galway Kinnell's "Vapor
Trail Reflected in the Frog Pond"—now seem pat and presumptuous, for
we can see that they actually say much less than they should have said. But
the grim monotony of this volume is necessary to its effectiveness, and
not many readers are going to go through it from first word to last as reviewers must do. Carolyn Forché has succeeded well in assembling what

amounts to a reference book, one that could be especially helpful to history teachers, who must remind students that behind the dates and the place names, behind the battles and truces and diplomacy, lie immensities of personal grief so painful that all the poetry they inspire can only hint at them.

We can gain an inkling of how large the whole body of protest poetry must be by looking at *A Gathering of Poets*. This anthology was occasioned by the anniversary of a single incident—and certainly not one of the most egregious in the context of contemporary global oppression. Kent State University's Official Catalog Statement describes the incident with this paragraph: "Shortly after noon on May 4, 1970, on a grassy knoll beyond Taylor Hall and the Prentice Hall parking lot, a contingent of Ohio National Guardsmen opened fire for a period of thirteen seconds, striking thirteen Kent State University students, some of whom were nearby, others of whom were distant. Four students were killed, one was permanently paralyzed, and others were wounded in varying degrees of severity." As a historical event this massacre is probably not even as important as the mutiny aboard the battleship *Potemkin*, but it has become symbolically important to much the same extent as that famous protorevolutionary episode, and it has made an indelible mark upon the American conscience as well as upon our foreign policy.

There was a memorial gathering at the university in May 1990, and that occasion gives this volume its motive as well as its title. But the poems included are not addressed solely to one incident. There are eight sections in the book, only two of which are directly concerned with the violence and its twentieth anniversary; the other poems are ones that—to editors Maggie Anderson, Alex Gildzen, and Raymond Craig—now seem related because of the intensity of national feeling the deaths of these students brought about.

As in *Against Forgetting*, some poems are present whose relation to the context is unclear; Judith Rachel Platz's "Crossing" is a generalization about loss of innocence that seems as much out of place here as Tudor Arghezi's "Psalm" (a poem about an intensely personal religious experience) does in the Forché volume. Neither am I convinced that the 1970 tragedy adds significance to Donald Hall's "Tomorrow," a memoir of the eve of the Second World War, nor that Galway Kinnell's "The Olive Wood Fire" has much to do with the topic at hand.

When they are most directly concerned with the massacre, the poems in *A Gathering* have the most impact. In "Contemplation on Blanket Hill," Gary Scott sees the event as defining generations, marking the differences in trust of government that he and his father are willing to give:

> somewhere between his time and my time
> disbelief died
> I have never stood anywhere and said I can't believe
> this happened I still can't believe this happened I can't
> believe this happened here

In "Enough," Mary M. Chadbourne imagines, trying to pierce through the impersonality of the violence, that one of the guardsmen who fired his weapon personally shepherds the bullet inch by inch toward the young woman who is its victim. It is partly because of their lack of artifice that I find her lines moving:

> Watch the bullet as it leaves the barrel,
> watch him, as he sees it stopped midair.
> His eyes transfixed on *his* bullet, suspended there.
> Laying down the gun, there is nothing else.
> Only this young man, this day, and his bullet,
> which he slowly walks beside, his hand
> cupped gently behind it, as if guiding,
> keeping it true.

The lines are rough-hewn (a dangling participle in the fourth line, for example), but they pulse with feeling—as do the contributions by Joseph Hansen, Jeanne Bryner, Mort Krahling, Michael McCafferty, and others. These are poets less well known than contributors such as Rita Dove, Kelly Cherry, William Stafford, Alice Walker, and Marvin Bell, but perhaps literary celebrity works against the more famous. Perhaps we expect too much of them in this situation—though maybe not. I believe that Lucille Clifton's "after Kent State" would be offensive, disrespectful, and false to history no matter who wrote it:

> only to keep
> his little fear
> he kills his cities
> and his trees
> even his children   oh
> people
> white ways are
> the ways of death
> come into the
> Black
> and live

But once more the question arises: do we have a right to expect good poems in these circumstances, poems that are powerful as much because of their art and beauty as because of the situation that gives rise to them? Is it the case here that the well-crafted utterance must be suspect, and that the poet who tries to produce a good poem is to be considered guilty of unwitting complicity with the oppressors? It seems farfetched to say so in broad and open terms, but this thought gnaws at many of these poets. Again and again they address the problem of whether writing a finely tuned poem is not in some sense a betrayal.

Kelly Cherry's "The Fate of the Children," after telling us about atrocities in Cambodia, Czechoslovakia, Russia, and Vietnam, casts the dilemma in these terms:

> None of this is poetry; it is fact.
> And not only fact, but act.
> And not only act, but raw fat and warm blood, hope expiring
> like breath, and shadow
> beating a menacing tattoo on the wall of the house in a high wind,
>   like an overgrown bush,
> and I refuse to pretend it is poetry,
> seeing it is not even food.

In "Oh, By the Way," Ed Ochester tells us, "The overexamined life isn't worth living." One of the editors, Alex Gildzen, admits in "the gathering approaches" that "I sit my ass down / writing these words / wondering / if they're a poem / wondering / if I'll read this / wondering / how many friends / will send more poems." Brenda Hillman in "White Deer" feels inadequate to the situation because, she says, "I've taught too much literature." And in "May 4, 1970" Donald Hassler gives this guilt feeling (which seems to prey on academics in particular) its most elaborate setting:

> We have wasted our lives as James Wright said
> He did on bookish matters. We are lost
> In John Barth's funhouse. Design of Robert Frost
> Has been our creed, and now four kids are dead.
> We talk too much. Our wives have learned to dread
> The nights of mental exercise. The cost
> May be too great as wrinkled sheets are tossed
> Away for waste, and now four kids are dead.
> But what else could we do? The sonnet form
> Won't let us drive our horses roughly shod
> Or bull our way through virgin fields of hay.
> Analysis is all that we can lay
> Against the darkness and an absent God.
> We save what we can in a wasting storm.

The intrusion of agricultural imagery into the sestet of Hassler's sonnet, the rough-shod horses and the virgin hay, exemplifies a difficulty many of these poets encounter: they find it hard to keep focused on the event itself, wandering off into autobiography, political speculation, or ritualized propaganda. Whereas Lucille Clifton seized the occasion as an excuse for racial—or racist—statement, C. K. Williams takes the opportunity with "In the Heart of the Beast" to vent raw hatred:

this is fresh meat right mr nixon?

this is even sweeter than mickey schwerner or fred hampton right?
even more tender than the cherokee nation or guatemala or greece
having their asses straightened for them isn't it?

When Denise Levertov entitles a poem "The Day the Audience Walked Out on Me, and Why," we can all predict, without reading the poem, the reason for the audience's desertion: Levertov dared to tell the truth and these wrongheaded citizens couldn't bear to hear it.

Other poems in *A Gathering* that now seem self-serving include those by Edward Field, Alicia Ostriker, Yvonne Moore Hardenbrook, Paul Metcalf, and Jean-Claude van Itallie. The most puzzling contribution is Allen Ginsberg's "Cosmopolitan Greetings": written in obvious imitation of William Blake's proverbs of hell, its intended purposes and the motive for its composition remain unfathomable. It is a list of pseudomystical mumblings only the most dazed trance state could ever persuade to significance: "Observe what's vivid," "Advise only myself," "Mind is outer space," "Stay irresponsible," and so forth. (My perverse favorite among these dicta is "Consonants around vowels make sense," because it implies that words with the other arrangement, like *only*, *ally*, and *oboe*, are devoid of meaning.)

I suppose that common sense is not what is called for by either the occasion of the Kent State massacre or its anniversary, but when we find such thinking in some of these poems, it strikes a wonderfully clear note. After the bellowing of C. K. Williams's poem and the histrionic posturing of Sharon Doubiago ("You lie dead in the street. / I stretch the full length of my body / onto you"), Steve Posti's note of caution in "We Myopic" is refreshing. It will not be the students, townspeople, professors, or guardsmen who shall make sense of what happened, he tells us, because they are like lovers and "hold such different / memories / of the same event." Each of them brings a ready-made point of view to bear. "However, history / is not written / with such a fine and intricate typeface."

Jeff Oaks's "Determination"—one of the most effective poems in *A Gathering of Poets*—works so well because it is quiet in tone: allegorical but resonant, resolute but understanding. It is also forgiving, and forgiveness (when it becomes possible) is the most fitting memorial we can raise to the fallen.

> Among the feathers and grass
> the flies dance all day

over the sparrow pulled apart
and scattered in our front lawn.

I am determined not to say
"if only I'd come here earlier . . ."
It would spoil the dancing
I am determined to call transformation.

I am determined not to hate
the cat when he comes in tonight
and lies down beside me.
And, later, when he does come in,

a little dried blood on his chin,
I say good things: how quick
he must be to catch a bird,
how patient and quiet, how tired

he must be, the bird having fought
him terribly for its life, all
it has, all it had,
even as I have, even as I would.

Theme anthologies may be useful, as in the case of *Against Forgetting*, or they may be necessary to occasions, as with *A Gathering of Poets*. There might be a thousand reasons to put together poetry anthologies, and most of them would look plausible. But I must admit that I encountered two anthologies of poetry for men with some skepticism, not being able to guess at the editors' justifications. Are not most poetry anthologies already well supplied with hairy legs and baritone voices? Have males really become a protectable minority?

The program that informs *The Rag and Bone Shop of the Heart*, edited by Robert Bly, James Hillman, and Michael Meade, seems to be therapeutic. Anyway, that's how I understand the editors' declaration that they have "come to think that working in poetry and myth with men is a therapy of the culture at its psychic roots." The import of this volume might be summed up with a line endemic to made-for-television movies: "Hey, go ahead and cry, big fella, it's all right."

But if anyone ought to weep, it is the shade of W. B. Yeats, whose famous line (minus one crucial word) gives the book its title. His poems "A Dialogue of Self and Soul" and "A Prayer for My Daughter" have been mutilated, chopped down to fit the programmatic notions of the editors. Hart Crane and Theodore Roethke and Galway Kinnell meet the same fate, having their poems curtailed, and the editors have even had the gall to rewrite poems by Louis Simpson and Walt Whitman. But they are especially savage toward Yeats; not only are his poems shortened, but "The Second Coming" is given this jaunty headnote: "Yeats says, 'Why deny it? Christ's dark brother is on the way.' " To me this is like prefacing the Gettysburg Address with "Lincoln says: 'Times are tough, folks, but there's light at the end of the tunnel.' "

If editors are willing to brutalize poems in such a Procrustean manner, they would seem to be fitting all works into a fairly severe program. But the purposes of *The Rag and Bone Shop of the Heart* are so flexible as to seem arbitrary. The volume is divided into sixteen sections, some that make good sense and some that are hazy, to say the least. In a book of poems for men we should expect to find selections devoted to war and love and children. But we hardly expect to discover a section entitled "The House of Fathers and Titans," and we are hardly enlightened when its brief prefatory essay by Michael Meade begins with a sentence as fuzzy as pink bunny bedroom slippers: "Walking into the house of fathers means beginning in questions and entering into mysteries." There are lots of sentences and paragraphs like this one in the book, and to me they all give off the unmistakable aroma of snake oil. Worse, they slant or reduce or obfuscate or turn into propaganda the integrities of the separate and quite diverse poems, so that these may come out sounding like psychotherapy counseling, vague and murmurous and intellectually empty.

Like *Against Forgetting*, *The Rag and Bone Shop of the Heart* contains poems about language and poems that exemplify language usage of one sort or another. James Hillman offers this justification: "By teaching men to speak well, men learn to speak up and speak out. Isn't this precisely what is needed, according to Confucius, to refound society?" And so Keats's "To Autumn" is included and praised because its language is "elegantly composed of precise images," and therefore worthy "despite the romantic emotion." Why *despite*? Why shouldn't the most gorgeous of English-language poets be celebrated *because* of his romantic emotion? Or would Confucius disapprove?

Let us admit once more that the rationale of an anthology need not be logically consistent or even comprehensible for the volume to be successful; maybe all that is necessary is a solid selection of poems. Yet here too *The Rag and Bone Shop of the Heart* is erratic. There are some good poems, of course, and I am especially grateful for the inclusion of César Vallejo's "The Anger That Breaks the Man into Children," with this startling first stanza that determines the form and the equally powerful effects of the following three stanzas:

> The anger that breaks the man into children,
> that breaks the child into equal birds,
> and the bird, afterward, into little eggs;
> the anger of the poor
> has one oil against two vinegars.

Clayton Eshleman and José Rubia Barcia have made a strong job of translating Vallejo's difficult Spanish.

Other striking poems include Sharon Olds's "Saturn" and "The Guild," Li-Young Lee's "The Gift" and "The Weight of Sweetness," Anne McNaughton's cheeky "& Balls," Ruth Stone's funny "Cocks and Mares," and nifty pieces by Richard Wilbur, Thomas McGrath, Robert Hayden, Jane Kenyon, and earlier poets such as Dylan Thomas, Li Po, Wordsworth, and other immortals—among whom I do not include Bob Dylan, represented by two poems, both silly (though one of them, "Quinn the Eskimo," is purposely so). Other notably empty verses include Nikki Giovanni's "Ego Tripping," Louis Simpson's "Big Dream, Little Dream," David Ignatow's preachy "No Theory," Haki R. Madhubuti's "Men and Birth: The Unexplainable," Thomas Wolfe's bathetic "For, Brother, What Are We?"—and a sockful of like efforts. Any large anthology (this one tips the scales at 536 pages) is bound to contain a few clinkers, but here there are too many—and too many by Robert Bly. Even Bly's translations are disastrous; his version of Goethe's Erl-König ballad is rhythmically spavined, and a grammatical error ("there is still some dark remains") scars his version of "Across the Swamp" by Olav H. Hauge.

For me the ultimate emblem of New-Age-Sensitive dolefulness comes with Gary Snyder's "Changing Diapers." Rarely has such sentimentality been wedded to such lack of taste, and when in the year 2094 someone brings out an anthology called *Embarrassing American Poems of the Twentieth Century,* this one will vie for pride of place:

> How intelligent he looks!
>   on his back
>   both feet caught in my one hand
>   his glance set sideways,
>   on a giant poster of Geronimo
>   with a Sharp's repeating rifle by his knee.
>
> I open, wipe, he doesn't even notice
>   nor do I.
> Baby legs and knees
>   toes like little peas
>   little wrinkles, good-to-eat,
>   eyes bright, shiny ears,
>   chest swelling drawing air,
>
> No trouble, friend,
>   you and me and Geronimo
>   are men.

One of Snyder's implications is surely debatable: that Geronimo became a rifle-toting macho man because his daddy used to change his diapers. These shymaking lines are followed by quite a nice effort, "At the Washing of My Son," by David Ray. It harshly disserves good poems to be abutted by lousy ones in anthologies; the poo-poo aftertaste of Snyder carries over into Ray's poem.

And no poem or poet in this book escapes injury from the pretentious prefaces to the various sections. Perhaps my favorite example of orotund inanity occurs in Bly's preface to the section called "I Know the Earth, and I Am Sad":

> The growth of a man can be imagined as a power that gradually expands downward: the voice expands downward into the open vowels that carry emotion, and into the rough consonants that are like gates holding that water; the hurt feelings expand downward into compassion; the intelligence expands with awe into the

great arguments or antinomies men have debated for centuries; and the mood-man expands downward into those vast rooms of melancholy under the earth, where we are more alive the older we get, more in tune with the earth and the great roots.

I take these sentences to be an example of Deep Image philosophy or New Age psychology or Rapture mythology or whatever, and although I find them distasteful, I would not dream of denying that many people consider them not only suggestive and exciting but profound. Mysticism comes in many exotic flavors, and if I prefer that of Dante and Blake to that of Robert Bly and Khalil Gibran, I may well be in the minority. Bly's work has been a contagious poetic influence in America for several decades, and now his oracular prose lucubrations have gained a wide following. But then, so did those of Madame Blavatsky and Jimmy Swaggart.

Among Bly's followers I think we may confidently count Fred Moramarco and Al Zolynas, the editors of *Men of Our Time*, another anthology of male poetry. Their acknowledgments pages express gratitude to Bly for help in choosing poems, and their introduction refers to him as someone who has "identified as the primary submerged emotion of contemporary men . . . grief between fathers and sons." Various sections are arranged pretty much along the lines of *The Rag and Bone Shop:* "Men at War," "Men and Women," "Fathers and Daughters," and so forth. Surprisingly, though, there is little overlapping between the two books: Richard Wilbur's marvelous "Boy at the Window," Robert Hayden's familiar "Those Winter Sundays," Etheridge Knight's sad "Feeling Fucked Up," and one or two others. Another surprising thing is the fact that *Men of Our Time* is the superior anthology.

One reason for its superiority is that we are spared those pompous prefaces that so perfectly exercise their ability to cloud men's minds. And Moramarco and Zolynas give us whole poems, not mutilations, though in some instances individual lyrics are lifted from lengthy sequences. Mostly, though, they simply make a preferable selection. Not perfect, by any means: any anthology that includes W. S. Merwin's boring "The Houses" has lapsed—but if it also includes John Frederick Nims's "The Evergreen," then we may view it as having atoned. If it goes on to include Robert Peters's "The Butchering," Michael Waters's "The Mystery of the

Caves," David Ignatow's "A Requiem," Li-Young Lee's "Water," Henry Taylor's "At the Swings," Philip Levine's "You Can Have It," W. D. Snodgrass's "A Friend," Jim Wayne Miller's "Down Home," and dozens of others as good or almost as good, we may describe the book as a winner despite its groaners.

The Rag and Bone Shop includes a section called "Zaniness," but only Russell Edson's three poems are really zany; the others, including Yeats's "High Talk," are stodgy. *Men of Our Time* has no separate section of humorous poems but does contain William Matthews's "Change of Address," James Plath's "Standing in the Reception Line at the Wedding of My Ex-Wife," Patrick O'Leary's "Vasectomy: A Poem in Two Parts," Charles Bukowski's *"O Tempora! O Mores!"* and three happy poems by Ron Koertge—whose "Girl Talk" is one of the funniest poems I know:

> During "The Desires of Monique"
> my friend and I were chatting
> about the alarming number of men
> who tore off Monique's flimsy panties
> with their teeth.
>
> The theatre was shrine-like—
> vast, smoky, and dim—so we confessed
> that neither of us had ever
> chewed away any underwear.
>
> We agreed, though, that perhaps age
> and experience could explain that.
> In the 50's there was something
> called a panty girdle and, believe me,
> after gnawing on a panty girdle
> for a while, a person gets full
> and has to ask for a doggy bag
> to take home the rest for later.
>
> On the screen, Monique dreamed
> of her voracious lovers. There they
> were—laughing, waving, flossing.
> This is where we came in, but leaving

> we vow that the first one to devour
> an entire pair will call the other
> immediately.
>
> That is the kind of friends we are.
> We talk on the phone for hours
> and we tell each other everything.

I have included this poem in a number of public readings and can testify
that it delights audiences, men and women alike. They are caught off-
guard by the change of voice in the last stanza, but they do come round
to enjoy the notion of a poem about male friendship closing with a mod-
ulation to female tonality.

Perhaps the reason *Men of Our Time* is more successful than *The Rag
and Bone Shop* is that it only presents the poems and doesn't take them as
sermon texts. Or maybe it is because the editors of the former are less
heavy-handed and more lighthearted. For instance, Moramarco and Zolynas use James Broughton's "Defective Wiring," one stanza of which seems
almost directed at the portentousness of Mr. Bly and his friends: "Have you
ever tried to / take the world in your arms? / It resists being fondled."

Like *Against Forgetting* and *A Gathering of Poets*, *Men of Our Time*
presents a number of poems about personal guilt, and here such feelings
seem more than ever insufficiently motivated. Simply to have been born
into the masculine gender gives some poets reason enough for self-
condemnation, as Philip Dacey's "Crime" states most succinctly:

> She lies at the side of the road, naked,
> having been raped, beaten, tossed from a car.
> You made her up. She is your soul's image.
> Who are the men speeding away? You are.

Dacey's quatrain is allegorical, of course, and delineates his perception
of the way men mistreat and maim the feminine parts of themselves,
their Jungian animae, if you will. It doesn't *merely* say that all men are
rapists by nature, but it does say that first, and if a reader does not assent
to the propositon then the other terms of the allegory go begging.

As in the other volumes we have looked at, in *Men of Our Time* it is the quieter and more thoughtful poems that at last work best. Perhaps this is because theme anthologies include so many poems hellbent on making "relevant" statements that the decibel level becomes uniformly loud and monotonous; the quieter poems then gain the advantage of contrast. Some pieces with this quality are Paul Zimmer's lovely "Zimmer Imagines Heaven," Michael Waters's wistful "Lipstick," Antony Oldknow's tender "Talking with Her," and Robert Duncan's intricate conceit, "My Mother Would be a Falconress." To illustrate this kind of poem, I'll choose another allegory, modest but hugely implicative, realistically detailed but mystically intended. Consider Louis Jenkins's prose poem "The Ice Fisherman":

> From here he appears as a black spot, one of the shadows that today has found it necessary to assume solid form. Along with the black jut of shoreline far to the left, he is the only break in the undifferentiated gray of ice and overcast sky. Here is a man going jiggidy-jig-jig in a black hole. Depth and the current are of only incidental interest to him. He's after something big, something down there that is pure need, something that, had it the wherewithal, would swallow him whole. Right now nothing is happening. The fisherman stands and straightens, back to the wind. He stays out on the ice all day.

I believe that my observation about quiet and thoughtful poems holds up even for such a book as *Fast Talk, Full Volume,* in which the aesthetic doctrine of loudness is carried through with excruciating thoroughness. Where other poets might seek to emulate Robert Frost or Robert Hayden, Ezra Pound or Langston Hughes, the poets in this collection have taken the relentless shouted blather of AM radio for poetic model. Almost all the poems are written at the top of the voice. The title of Bernard Harris Jr.'s "Wake Up People!" might serve as an epigraph for the volume; the current fashion in much African American poetry seems to be to open with a shout and then get louder.

When Susan Anderson begins "Notes on a Storefront Church" with "Preacher deaf from the steel mill scream," I have real sympathy for this minister, having just read ninety-one pages of poetry mostly like Kenneth Carroll's "Never Piss Off a Poet," which starts with these lines:

don't try to play me chump!
cause i'll meet you in a back alley
on a rainy moonless night
wit a loaded verse in my pocket
push a sawed-off simile 'gainst your nose
as a dog that looks like your sister
drains the last swig from a dead thunderbird bottle

In "Party Over Here and There, Y'all," Darrell Stover praises ancestors who acknowledge each time a black "Voice is Raised in Outrage and Protest / To scream the Truth / Stingin' like Sonia // Slicin' like Farrakhan." His piece ends with onomatopoeic lines intended to suggest specific musical phrases: "DOOEWDOOEWDEWDEWT / DOO-EWDOOEWDEWDEWT TCH!"

Such musical effects are fairly common in this collection: the aforementioned Bernard Harris Jr. reports on hearing "the illest be-bop-hip- / hop-non-stop-rap record around"; Keith Antar Mason's "A Boy's Poem" quotes Aretha Franklin ("Don't send me no / doctor—fillin' me up"), Kweli Smith's "Billie's Birthday" quotes Holiday's "Fine and Mellow" ("my man don't love me / treats me awful mean"), and Reuben Jackson's "For My Neighbor" quotes Lionel Richie ("easy like a / sunday morning"). Only Wanda Coleman with "Walkin' Paper Blues" essays a formal blues poem, but blues and jazz musicians are celebrated by many of the poets represented here. The names most often invoked are Miles Davis, John Coltrane, Holiday, and Jimi Hendrix, but we also hear of Cannonball Adderley, Thelonious Monk, Ray Charles, and even Mahalia Jackson. Is it merely accidental that none of these poets mentions Duke Ellington?

I'm not sure that it is. Rabia Rayford's poem, "Wouldn't It Be a Shame (Where is Motown?)," presents the anthology's most explicit exploration of feelings about music, and her lines suggest to me that perhaps Ellington's music is considered "too white" to be authentic. The poem is built upon a fancy that "black music" might die out and that all that would survive would be rock ("the Average White Band") or—worst of horrors!—"Classical Music": "Aaaaaarias and / Italian lyrics / *Per la Gloria*, but no R E S P E C T." It would, of course, be disastrous to lose any of our hard-won musical idioms, but black music is in little danger of extinction. Ice-T is doing quite well, thank you; it is the St. Paul Chamber Orchestra that has disappeared. So let us put the proposition the other way about. What if classical music disappeared—as it is the more likely to do? Perhaps Rabia Rayford, like Chuck Berry, would be content to jettison Beethoven and Tchaikovsky, but is she also willing to get rid of Chevalier St. George, William Grant Still, *Treemonisha*, and such fine contemporary black composers as George Harper? This narrow-minded identification of a limited number of styles as being the only legitimate "black music" is one of the main reasons we never get to hear the more serious ("classical," if you like) compositions of Charles Mingus and Fats Waller.

That is the trouble with a poetry that has little content but much Attitude, with pages that are almost nothing but shockshuck and aggressojive. Such writing is mere emotional reflex triggered by rhetorical cliché, and it produces lines that are hasty, often insincere, and sometimes unwitting self-parodies. When in one stanza of "Wouldn't It Be a Shame" Rabia Rayford attempts to get us to imagine the worst fate that could happen, she may wind up persuading many readers it would be the best:

> What if wailin'
> And moaning
> Shouting
> and
>   SCREEEEEEEAMIN'
>   was forgotten
>   as an ART FORM?
>   No Pleeeeeeeeeeaaaaase Babeh, Babeh
>   No Ow! Wit You Bad Self
>   No Come on now HUH!

One may understand the aggressiveness that inflames these pages as being in some degree defensive in nature. Rayford's notion is not after all a complete fantasy; in the long term those kinds of music she now identifies as best expressing black feeling will indeed die out. This year's Hi-Flash becomes as quaint as last year's Funky Chicken. J. S. Bach may lose his contemporary consumer audience, but a hundred years hence and forever after he will be listened to with reverence by *musicians* black and white alike. From them he gets, Babeh, R E S P E C T.

Darrell Stover lays open this cultural dilemma in "Dash": "We are that dash in African-American / There are those of us pulled to the right to dwell as Americans / and those of us pulled to the left to dwell as Africans / The choice is conscious / But as that dash we are challenged / Our allegiances in daily dalliances called to question constantly." The poem climaxes with a series of puns on its title ("A dash of this / A dash of that," "Don't dash our hopes and dreams / Dash our differences") and ends on a note of hope: "Now dash / Dash / Dash on!"

Mariah L. Richardson's "English as a Second Language" also takes the culturally divided psyche for subject matter, but her poem ends wryly rather than hopefully. She grew up speaking the "black' english" of her neighborhood but then had to learn a more "proper and polished" style of speech. Now, she claims, she "cannot hold / a decent black conversation / without stammering / in search of words." That adjective "decent" holds a rich cache of ironies which look especially prickly because they come after her sample of the way she used to be able to talk:

> "Hey, like I be thinkin
> wid my black self and
> shiiiid. . . . I be wondrin
> why them teachers
> be sayin that
> I cain't talk
> when my words
> are electric   like me."

There is more than a touch of Brer Rabbit in Richardson's claim that she can no longer speak black English, and her point is made the more acutely for being made with quiet slyness.

Once again, the modulated lines carry the day, especially in a volume that contains so few of them. One of the quietest and best in *Fast Talk, Full Volume* is contributed by the editor, Alan Spears. His "Poetry and Other Self-Inflicted Wounds" is a surprising examination of the influence of "too many English war movies" on contemporary romantic relationships. It is a poem that does not insist on either reader or writer being black, and it tries to see both sides, male and female, of a problem. Those melodramatic English films instilled, Spears says, "a rigid sense of chivalry" that made a senseless massacre "better than a sensible retreat on any day." The women too fell prey to the code, having to lie still and "think of England" during loveless sex. The twist is that Spears pictures the male in this situation: "It was his dreadful labor / to read the pained expressions on the face below / and wonder if she had ever loved him at all?" The poem ends on a defensive note, taking into account recent feminist complaints about male insensitivity: "But despite all evidence to the contrary, / you would be wrong to think that men don't feel."

"Despite all evidence to the contrary"—what a plaintive phrase! If documentation is needed that feminism is making some headway in the African American community, Spears's lines may be offered. Stronger evidence might be Toni D. Blackman's "For My Brothers Who Chant the Pussy Song." In this poem irresponsible sexual behavior is seen as something forced upon the black male by white society: "those concepts / with which they have / brainwashed us." This idea is at least as inaccurate as Lucille Clifton's notion in "after Kent State" that black people are less prone to violence than whites. When it comes to violence, disrespect, knavery, viciousness, and irresponsibility, we're talking about *real* equality between the races. But Blackman turns her complaint inside out and offers it as a possible source for racial pride:

> sex
> is not for
> our people
> we cannot allow
> it
> to happen
>
> we
> must
> make love!

Maybe this message will get through. A piece of good news is that I heard the same sentiment—in fact, the same words—recently in a popular rap song. The bad news is that as poetry it has no staying power.

Couched in undistinguished language and undeveloped reasoning, it washes away like radio chatter and leaves little or no trace upon the psyche. Without more diligent process of thought this sort of wish is empty sentimentality, as saccharine and swiftly fading as almost all popular music.

I have listed some of the musical names that serve as cultural touchstones for the poets in *Fast Talk, Full Volume,* and there are other names too: Etheridge Knight, James Baldwin, June Jordan, Maya Angelou, Malcolm X—even Jay Bias. But almost all the heroes are contemporary or fairly recent figures. There are thirty-five poets included in Joan R. Sherman's fine anthology *African-American Poetry of the Nineteenth Century,* and not one of them, not even Paul Laurence Dunbar, is mentioned in the Alan Spears gathering. Again, there may be a question of the older poets being perceived as "too white" in manner. Or it may be that the young poets don't know much about their forerunners; I will confess that I do not, and have found Sherman's collection a useful and welcome introduction. Or it may be that the old poems simply do not speak *as poetry* to young readers these days.

That's a sad possibility but an understandable one. The kind of poetry that nineteenth-century American poets wrote has largely fallen out of fashion with white readers as well. There seems to be a wide cultural gulf between, say, Longfellow and almost any contemporary poet you'd care to name. The rift shouldn't be inevitable; after all, most of the subjects of contemporary poetry are the same as those of a century ago: nature, cultural achievements, love, history, political injustice, suffering, war, and so forth. But poetic idiom has changed, and for many readers (especially young ones) idiom is a dominant characteristic.

Well, it *is* a long way back from Keith Antar Mason's lines "playing with her clit / I turn magical for myself" (in "On Nigga Terms"), to James Monroe Whitfield's quite different celebration of a black woman:

> A vision as of angel bright
>   Sudden appears before my face,
> A beauteous, fascinating sprite,
>   Endowed with every charm and grace.

Majestic Juno's lofty mien,
  With beauteous Venus' form and face,
And chaste Diana's modesty,
  Adorned with wise Minerva's grace,
United in thy form divine,
With most resplendent luster shine.

Partisans of Mr. Mason's poetry may likely find Whitfield's lines un-
genuine, silly, derivative, clichéd, empty, and above all too thoroughly in-
debted to the genteel white poetry of the period. It is inexpressive, they
might say, of the souls of black folk. Who are Juno, Diana, Minerva? Ancient Greek goddesses? What have they got to do with anything?

The evidence will show that Whitfield's Greek goddesses have great
emotional significance for him, and that as poetic symbols they serve
him as powerfully as the magical clit serves Keith Antar Mason. The
terms have changed, but what to a contemporary reader might look like
courageous and gritty writing on the part of Mason would look to Whitfield like a barbaric indecency unbecoming the dignity of a true poet.
And he was no Uncle Tom, this James Monroe Whitfield; he was a black
separatist who explored in Central America looking for land upon which
to found a black colony. He seems to have been largely self-educated, yet
he took himself seriously and welcomed the moral responsibilities that
he saw in the role of the poet. His work is suffused with bitter sarcasm,
and in "How Long" he dared to attack the hypocrisy of the white clergy
that applauded European revolution while countenancing American slavery. He had a great deal more at stake than any poet in *Fast Talk, Full
Volume* is able to risk when he published the following (from "How
Long"):

And while from thirty thousand fanes
  Mock prayers go up, and hymns are sung,
Three millions drag their clanking chains,
  "Unwept, unhonored, and unsung";
Doomed to a state of slavery
  Compared with which the darkest night
Of European tyranny
  Seems brilliant as the noonday light;

> While politicians, void of shame,
>   Cry, this is law and liberty,
> The clergy lend the awful name
>   And sanction of the Deity,
> To help sustain the monstrous wrong,
> And crush the weak beneath the strong.

These lines also exhibit Whitfield's considerable skills as a technician, yet I have the feeling that no matter how acutely I might analyze his metrical and rhythmical accomplishments, or how strongly I might praise them, contemporary black readers are going to prefer Rabia Rayford's hopscotch rhymes in "Name Change": "Of Mer ke dees cars / And Soo She bars / /'n razor lines up / aquilines."

I would be joyous to think I am wrong in my surmise, but I can't help gaining the impression that contemporary black poetry as represented in the *Fast Talk* collection doesn't really desire to communicate broadly, that it takes pleasure in ethnic exclusivity. The danger is that if this single idiom alone is regarded as the one true black poetry, an ability to understand other poetic styles will be lost—and lost along with it access to a large and rich part of African American cultural heritage.

This is an honorable heritage, one perilously achieved, paid for in blood, and not lightly to be disregarded. Present-day black poets like to complain of their hard lot (as do all poets, now and forever), but the poems in Joan R. Sherman's anthology were written by those who were forced to suffer slavery, brutality, frozen indifference, poverty, illiteracy, crushing day labor, and—in a surprising number of cases—blindness. Much of their verse is as courageous and outspoken, and often as bitter and mordantly witty, as anything written in our time by Amiri Baraka and Etheridge Knight. (Consider, for example, Elymas Payson Rogers's lines spoken by a personification of slavery: "Of politics, I am the pope / To whom each candidate must stoop, / And there devoutly kneeling low / Do homage to my sacred toe.")

But it requires practice and patient attention to read nineteenth-century poetry, and not all the poems in this anthology are good ones. The odds against such poets as Charlotte L. Forten Grimké, John Willis Menard, and even George Moses Horton were too great. Editor Sherman shows wisdom in not overselling the verses; she says of Menard's work that the "language is banal, the imagery stale, execution clumsy, and sentiments repetitive and spiritless." Strong condemnations these, and yet it won't be all that long before such description is applied to the greater part of the poetry produced in our own decades.

It is more inspiriting and much more interesting to talk of the triumphs these poets scored and to note some of the characteristics that make their work different from contemporary work. A number of nineteenth-century black poets wrote long narratives such as Frances Ellen Watkins Harper's *Moses*, George Boyer Vashon's *Vincent Ogé*, James Madison Bell's *A Poem Entitled the Day and the War*, and Albery Allson Whitman's *Not a Man and Yet a Man*.

If I could judge from excerpts I might well place Albery Whitman's achievement in the long poem on a par with that of William Gilmore Simms. The work of Frances Harper is less accomplished, but it can boast the broad and fervent ambitions, the reach for narrative scope and historical understanding, and the energetic naïveté that we admire in the films of D. W. Griffith and in the paintings of such folk artists as Erastus Salisbury Field. We may smile tolerantly when an Egyptian overseer in Harper's *Moses* speaks in lines that seem to have been scripted by Cecil B. DeMille—"Back / To the task base slave, nor dare resist the will / Of Pharaoh"—but the verve of the story and its stout purposes carry us along. Harper's lines are overripe with romantic clichés, but her obvious enjoyment of them is sometimes infectious, as in these lines that describe Moses' vision of the Promised Land he will never enter:

> He stood upon the highest peak of Nebo,
> And saw the Jordan chafing through its gorges,
> Its banks made bright by scarlet blooms
> And purple blossoms. The placid lakes
> And emerald meadows, the snowy crest
> Of distant mountains, the ancient rocks
> That dripped with honey, the hills all bathed
> In light and beauty, the shady groves
> And peaceful vistas, the vines opprest
> With purple riches, the fig trees fruit-crowned
> Green and golden, the pomegranates with crimson

Blushes, the olives with their darker clusters,
Rose before him like a vision, full of beauty
And delight.

I do not offer this passage as a model; a young poet would be ill advised
to try to write in this manner today. Yet I will plead for appreciation:
Frances Harper is expert in the idiom of her own generation, living at a
time when Thomas Campbell was perhaps too assiduously admired but
when adjectives like "emerald" and nouns like "riches" still carried force.
Her sonorous blank verse is stately but fluid, and her use of "chafing"
seems quite original, as do the happy ironies of "opprest."

Like our contemporary African American poets, those of the nineteenth century celebrated their cultural heroes: there are poems for and
about Toussaint L'Ouverture, William Lloyd Garrison, Frederick Dou-
glass, Booker T. Washington, Paul Laurence Dunbar, and Harriet
Beecher Stowe. What I hadn't expected was the number of poems devoted to the achievements of white poets—not only Whittier, but also
Longfellow, Swinburne, James Whitcomb Riley, and even Edgar Allan
Poe, whose sentiments on the subject of slavery were hardly liberal. It is
true that black poets of the time could find few other black writers or
artists to eulogize, but the fact remains that their passion for art was
greater than whatever feelings they may have had about skin color or the
detestable treatment they suffered at the hands of whites. In other words,
for many of these poets *poetry* came first, and they used the art to ennoble and embellish their political thoughts and urges. I can't help feeling
that this usage is often reversed today: mere Attitude is sometimes regarded as the first prerequisite for being an African American poet, and
love of the art and mastery of the craft count for little, if they count at all.
This idea is common to young white poets as well, but it would seem to
be all too easily exemplified by many of the selections in *Fast Talk, Full
Volume.*

African-American Poetry of the Nineteenth Century is designed, I would
think, as a textbook. It has the familiar paraphernalia: biographical head-
notes, textual and critical bibliographies, a brief but informative introduction, and footnotes that tell us who Apollo and Nero are, as well as
George Washington and Andrew Jackson. I would hope, though, that its

selections are read for more than their historical values. I would hope that readers can enjoy as poetry such pieces as Alfred Gibbs Campbell's clever and shaped "Song of the Decanter," Joshua McCarter Simpson's nifty parodies of popular songs, James Monroe Whitfield's headlong tetrameter rhythms, the wide metrical variety of Elymas Payson Rogers's "A Poem on the Fugitive Slave Law," the wicked humor of James Madison Bell's "Modern Moses, or 'My Policy' Man," and the infectious dance measures of James Edwin Campbell's "Mobile-Buck."

I will end by quoting yet another fine piece. I have spoken often in this essay-review of the striking contrasts that the quieter poems lend to theme anthologies. In "The Poet," Paul Laurence Dunbar praises the quiet poem, too—but, with customary prescience, he foresees that, in the short term, the loudmouths will carry the day:

> He sang of life, serenely sweet,
>   With, now and then, a deeper note.
>   From some high peak, nigh yet remote,
> He voiced the world's absorbing beat.
>
> He sang of love when earth was young,
>   And Love, itself, was in his lays.
>   But ah, the world, it turned to praise
> A jingle in a broken tongue.

Figured Carpets:
The Collected and the Selected

Henry James's teasing novella, "The Figure in the Carpet," is built upon one of his most tenuous conceits, and for this reason is one of his most elegant and suggestive stories—a piece of music, really. It concerns, as you may remember, a young writer's preoccupation with an older author named Hugh Vereker. The veteran novelist has dismissed the other's newly published review of Vereker's work as being clever but irrelevant, as having failed to make out the unifying design (which he calls his "little point") that ties all his work together into a whole greater than the colligation of its parts. Vereker attempts to explain: "By my little point I mean—what shall I call it?—the particular thing I've written my books most *for*. Isn't there for every writer a particular thing of that sort, the thing that most makes him apply himself, the thing without the effort to achieve which he wouldn't write at all, the very passion of his passion, the part of the business in which, for him, the flame of art burns most intensely? Well, it's *that!*"

Vereker's hint sets in motion the quest of the young man and his friends to discover the novelist's grand hidden design, and their quixotic mission comprises the story line of this novella so delicious with slyness and irony. A poetry reviewer is likely to feel some sympathy with James's overearnest young questers when he is confronted by those volumes by poets that present, in collected or selected versions, the labors of a great deal of their lives. When he reads through the lines that decades of meditation have accumulated, might not he miss the poet's "little point"? Might not he fail to find the poet's "very passion of his passion" and so render his own judgments, however well-meaning and clever, trivial and even distracting?

A fear of such failure is not confined to critics and reviewers. The same uncertainty about the meaning of their whole work troubles the poets themselves. In his book of new and selected poems, *What I Think I Know,* Robert Dana broaches the question in "I Used to Think So":

> What is it once heard
> that will not come back in an act of memory
>
> in which the day is as soiled
> as the glass of these institutional windows
> facing the passion of trees?
>
> To lose it.
> Perhaps that's the whole idea after all.
>
> Not to stand
> months hence
> caught in the doorway of a blue photograph looking strange.
>
> I want to start over again
> every day of my life.
>
> Do I?
> I used to think so.

Uncertainty is one of Dana's constant themes, as the title of his collection indicates, but often it is not possible for a reader to find the sources of this uncertainty. Perhaps Dana himself cannot always identify the roots of his fretfulness, but even when he can he will likely as not refuse to divulge them. In an earlier part of "I Used to Think So" a female is alluded to:

> As she leaves,
> and the door jerks to a close,
> I listen hard into the stillness,
> into the building's actual weather,

hearing nothing that loves me,

as if each detail
had to be tricked into meaning.

The last two lines have immediate application for a reviewer examining a large number of poems like this one. The "she" here is not referred
to before the single line containing her pronoun and is never referred to
again. She is important to the speaker, a key part of the story of the poem.
But the poem is not going to tell us the story; Dana has deliberately suppressed it. We are free to imagine all sorts of things about the relationship
between the woman and the speaker—a failed marriage or love affair,
mental illness, an aborted fetus—almost anything. While such an exercise might be amusing, it is not helpful in determining what the poem is
actually about, and until a reader knows that, any emotional response to
the work is muffled. Rhetoric cannot make up the deficit; when it is indicated that we are supposed to feel something, we want to know why the
poet attempts to elicit our emotion.

Dana's poems are filled with such frustrating hints and details that
lead to culs-de-sac. In "Driving the Coeur d'Alene Without You" occurs
this baffling datum: "I tell you, / the dumb stain on my
shirtpocket / could pass for loneliness." In "Mnemosyne," "A trap
springs / in the rat-infested grapes // Harry's fingers ribbon with
blood // I remember Harry / sweet drunken Harry." The poem that
calls itself "This Isn't a Story" is accurate in its description; the lines
merely pile up a list of seemingly unrelated facts and then finish with a
longish description of an old photograph of the speaker's father. In the
middle is a striking bit of information delivered in a manner more dead-
pan than even a typical White House spokesperson can usually muster:
"My daughter's / marriage is in trouble. / There's no story at all, / really."

The figure in Robert Dana's carpet may be a distrust of such a figure
or a disbelief that it would have validity even if found. Some of his titles
imply as much, at any rate: "A Note from Nowhere," "The Unbroken
Code," "The Lie," "Not Quite," "Starting Out for the Difficult World,"
and the title poem, which turns out to be only a fragment in a suite of
fragments called "Five Short Complaints."

It is not fair to judge a poet's performance by his philosophic premises unless these are stupid or brutal or contrary to indubitable fact. Though a distrust of the power of art, and particularly of the art of narrative, to inform and enlighten us may seem a self-defeating stance for a poet to assume, still it is a legitimate one. The trouble is that a volume of selected poems has not only a purposeful consistency but a certain insistency too, and the searcher-out of carpet-figures is going to judge one figure more comely than another. Dana's book offers no fewer than eighty-four poems, and if only half of them treat of his characteristic self-skepticism the effect is bound to be a bit dispiriting.

No complete judgment of a poet's selected works will be purely aesthetic in nature, however sternly a critic may try to make it so. When a poet brings out a collected or selected volume he or she is asking that an estimate be made of the philosophy the pages embody; the hope for an understanding of broad purposes is one of the motives for publishing such a selection. I find Dana's distrustfulness stultifying if taken in too-large dosages.

And I don't think that my reaction is mere personal caprice, for those of his poems which do deliver intelligible narratives, those that do give out sufficient information, are superior to the deliberately inchoate and suppressive efforts. The first two stanzas of "Pop: at Checkers" are lovely, and such poems as "A Winter's Tale," "A Letter from Divizio, Patient, Pilgrim State Hospital," "At the Vietnam War Memorial, Washington, D.C.," "On the Public Beach, St. Augustine," "Black Angel," "Victor," and "These Days" are successful because their phrases have a structure to attach to and a clarity that can move readers. A middle passage from "Black Angel" is wonderfully effective:

> This poem is an adagio. A slow
> yearning of winds and strings.
> Like the hot August night I got
> drunk with friends, and laughing
> and sweating, we linked arms and lay
> back in the deep wine, the cool
> Einsteinian space of summer grass,
> streaming upward like angels,
> past trees, past crumbling eaves

and stars, rising like music farther
and farther out the closer home.

The narratives of lyric poems are not supposed to be prolix reports as
gluey with data as the pages of Theodore Dreiser. They are supposed to
be compressed and suggestive, attacking their subjects and themes
obliquely. But there is a middle way between the verbose treatise and the
incomprehensible code message, and when Robert Dana finds it, he can
write a poem both thoughtful and intriguing, allusive and comprehensible. Here is "True Story":

> What does the morning say
> I wish I hadn't heard before,
> the wind still for the first
> time in days, the little maple
> standing like sodden bronze
> beside the garden. Beneath
> it, the green roses of the cabbages
> unfold, zucchini spread the
> canopies of their first true
> leaves.
>   Tell me again how your
> uncle Willie sold his acre
> of downtown Wichita for five
> bucks and a shot of booze.
> And how, where oil-rockers
> dipsy-doodle in the wheat,
> fire of sex or soul could fry
> a young girl's hair to ringlets.
>
> If the rich talk only
> to the rich, then it's true:
> we are whatever's left of us.
> In the scrub, the cardinal
> whistling like a rubber mouse.
> But nothing's so exotic here
> as the emptiness of ordinary
> day. It falls through the eyes

of my cat, turning slowly, like
flakes of sunlight in the air.

One phrase from this poem, "the emptiness of ordinary / day," could almost stand as an epigraph for Dan Gerber's new and selected volume, *A Last Bridge Home.* Many of Gerber's poems describe exactly such a condition, *listlessness* being a theme that he returns to again and again. "July, my sweet" offers one of his briefer accounts:

> The whole town was
> a fly on a screen door
> waiting for weather
> grit under heel
> on the sidewalk
> a sleeping turtle
> in the weight of heat
> tattooed muscle
> the ding-bell machine
> lead milk bottles
> and melting girls
> blanking under heavy trees
> the falling moon

It would be difficult to think of another piece of writing in which a carnival is described so unenthusiastically. Or so sketchily—its presence is barely noticeable in the poem. And what the word "blanking" means in this context is impossible for me to surmise, but its effect on the poem is undeniable; it adds to the dull drone.

A number of other poems in the book address this paralysis of will, sometimes employing the figures of landscape as in "July, my sweet," sometimes describing it in terms of psychology as in "The Tragedy of Action," sometimes making it a character portrait as in "All of This." Gerber establishes this weary half-somnolent mood pretty often as a trope for immanence. In his dusty sunlit rooms and nearly featureless exteriors, something may be about to happen. Perhaps a transformation is being prepared for, and these spaces that are as silent as Chirico's and as empty as Giacometti's may become arenas of revelation. This idea and its accompanying poetic strategy one might well recognize as being characteristic of the work of Robert Bly and James Wright—and such Gerber poems as "Snow on the Backs of Animals" and "Drinking Coffee" call these poets respectively to mind. "Burning the Last Logs of Winter" is so uncomfortably close to the manner of Wright that it is hard to say whether it is a homage or merely an imitation. But it is still an effective poem, so maybe the borrowing can be justified:

> A spring wind rattles the window,
> and the farmer turns fitfully under the moon.
>
> Tubers sprout below the frostline.
> Soon the fields will be plowed.
>
> What snow is left whitens the gullies
> like sweeps of canvas waiting for paint.
>
> I awake and my parents are together again
> as if they'd discovered that death was a dream.

Most of Dan Gerber's somniferous mindscapes do not burst into pear blossom as neatly as in this poem. He tells us in "Why I Don't Take Naps in the Afternoon" that the long static afternoons he describes are images of infinite time: "Eternity. / We are living in eternity." His skill at drawing long preternatural silences and lackluster incidents might persuade me about eternity, but can we really call it living?

> The clouds break open, the sun about to set.
> Nothing you can do about it. You walk from your
> hotel, down rain-washed streets, glistening in places.
> The cafes are closed, or you feel they should
> be closed. The life in them doesn't concern you.

Like Robert Dana, Gerber is more interesting when he includes information and establishes story lines than when he does neither. The longish poems in *A Last Bridge Home* are almost invariably more intriguing than the shorter ones. I suppose "The Poor Farm" must be classified as a mere anecdote, but its characters and dialogue draw us in; the same is true of "Incident at Three Mile Road." Even with its sometimes bollixed diction ("Two weeks ago, pneumonia ganged up with a / rare blood disease"), "Speaking to Horses" is a good poem, though certainly no better than "The Third Week in July." The latter is a simply casual narrative about the joy of farm labor, specifically that of loading and hauling hay bales: "We develop a rhythm, building the / load, knowing that though the years seem short, / the day is long, and there's nowhere else to be."

It may be that inside the taciturn Dan Gerber there is a garrulous narrative poet waiting his turn to speak, but if that is the case, the storyteller is going to have to hang fire. Gerber's talents and the temperament he has sharpened them with seem resolutely turned in other directions. Though I cannot help regretting often the loss of the larger gesture and the wider scope contained in his narrative poems, neither can I deny the admirable impressions that some of his short lyrics make. The gnomic scraps of phrase that constitute "Zone" create an atmosphere as subtle and disquieting as in a painting by Yves Tanguy:

> In the desert   the snake
> sleeping on the rock
> lives by the heat it absorbs
> Nothing in itself
> but the terror you grant it
>
> An obscure notion of time
> the circles around a chimney rock
> the floor of an ocean of air

The difficulty with such subtle effects is that the poet has to keep standing precariously on the tips of his toes to achieve them. When he loses his concentration just a little he comes down with a flat-footed thud—as in this stanza from "In the Winter Dark":

> Do these smoldering logs, waiting
> to be stirred back into flame,
> become the compulsion to build cathedrals,
> pyramids, tombs,
> the great buried silos of North Dakota?

Probably they are less likely than Dan Gerber supposes, these imputed architectural ambitions of his hearth-fire logs, and to include such silliness in the context of this particular poem betrays a desperate striving for the surreal effect. We could do with a little less tone-painting and a little more reporting.

But if Gerber is sometimes too reticent, Stephen Berg is too talky by half. There may be some good poems in the pages of his *New and Selected Poems* but most of them are buried inside long sloppy perorations that seem to begin at random and end at whim. Berg's passionate earnestness is not in question, for he has the sincerity of his obsessions. Unfortunately poetry is not one of them.

In fact, where Robert Dana shows a distrust of the art of poetry, Stephen Berg possesses a frank dislike of the stuff, and especially of his own. The twenty-ninth line of a piece called "And the Scream" admits that "Nobody would call this poetry." "At the Door" sets down a singularly barren declaration: "They say each person has a story / but that isn't true." In "Wanting to Be Heavier" we are told that "All the words have died out." "Through Glass" iterates that the search for meaning is useless:

> Queasy nothingness shapes caught in windows
> flash, squirm.
> Wonderful distant mirrors of no mind,
> go fuck yourselves, go fuck your absent answers.

It stands to reason that a poet who dislikes poetry will execute feckless slipshod work, and Berg seems to take a perverse pride in doing so. He describes his method of composition in "A God" with cheerless sang-froid: "Alone at night in my room, / typing these words, / baffled by what they will be / . . . I go back."

I believe we must take him at his word; he really has no idea where a poem is going when he begins. And he certainly has not the faintest notion when he has arrived: his closures are his weakest sections, tacked-on afterthoughts or reversals of direction or digressions so wayward that they might be the openings of new poems. "Why Are We Here?" is one of his best efforts, but the final fourteen lines, an account of a museum visit, carry us far away from the subject of the poem and leave us stranded. "It Is" finds an image of raindrops that brings together vividly different strands of thought and feeling, and the poem should end with this image. But Berg lumbers on for four more lines, lecturing about what has already been experienced. "Sister Ann" doesn't even attempt to close; it just quits, as if the printer had run off the page.

Sometimes his dislike for poetry seems to verge upon contempt. How else shall we explain his reliance on clichés and bland assertions that at every turn undermine any attempted seriousness and earnest purpose? Here are a few that slide lugubriously down the page, leaving in desperate shambles poems with some promise of emotive development: "a loneliness nothing can cure," "I am here / and not here," "Tell me what your life is like," "We want everything," "you have / to say something," "the aloneness of life, / how strange and miraculous it is," "Having a lot of money means everyone loves you," "Is there anything we can say we know?" These phrases are only a few of the most egregious. Some of them may be intended as irony, but Berg's tone is so flat distinction is lost.

I will forbear talking about all the pronouns that have ambiguous references or none at all; they are as thick in this volume as dust motes in a busy sawmill. But I cannot so easily overlook grammatical solecisms that freshman composition students get their knuckles rapped for committing—as in, for example, "The Rocks": "He lay the screen on the floor."

The obvious question that arises is why anyone with so evident a distaste for poetry should set up as a poet. I can venture only the guess that Berg would not describe himself as a poet. Most of the responsibilities we usually ascribe to the figure of the poet he seems to have abjured, and without regret. For neither the craft of verse nor the care of language does he show any concern—and this is sad, because he obviously has some aptitude for the vocation. Perhaps he would assent—though with a different interpretation—to Jean Cocteau's description in his film *Orphée* of a poet as "someone who writes but is not a writer."

As evidence of his talent, I would like to present "Last Elegy." It really is too long to quote in a tandem review, but I have said so many acer-

bic things about Berg's work I feel he deserves the opportunity to display
in full one of his best performances:

Surgeons cutting a hole
in my father's skull
with one of those saws that lift
a plug out of bone also took
a big lump off my spine
in the dream I don't understand
that flickered back
the day before he died.
We were at the shore following
a golf match on TV,
eating, napping. His drained
gray face didn't reveal
any sense of being here,
any desire to live.
The money he made,
the failure he thought he was
in love, in business,
intensified his mood
after the heart attack.
The sky blew flat, smeary gray,
a few fly-like figures
paced the cold beach. Millie,
Clair, Margot, Mom and I
didn't know how to stop his
staring out of nothing into nothing,
so we watched hard
Nicklaus miss two easy putts
and other famous pros tee off
with that quick fluid swing
they have, then stroll down
the fairway to the ball,
the entire world manicured, green.
To say "I love you"
meant "I know I'm dying,"

but you said it,
at least I think I heard you
whisper it to me. Or was it to yourself?
I kept my eyes on the screen.

This poem contains some of the traits that in other poems have to be denominated faults—the flat diction, the long digression, the rhetorical question—but here Berg's control is operative, and his respect for his subject matter makes some of his bad habits work in his favor. The digression about television golf turns out not to be a digression, and the rhetorical question is not merely rhetorical.

I can recommend other poems also. "Desnos Reading the Palms of Men on Their Way to the Gas Chambers" is truly powerful; "Remembering and Forgetting" is another moving elegy for Berg's father; "Why Are We Here?" is good, except for the jerry-built closure; "Visiting the Stone," "Summer Twilight," and "Talking" are admirable. Other poems have strong feelings and graceful moments, yet the dominant impression one receives from *New and Selected Poems* is of an exhausting sullen anger—not only at the sorrows and brutalities of the world, but also at our attempts and our need to speak about them. The final long prose poem, "Homage to the Afterlife," is symptomatic of the insurmountable furious despair that is present almost everywhere in these pages. This piece takes a groggy pleasure in lapsing into incoherence: "Without me, I wanted this to I have to confess help I mean possibly console in some way but halfway through I knew it was wrong knew it couldn't too many motives too much blind greed stupidity the needs hungers moral violence of having a self unable to give beyond its who knows beyond its need to be rid of itself." There are sixteen pages of such babble, much of it not even as comprehensible as this passage.

One has to say of Stephen Berg that he doesn't go easy on himself. Perhaps he is unable to do so, but his work might be more palatable if he went at it with less oppugnance.

In the poetry of Vassar Miller we can find as much philosophic uncertainty and doubt as in Dana, Gerber, and Berg; *If I Had Wheels or Love* can be read almost as a diary of her struggles with her religion, of a straying from faith and a continual glad or sorrowful return to it. But her quarrels with herself have recognizable parameters: the doubts and fears are those traditional in genuinely religious personalities, the same ones we find in John Donne and Gerard Manley Hopkins and Blaise Pascal. Miller is like those poets in that the boundaries of her questioning are well defined, and her security about the worthiness of her art is as steady as her mastery of it is evident. The landscape of her poem "Adoration" is as unpopulated and mostly as silent as those of the three dour poets we have been examining, but what a startling difference! Here is firmness of statement, lively diction, enjoyment of detail, and refreshment for the eye:

> The afternoon is beautiful and silent.
> The white garage lifts like the cloudy pillar
> Into the sunlight. The tree rears taller,
> Its foliage ruffled like a green swan's plumage,
> A sudden bird goes skimming through the sky
> As noiseless as a fish swims in the sea,
> When everything is far and near at once,
> Remote as memory and luminous as now,
> Till mind is cut adrift and like a web
> Shimmering rides the heat waves up and down.
> Nothing is half so tenuous as flesh,
> Which, on the lightest pretext, steals away
> To sleep in the cocoon of summer heat and haze,
> When a jay's scream might tumble the brick wall
> Next door to slide into the forests of the grass,
> The afternoon so beautiful and silent.

The senses are engaged by these lines, the mind is intrigued, yet the poem never loses a hypnotic mood that is half waking, half dreaming. "Adoration" has all the precise but dreamy clarity of a Debussy piece like "La Plus Que Lente"—and all its gentle liveliness too.

It is much too simpleminded, I suppose, to ascribe to Vassar Miller more strength of character than we usually find in the work of contemporary poets. The short biographical notice at the end of this volume tells us that she has been afflicted with cerebral palsy since birth. I could name almost without thinking two score poets who would heap up gross literary capital from such a handicap, but Miller rarely refers to it in her poems. Her anguish—which is always genuine—springs from less obvious sources: from chagrined disappointment in love, from her unappeasable desire for God.

In one sonnet, "Love Song for Easter Even," she uses, in the manner of the metaphysical poets, erotic love as a trope for religious longing. As she lies on the springtime grass next to her loved one, she feels the debilities of her physique disappear: "I have quit / the binds and bonds of the body inside matter." Her flesh, she says, "seems infinite, / like Christ, can tread the tips of the grass like water. / Yet you dart past my touch like Him, smooth fish!" Three sad enormous pressures distress the poet here: her love for her friend lying so close to her, her impatient despair about her stricken body, and her continual desire for the assurance of Christ's presence. But the poem never loses sight of the joy of this fleeting moment, and Vassar Miller maintains—somehow—her wit and good humor.

These latter traits must have helped to sustain her over the years, and she has learned to use both of them to the great advantage of her poetry. Her way of life must be rather monastic, though, as she implies, more so by accident than by choice. Yet she is no nun, as she enjoys pointing out in "On Not Making a Retreat," and one of the reasons she is not is because of the clunky footwear the vocation entails:

> The nuns walk by in twos,
> Lightly, in heavy shoes.
> The nuns send praises thronging,
> Their strong wills leashed and longing.
>
> Their voices rise and fall
> Washing against the wall
> Of the world day after day
> Till it has worn away.
>
> . . .   . . .
>
> I passing by, austere
> As they whose home is here,
> My lonely feet refuse,
> Lightly, their heavy shoes.

There is much more to this poem than a joke about shoes, of course; other stanzas draw a rueful distinction between celibacy as a choice and as an unwanted circumstance. But the joke underlines the courageous cheerfulness that we find also in "On Opening One Eye," "Thus Saith the Lord to the New Theologians," "Church in Heidelberg," "Morning Person," and a good number of others.

Miller shares also with the seventeenth-century devotional poets a predilection for wit and paradox. Her early poems are filled with the latter, serious and playful and playfully serious. "Lady of Leisure" is a nifty sample of this sort of verse, though it sounds more like E. A. Robinson than Richard Crashaw:

> Life never gave her any tasks
> Lest labor should unnerve her.
> People, she thought, were but the masks
> Put on by life to serve her.
>
> Existence was a blessed blur,
> Time made a happy hum.
> Waiting for life to wait on her,
> She waited what might come,
>
> And waited. Sure enough, one day
> Life, servant born and bred,
> Tripped in with death upon a tray
> Like John the Baptist's head.

The confidence required to write poems like Vassar Miller's has to come at least partly from a faith in the purpose and efficacy of the art. Poems about poetry are not frequent in this volume, but they are present, as they seem to be in all the collections of our contemporaries. The fact that this author often identifies the act of composition with the act of praying gives her an authority that others lack; she acknowledges this principle in several places and her title poem, a villanelle, uses this line as one of its refrains: "I could make prayers or poems on and on."

There are important differences between private prayers, devotions that are made in churches and in the confines of personal chambers, and literary prayers that are set out for public gaze. But there are important similarities too, as the sonnets of Donne and Hopkins show. The literary prayer is at pains to record the struggles of the soul as well as the victorious or disappointed conclusions that are attained. For this reason and for others equally germane, I would remark a sequence of twenty-two linked sonnets, "Love's Bitten Tongue," as one of Miller's most important and enduring achievements. In this sequence, lament about the silence of God gradually gives way to a vision of Christ. This vision changes in character, from Christ seen in His painful human guise to images of Him in triumphant splendor, a splendor that is the more distant from the longing heart as it is the more transcendent.

Before she sees Christ as a person, the poet asks to be rescued from the oppression of her ego: "From what I am not make me what I am." It is never clear to her whether this cleansing is completed, for the last lines of the sequence repeat the same phrase. Next she describes Christ in His earthly, His extremely homely, predicament:

> A stranger to Your mother thirty years
> After her rapture of angels gave way
> To neighbors' titters and their outraged jeers,
> Stranger to Yourself, forever an orphan,
> Calling God Father because You were lonely. . . .

The poet then recounts a history of her longing for Christ, from her time as "a Texas child on edge in my bed" through the years when she could shelter "never Your words but Your silence / Housing my mind to be housed in my heart, / Or rather housing heart and mind in balance." At last she brings us to the revelation of the present moment, but even at this ending her joy is not unmixed. The search of the desirous heart goes on:

> So You have opened me to woe and wonder
> Much sharper than woe, far keener than pain
> Pitching the techniques of thought that might pander
> To the gimmicks of mind, but split open mine
> That prays, "What shall I do, Jesus? How deal
> With those flesh-splitting throbs, pain, dread, rapture
> Which rupture my being drooping and dull

To the literal Word, ecstatic scripture?
How may I do it, Great Alpha, Omega
Unless I bow, acolyte to my ego."

"Love's Bitten Tongue" is furnished out in high baroque style: here are gilt and crystal and plaster scrollery, trumpet flourish and clarino trill. But all the ornament, all the bold declarations of the statements, are justified by the poet's hard-won honesty and the exigency of her yearning, and the intensity and lustrousness of these poems also proceed from a more intimate conception of poetry that Miller has couched elsewhere in more modest fashion. A gently teasing, mostly parodic poem called "Or as Gertrude Stein Says . . ." poses a question, "How shall I write a poem about today?" Miller answers herself with these lines:

When the sky is as blue as itself,
and the tree is as green as its leaves—
a poem is only
taking a child's downy skull
gently between your hands
and, with not so much breath as might startle a gnat's wing,
whispering,
"Look!"

Julia Randall shares with Vassar Miller so many personal concerns and so many artistic resemblances, it is not surprising to find that one of Randall's poems, "The Writer Indulges a Hobby," declares ideas about poetic composition quite similar to those in the lines just quoted. The hobby Randall's poem speaks of is mushroom gathering, and she reflects upon how the concentration required in its pursuit leads to a quiet awareness of the details of nature—and of the simplicity of statement necessary for their description:

To the eye grown quiet on its spot,
fields open out their greens,
and every green his shape,
and every shape his shadow moving slow,
a nothing, a steeple-head in the sun's eye,

an ant on the steeple-bush, and in his jaw
a grain, and in that grain a cell . . .
It is only to tell
over again, how much we overpass,
walkers on dust, walkers on grass.

Randall's new and selected volume, *The Path to Fairview*, shares with
If I Had Wheels or Love faith in eros and agape, in the purposes and efficacy of art, in nature, in God. Both poets are masterly with forms and
their prerequisites, rhyme and meter, and both can also write a sprightly
but never careless free verse. Yet the two volumes are different, not
merely in subject matter and diction and tone, but in essential character.

One of the reasons for the differences between the poets is influence.
I have indicated that Miller owes a debt to the great devotional poets, to
Donne and Vaughan and Herbert and Hopkins. Julia Randall writes devotional poetry too, as well as other kinds, but the great beneficent
shadow falling upon her page is that of W. B. Yeats. In stanza after stanza
we can hear Yeats's meter, syntax, and diction; Randall even makes free
with some of his characteristic images. The epigraph to a deeply felt
suite called "Advent Poems, 1963" is from Hopkins, but Yeats's presence
in it is unmistakable. Here are two stanzas from the third section:

It is silent under the steeple, cold enough
To crystallize the little light. The dead
Would tremble at that sign: one star, one note.
The stone could melt, the tree leaf: they do not.

The shroud of mourning coats me like a ghost,
And like a ghost, bone white, I gleam and sing
The folly of warmth and song, and of love most,
And the folly of grave comforting.

There is nothing more pernicious about influence than about any other
quality a poem might exhibit. The reader must distinguish between
homage and theft, between imitation and the purposeful, successful ab-
sorption of another's means and manner. Despite the almost omnipresent
Yeatsian sound that Randall's lines make, we would never confuse her
poems with Yeats's any more than we would suspect a verse of Vassar

Miller of actually being by George Herbert. Randall has appropriated some of Yeats's formal qualities, but her thoughts and feelings and final effects are her own.

Another difference that separates Miller and Randall is in their varying conceptions of the figure of Adam and the vision of Eden. Miller refers but sparingly to the former, and usually in the sense of our proverbial phrase "the old Adam." She emphasizes the fallen Adam rather than the unfallen, and she has no faith that humankind can again attain our original innocence. In fact, her sonnet "Fiat" characterizes Edenic longing as a dangerous weakness, if not an actual error:

> Eden is closed forever, if it was
> Opened to us anytime anywhere,
> And we who try to find it have more cause
> For grief, I think, than Adam, forced to wear
> The skins of guileless animals outside the gates
> And watch Eve sweating, no longer clothed only
> In delicate nakedness, lust and hates
> Stuffing them both full, however finely.
> At least they knew their state and did not try
> To get back in. They saw the burning angel
> And did not bait his flame. They had to die
> And so walked toward their deaths austere and
> Single. Yet from those gates we come back emptyhanded
> Over and over foolish still, and branded.

The notion of Adam is perhaps the longest and brightest thread in the figure of Julia Randall's carpet. Her 1968 collection was called *Adam's Dream*, and our first father shows up in poem after poem. She even names a *dog* Adam. But Randall's Eden is not Miller's forever lost and sorrowful ground; it still exists in our natural surroundings, and Adam and Eve are still with us as fresh and forceful presences. The tragedy of the Fall is acknowledged, but Randall is more interested in the conditions and cast of mind that led up to it. Repeatedly, she attempts to reconstruct the psyches of the innocents and to pose to them the questions they must have had to face. Sometimes, as in these lines from "Recipes," she looks at the old dilemma with wry humor:

> The strict constructionists say man
> strutted on two legs of his own
> all around Eden. Maybe he did,
> sharing his recipe with only God, and his spare rib
> with woman.
>
> She found apples
> good eating. Naturally she shared.
> She discovered blood,
> guts, seasonings; how to make stock; how best to grow
> salads and sesames; and how to raise
> bread. One son discovered how to raise the dead
> but he never told.

The humor here may be fairly described as feminist, I think; it is neatly pointed with puns like "guts" and "seasonings" and "raise," and Eve's dryly fond characterization of Jesus is particularly delicious. But the lines are free of pamphleteering and have more of the telling wit of Jane Austen than of the strident hectoring of some lesser talent who might offer polemic sans poetry.

The Edenic trope is important to Randall in stronger measure than in any other poet I can think of, living or dead. She seems able to *think* in Edenic terms—at least, her poems are as convincing as if she can. In "Adam's Dream" she re-creates the drama of Genesis in her own life:

> Once I lay
> where Adam stood.
> Day's eye, night's lid.
> And dreamed a dream out of my side
> and woke and it was blood.
>
> Once I stood
> where Adam lay.
> Night's lid, day's eye.
> Stood up in my blood and wept
> over Adam where he slept.

It is necessary to read this poem whole to appreciate the fitness of these lines and the tight slant music they make. "Adam's Dream" is a paragon of Randall's special excellences: here she sees herself able to participate in the Edenic experience because in her view all human history, civilized as well as prehistoric, was prefigured in Adam's mind, even if he was unaware of it consciously.

> Silver cities rise and fall
> for Adam's dream.
> Mountains crumble, planets cool
> for Adam's dream.
> Adam's neighbor, Adam's son
> watch the sea swing up and down,
> roast and shiver, spit and turn
> for Adam's dream.

Our origin is always present with us, no matter how far we have come from it and by what sullied ways. I think that Randall would not only assent to Hopkins's line from "God's Grandeur," "There lives the dearest freshness deep down things," but would extend the thought and familiarize it with her humor. She seems to do so in "Album Leaves" when she glances with double intent at the structure of the DNA molecule: "Spun on a double thread? They bring the news / from Genesis: we replicate by twos. / But still, we do not share our parents' views."

We may try to share those views, but time and all its accidents have intervened. We live in a fallen state and must admit the fact in order to get along from day to day. "End of Leave" contains such an admission, in lines as wry as they can get without becoming bitter:

> To live as a green thing
> is to live alone. Human action
> requires a gray suit, a raincoat,
> a comb, a contraceptive, and a hat.

Vassar Miller glanced at the dream of Eden we fallen beings possess and found it a torture, an image of happiness forever out of our tantalized reach. Randall agrees with her in the matter of the dream's inaccessibility, but avers that the hope of attaining it is one of the sustaining pillars of our lives. In "Le Goût d'Ailleurs" she tells us how she still aspires while nonetheless assenting to the hard facts:

> Is this the charge from Eden,
> not to stay? Whatever bade,
> I balance in my sixtieth year
> (remembering who the angels were)
> the coming and the going there, the path
> by Rothay and the path by Alph,
> the lubber and the sailor self.
>
> I keep a picture of the Yellowstone
> tacked to the wall, and that must do
> for regions where the muscles shy
> and breath comes small, and death
> comes fresh. I'll tie
> the roses up, like Eve, make where we are
> be east and garden, or be west and shore.

Not all of Julia Randall's poems are about Adam and Eve, though I feel confident that there is none in this book that stands untouched by the Edenic theme. Even so, I would not dare to say that I have grasped the whole shape of her intention.

I would not say of any poet I have spoken of, here or elsewhere, that I actually perceived with moderate comprehension the figure in his or her carpet. Perhaps Henry James's young man—who claimed to have discerned the design embedded in Hugh Vereker's fiction, but whose untimely death prevented his revealing that secret—was deluded about his perspicacity. To trace the figure in the carpet may be beyond the capacity of any critic or reviewer. After all, James tells us in the preface to his novella of his "habit of having noted for many years how strangely and helplessly, among us all, what we call criticism—its curiosity never emerging from the limp state—is apt to stand off from the intended sense of things, from such finely arrested matters, on the artist's part, as a spirit and a form, a bias and a logic, of his own." But though the critic may not be able to find them, James never doubts that this spirit and form, this bias and logic, are there to be found. James's purpose was to come to an appreciation of these, whether they are totally discernible or not. "What I most remember of my proper process [of the composition of "The Figure in the Carpet"] is the lively impulse, at the root of it, to reinstate analytic appreciation, by some ironic or fantastic stroke, so far as possible, in its virtually forfeited rights and dignities."

For all of the poets discussed here the act of composition is an ironic act, since the delivered poem is always so much less than the intended and partly imagined one. But the courageous poet can find the irony bracing rather than dispiriting, can endure the guaranteed lack of success by taking enjoyment in a process of creation that is as close as you and I can come, by any secular means, to those first acts of naming and creation in the Garden. That is how Julia Randall puts it in "Nearly Anon.," her poem about an unknown Renaissance composer:

> We know, from his *Fantasia,* he had talent, know he knew
> how breath and gut can conjure miracle
> at work, how in our dark environs we repeat
> that first enlightening act, to make
> music of time—the day, the night, the first tree
> in the midst of the garden, which we nearly ate.

Once upon a Time:
Narrative Poetry Returns?

*E*very poetic manifesto contains two implicit propositions that color whatever theory is being expounded: "My friends and I are doing it right; everyone else wanders in blind error, stumbling and hopeless." The Imagists felt that way, and so did the Futurists, the Vorticists, the Abstract Poets, the Cambridge Platonists, the Welsh bards, and the troubadours. Nowadays the New York poets, the Language poets, and the New Formalists are odorous with this familiar, almost irascible, esprit de corps.

It is not surprising, therefore, as narrative poetry is making a comeback, its proponents are also generating manifestoes. One of its most spirited defenses is an essay by the poet Alan Shapiro, "In Praise of the Impure: Narrative Consciousness in Poetry," which appeared in *Tri-Quarterly 81* (Spring/Summer 1991). Shapiro hails the "resuscitation of narrative by poets" and names some representative practitioners: C. K. Williams, Frank Bidart, Robert Pinsky, W. S. DiPiero, James McMichael, Ann Winters, Eleanor Wilner, and Mary Kinzie. Readers familiar with the work of these poets should see immediately that the essayist will have to propose an extremely flexible definition of narrative to include such a variegated array of versemakers; it is hard to see how C. K. Williams has anything in common with Mary Kinzie, or to find any other poet who writes like Frank Bidart (or would aspire to do so).

Shapiro's definition is indeed inclusive, as most reactionary definitions are. Narrative poetry, he believes, is that form which implies, remarks, and strengthens its social and historical connections with its audience, while nonnarrative modernist verse isolates, expresses, and celebrates highly discrete moments of intense perception. Modernist poetry is characterized by the "Poundian ideal of the image flash which liberates the mind from time and space constraints," while "narrative is the figure inscribed upon the ground of being, marking our provisional position as individuals and cultures in relation to unknown origins and unknown, unknowable ends."

There is something desperate in this formulation; the words *provisional, unknown,* and *unknowable* and the essayist's resort to Heidegger's catchall concept, "ground of being," tell us that he fears making his definition of narrative too narrow to include all the contemporary poets he admires. In fact, he has fashioned it so broadly that it can embrace almost all poetry, including modernist "image flash," and he begins his demonstrations by analyzing William Carlos Williams's "By the Road to the Contagious Hospital" as a narrative. He makes a good job of it too, even though he feels that he injures the poem by using this tactic.

So what will we find when we turn to Shapiro's own new collection, *Covenant?* If we let his thoughtful essay determine our expectations, we might look for work largely untouched by the modernist tradition, poems that tell stories in the good old comforting Victorian way. We do indeed discover a few poems that make use of older forms and modes; there are some interesting historical-literary meditations, like "The Sweepers" and "Virgil's Descent," and even a couple of tidy allegories, "The Visitation" and "The Experiment." But other pieces read like the story poems that a great many contemporary poets write. The details are unique, since the material is usually autobiographical, but the narratives have an expectable look about them.

For example, "The Lesson" comprises ten pages of short lines that tell of the speaker's loss of innocence in an encounter with a child molester. It is a smooth and beautifully readable poem, and its best point of interest is not the betrayal of the child but the characterization of the molester, a fellow named Rich who drives every day to a playground to pick up boys in his gold Stingray:

How's it hanging?
he'd ask us from the center
of the chrome-lined golden
nimbus we couldn't keep
from touching, drawing
our hands over the sloped
sides, the grooves and channels,
and the sleek wedging
where the headlights hid.
The whole car radiant
with everywhere he'd been,
everything he'd done.

Now that's a good way to tell a story: A single line of dialogue counterpoises a main character against a group; this character is spatially centered by means of a witty and understated metaphor; and there is a quickly drawn but convincing crowd scene as the boys flock around the car. Then, a deft sentence fragment informs us as much about the boys' fantasies and cast of mind as it does about the despicable Rich.

When the speaker is enticed into going for a ride with Rich, he hears some thrilling dirty words, he gets to see the Dick Stick—a rubber penis that fits over the stick shift—and he learns a new baseball grip, the "fuckyknuckle": "like this, with the seams, / let's see you do it, / now snap it down hard / this way, that's right, / that's the fuckyknuckle."

In the end Rich is confronted by an outraged mother who berates him in public and threatens him with police action. He runs off, "the back wheels / of the Sting Ray skidding / as it shrieked away," but he has left his mark on the boys. Even as the molester disappears the speaker has begun to practice the fuckyknuckle:

all I could feel
was my throwing hand,
the fingers flexing claw-like
and still more claw-like,
till I got it right.

I expect that Shapiro would describe "The Lesson" as a narrative poem because it tells a story, and it even contains some of the larger elements a short story will contain: setting and theme, as well as dialogue and expressive detail. However, even though it *tells* a story, "The Lesson" is not itself a story because it has only a rudimentary narrative structure and sketches in but a shadowy background. And this poem has theme too, a great deal of theme that it points at directly in the way that poems often do and that short stories usually do not. The proposition to be examined, then, is this: does anecdote + theme = narrative poetry?

If this equation holds, then Shapiro may justly claim to write narrative poetry in such efforts as "Maison des Jeunes," "Home Movie," and "Covenant," and maybe also in shorter works like "Owl" and "Marriage." Yet I am not certain that I would describe Alan Shapiro as a narrative poet. My reservations on this score are not judgments about quality; I do not regard a narrative poem as inherently superior to what I shall call a story poem. Robert Frost's "The Death of the Hired Man" and his "Home Burial" I recognize as narrative poems while thinking of "A Servant to Servants" as a story poem, yet I prefer the latter to the other two.

However he may be classified, it is certain that Shapiro is an excellent poet. *Covenant* is an example of that extreme rarity, a collection with some minor verses but no clinkers. "Seventh Month" reveals his dark and sometimes defensive wit; "Turkey Vultures" displays his enviable gracefulness in line and phrase; "The Visitation" shows him as deft in concealing scaffolding as in avoiding cleverness. His title poem proves that he can write narrative if he chooses to; here is evidence, in a scene of a brother and sister gossiping, of the poet's ear for dialogue:

> Listen, she would be saying, listen Charlie,
> her elbows on the table, both hands open,
> the body fashioned to the voice's weary
> What can you do? What are ya gonna do?
> in answer to some story of a cousin's
> sudden illness (And he was just my age, just
> like that one day he's shaving with the toothpaste),
> or a friend's death (That one, she didn't care
> how sick she got, she always had her hair done),
> his back pain, her arthritis, or the daughter
> who won't diet (And she'd be such a beauty!);

after his joke about the nurse, and hers
about the bedpan, Listen, they each say,
Listen, What are ya gonna do?

But Shapiro prefers to write story poems rather than narrative, and since I find the anecdote-plus-interpretation form unsatisfactory as genuine narrative, I am hard put to think of many contemporary poets I would classify as narrative poets. Mark Jarman comes pretty close; *The Black Riviera,* his fourth volume, contains many poems that tell stories and some that attempt to *be* stories. "The Death of God," a case in point, takes place in Los Angeles circa 1960, where a man "whose wife's enlarged heart was going learned of a drug / That would enlarge the mind." He takes the drug in hope of getting closer to his wife as her life force wanes and gutters. At first, he is elated, for the drug confirms him in his belief "that the body is a radiant intersection of enormous power, / Even his aging and shrinking body that had been apart from hers so long." He becomes convinced that he can cure her merely by touching her, "But she drifted just at the lip of death, / Like a child trailing her fingers along the top of a garden wall, / Turning the tips black with dead lichen and dust, and he turned away."

Then the husband renews his efforts, ingesting more of the drug, and for a time is able to tell himself that he is sharing with his wife the experience of death, traveling with her as she leaves this world. At this point he thinks he is granted an understanding of death, its place in the cosmos and its relation to the individual person. He discovers that death is "larger than the body, like the mind / Radiating from him on the tips of his senses and meeting the crowd of stars." The transcendent vision is heady stuff, and he remembers the god of his childhood and how that god "became a woman / Who held him and led him along a route he was glad to take, / Into the enlarging heart of the world, where prayer was answered / By a touch, a glad cry and deep sleep." But all his vision is delusion; the drug has betrayed him. Lost in his reveries, immersed in the self, he fails his wife in her direst hour: "They needed his voice— / Not the voice of infinite space—to call for help at the speed of light / From the small house in Greater Los Angeles, where God was going quickly."

Jarman tells this story gracefully and memorably, possessing a happy gift for proceeding from the concrete image to misty but effective abstraction in a hallucination sequence: "The highway crossed from the bulbous / Moon's face into the faint promise, like an aura, along the horizon." And strange as some of its imagery is, loose as the time sequence is, the poem is always clear, always visualized. Its theme stands out a little too obviously, but a reader comes to expect this in story poems— for poets are a theme-proud race, it seems, and they might all profit from studying certain fiction writers who exhibit a finer sense of propriety: Peter Taylor or Elizabeth Spencer or Henry James. Then the poets might learn to leave off packing heavy charges of message into small-bore anecdotes. The last five words of "The Death of God"—"where God was going quickly"—are mystifying, distracting, and exasperating. This sort of ambiguity does not provoke the question, "What does the poet mean here?" but instead, "What the hell made him toss that in?"

Still, I have allowed myself to become too vexed. Mark Jarman is good, one of the most thoughtful and adroit poets writing these days, a man with handsome ambitions. I recommend to everyone "The Home," one of the longest pieces in *The Black Riviera*, and a story poem whose ironies and telling reticences are worthy of Chekhov. The title poem is an autobiographical anecdote whose theme is not so rawly naked as those we encounter in, for example, "Liechtenstein" and "Testimony and Postscript," which have lovely moments but are undermined by artificiality.

"Story Hour" is one of Jarman's best efforts and, though it goes on too long (a recurring problem for this poet), one of the best poems I've read in months. The speaker remembers how, as a child drifting to sleep in his bedroom, he listened to the adults telling stories in the living room. He could not hear their words and feels that he was missing everything of the secrets about life that grownups know and will rehearse only to one another. Now, in present time, he thinks that they would speak to him if they could, and in the same terms he understood then:

> It is the story hour on the hilltop.
> The blue sea looks up at the sky,
> The foxtails point with the breeze,
>   The sinless, culprit breeze.
> And everyone's gone, except
> As this dream I wished to dream.

Having set the stage by coloring this hour of childhood as blue and calm and inviting as a Kate Greenaway storybook illustration, he imagines that the grownups do at last speak to him:

> "You wanted to hear us assure you
> That there was only one story,
> And that story a promise
>> Of never-ending love,
>> That you would love us
> Just as a child loves his parents
> And we would love you
> In the same, unchanging way
> And each other, telling the same stories,
> Long after you had grown and gone,
>> To no one listening
>> In his deserted room.
> The one story that is never told
> But thought of as if it had been,
> As a perfect story, none better,
> Is of a love nobody keeps."

The insight in those latter lines—"The one story that is never told / But thought of as if it had been"—is worthy of Henry James or Katherine Mansfield, and the imagined voice of the adults is palpably convincing: this is just how our parents would have spoken to us if they could have articulated the thoughts we knew they were thinking. "Story Hour" is a meditation rather than a story poem, but its discernments are as perspicuous as those in the best fiction, and are offered almost in the same way.

The Black Riviera is a strong book, stronger than Mary Kinzie's *Autumn Eros and Other Poems* but perhaps less fine. In both collections there is a great deal of psychologizing about character, close description of the movements of reverie and memory, and delicately limned reminiscence. But subtle as Jarman is, Mary Kinzie is subtler.

She is so subtle that to trace the contours of her thought requires a fair amount of effort—and more space than this review has at its disposal. "Strawberry Pipe" is a case in point. This poem begins with a long description, consciously Proustian I would suppose, of an heirloom china cup. Then, an unwieldly speculation about the relationship of generations to one another coalesces into a scene of the speaker's mother as a young woman swimming in a lake in North Carolina, and this memory links to another childhood incident in which the speaker as a little girl plucked a Golden Delicious apple, only to find it eaten all away inside by hornets. The apple serves as metaphor for memory and is a strained maneuver which brings back the description of the mother swimming; this latter account becomes a longish scene that gives way to a heavy conclusion, a lament about the tyranny of time and the uncertainty of memory.

Even from my clumsy outline a reader can tell that the poem tries to suspend a ponderous burden of theme by a fragile thread of narrative. When the thread snaps, the poem plunges into an abyss of murky meditations only tenuously connected. These meditations are often tiresomely lengthy, as in this description of the strawberries painted on the cup:

> Like shoots in the wet after a hard winter,
> There rise up, straggly as fur, gap-toothed as dill,
> These fern sprays that seem to tremble behind the leaves,
> Dark green, black-veined, of the strawberry vines.
> White flowers that will harbinger more berries
> Appear in paint beside what they become,
> Like parents in all our photographs before us,
> Which we confuse with those with us in them,
> Except that, then, it's they were the fragrant and pendulous
> Like tapestry rosehips, open pistachios,
> Like pebbles falling on a hot day to the bottom,
> And we, the dry-lipped paperwhites of spring.

This description continues for eleven more lines, and brings us to the episode of the mother swimming—by means of one of the most curious uses of a pun I've ever encountered. The cups are scrawled with a phrase, "Strawberry Ripe," that on the speaker's cup has rubbed away to "Strawberry Pipe." The word "pipe" reminds her of the tone of her voice as a child, and she imagines how it must have sounded to her grown-up relatives: "As though this were the grove where they had played / In the past, listening to my pipings." And so the scene shifts to the lake where her mother swims: "Across the water, one can hear their voices / (Even if the air were empty now)."

If we came across this passage in fiction we would mark it as a faulty transition, flimsy and arbitrary. It would not be successful in narrative poetry, and even in this story poem it finally does not work: we are able to recognize the crossover between auditory and visual imagery as a bit of a cheat, and we must decide whether the charm of the notion makes up for its implausibility as a structural element. It is in instances like these that a lyric or story poet might with some justice claim "principle of association," while a narrative poet might cry "Foul!"

Convoluted as "Strawberry Pipe" is, "Autumn Eros" goes it one better. This poem is so thoroughly overwritten, its vocabulary so extravagant, that at first I regarded it as an extended send-up on the order of W. H. Auden's "Mundus et Infans." It was with disappointed regret that I decided these lines were only sentimental. The subject of the poem is the first journey of an infant on the sidewalk in her stroller. The child is a late child; the parents are "old enough to be grandparents" and they hang protectively about the stroller, "flared in attitudes / Fending and succorant and faintly dazed."

These parents are infatuated with their baby, as of course they ought to be. But even such natural and proper infatuation does not justify the range of hyperbole in this description of the tyke:

> It is as if she burned the atmosphere.
> Like heat wicked from a star, or the gold ions
> Poured down from an angel's mouth and forehead,
> The look of flame licking her upturned face
> Licks at us, too.

Reading these lines, I feel more embarrassed than I do when asked to look at baby pictures. Maybe the emotions here were too powerful or too fresh for Kinzie to handle. In other poems her long sentences with their manifold fine distinctions hold together, but here she lapses into scrambled construction:

> Old enough to be grandparents, we
> Are met by her grandparents at the gate.

> They, too, have had their losses, seeing by stages
> Coarsen all their tender potencies
> And all the gleanings taken from their hands.

And here is another sentence from the poem even more puzzling than the latter: "Calm / Treads out the dark hairs on my father's hand."

I won't belabor the point. If a poet is going to go all gooey-sentimental, a poem about her new baby is a good place to do it. The real wonder is that even in this intoxicated panegyric to an infant there occur passages of sound insight and beautiful expression. At one juncture Kinzie entertains the idea that the baby is for her parents their "tiny Eros," with whom they are "quietly drunk." She wonders then if husband and wife did not formerly feel about one another the way they feel about this child:

> Once, perhaps, we felt so for each other:
> That we were the secret the other one was keeping,
> Even the air the other one was breathing
> In rhythm with the rain that bathed the planet,
> The food the other one drank in by gazing
> So if that gaze extinguished, we should die,—
> As, in a way, we have. Simply died out
> In our embering honeycomb of coal.

Yes, I know—this passage is a bit fruity also. But it is not empty gorgeousness, it is thoughtful and expressive gorgeousness of the sort we find in Shakespeare—and if we do not allow our contemporary poets Shakespeare's latitude, how shall we expect them to approach, however distantly, his power? Shakespeare's advantages, though, are what Kinzie sorely lacks in this poem: stronger narrative incidents, and more of them.

Despite Alan Shapiro's designation of Mary Kinzie as a narrative poet, *Autumn Eros* is almost entirely a collection of meditations. These are closely felt and closely (though not always logically) thought through, and the attention required to enjoy them is often ennobled by her lines. "Rosary," "Lunar Frost," "Stove Sickness," and "Learning the World" are good poems; "Dwellers in the Forest," "Mannikin," and "Angel Food" are even better. But Kinzie's infatuation with divagation, her habit of gnarling bunches of nouns into inseparable knots, and her gelatinous organization make some of her work hard going, especially the long poems.

The longest poem in Cornelius Eady's *The Gathering of My Name* is "The Sheets of Sound." This title refers to the manner of John Coltrane's saxophone playing during a period of time when the great jazzman filled every conceivable space in his solo measures with notes and ideas; it was dense, exciting stuff, and Eady tries to suggest the spirit of Coltrane's concept with ten sections of speedy lines full of leaps and startles and seeming digressions. The fifth section recounts an anecdote the poet knows only as hearsay, but it is important to his design:

> I heard a story, once,
> Told on Miles Davis and
> The young pup, John
> Coltrane,
> Who was seeking out
> The master's
> Wisdom, sort of
> Sitting at his feet,
> So to speak,
> And he asked Mr. Davis
> To reveal to him
> The secret of how
> To finish
> A solo,
> And Miles sort of
> Grunts like a
> Baptist mother,
> And he tells Coltrane:
>
> "Take the
> Damn horn out
> Of your mouth"

Eady makes no attempt to present this probably apocryphal episode as anything other than a casual anecdote, yet it has wit and point and some wide implications, and its casual manner is part of its substance. The rep-

etitions of the disarming phrase "sort of" and the interpolation of the line
"So to speak" are designed to parry any motion toward pretentiousness.
Here is no philosophic parable, no Zen koan, and the desultory atmosphere of the lines freshens their implications with easy understatement.
Coltrane was an earnest student of Eastern philosophies, and he did have
a propensity for guru-seeking. Miles Davis did indeed possess a deep distrust of abstractions and always relied on his traditional roots for the
basis of his music. He was a gruff and laconic talker, and Coltrane's zeal-
ousness must have seemed sophomoric to him as well as possibly delete-
rious to the younger man's art.

Eady's lines seem lazy, almost slovenly, upon the page, yet they give
us clear ideas of two different temperaments, two different philosophies
of art, and, while disavowing parabolic intention, they deliver something
close to a parable. A poem doesn't always have to wave flags and send up
rockets in order to make its points.

An even more taciturn poem, "West 3rd Street, the First Weekend in
June," verges on genuine narrative—yet it doesn't tell a story, it only describes a scene. The central actor we know only as "a neighbor," and we
are not told his age or anything about his background or demeanor. We
don't even know what his face looks like. But the action described is so
characteristic, so unguarded and revealing, that we feel we know a great
deal indeed:

> Across the street, a neighbor
> Carefully dusts his shoes off.
> Leaning out his window,
> He places one inspected pair
> On the fire escape, slowly
> Begins on the other, his ragged
> Yellow wash towel working
> At it, no polish here, just
>
> A critique of wear, a lifting
> Of dust from scuffmarks. He hauls
> The shoes in, shakes the towel
> Out, his head tortoises home,
> And he is rid of something.

The only word uncommon in the least is the verb *tortoises* and, for all its fitness and economy, one might argue that it disturbs the tenor of the poem, the other words being so ordinary, so smoothed-down with daily usage, and the action presented being so unremarkable.

But once the scene is set forth, of course, it *has* become remarkable, heady with implication, brimful of tacit narrative. It is a poem about poverty, urban life, disappointment, and the renewal of hope. The gentleman in the opposite window has gone out earlier to seek opportunity, all dressed up in the best he has got, the handsomest clothing he can afford. But he has met rebuff and frustration. Soon he will try again, but first he must slough off this present mood and make a fresh start. These muted few lines are as eloquent on the subject of courage as are some passages of Virgil.

They are certainly more eloquent than some of Eady's others. "The Wrong Street," for example, and "False Arrest," and "Spic." These are poems about ethnic injustice, a subject that invites eloquence, noble and impassioned utterance. But Eady's lines seem merely querulous, almost whining. Alan Shapiro is right to include historical awareness and historical connection among his requirements for narrative poetry, but the history has to be genuine, rediscovered, and thorough, not a weakly liberal gesture toward an existing attitude. Too many of us minority poets—African American, Jewish, Chinese, Southern, Canuck, Appalachian, Irish, Native American, female, homosexual—like to write poems that say no more than "My tribe has suffered more miserably than your tribe has suffered," and to view that formula as embodying historic truth. But until a history has been researched and absorbed as fact, meditated into philosophy, and at last dramatized in poetry, it is mere bromide. For too long now, recent poets have preached to the converted, taking for granted that whoever is willing to read a poem must already be in agreement with the author's historical conclusions. This moral flabbiness has undermined the historical consciousness of contemporary poetry.

My point is not political; I would not deny injustice as a theme for poetry, thus losing some of the best stanzas ever written. I would only suggest again that poets consider taking cognizance of the procedures of fiction writers who make copious notes about historical background and social conditions, provide dossiers for their characters, and attempt to fit the themes of their work inside the largest frameworks they can conceive. I'm asking for a great deal of labor, and yet no more than fiction writers routinely undertake. If poets complain that such elaborate preparation dampens their spontaneity and élan, I would only reply that they need to find more confidence in their own powers.

A great deal of groundwork must have gone into the composition of Brendan Galvin's *Saints in Their Ox-Hide Boat*. This book-length poem is an historical work in which the sixth-century Irish monk St. Brendan the Navigator recounts the story of his voyages across the Atlantic toward a new world. (He couldn't have known it as *the* New World.) This work is a true narrative poem even by my persnickety standards, and a fascinating story it is.

About 1,300 lines in length, the poem has an advantage for narration that shorter works lack. Galvin has room to draw character and present incident in detail, and he enjoys the breadth of an historical period for his canvas. Because we know relatively little of the culture of St. Brendan's milieu (compared, say, with what we know about Rome and France at the same period), Galvin must focus his purview narrowly while at the same time imagining his details fully and vividly. He has brought rare seriousness to his work.

Brendan is a holy man, but bluff and pragmatic. He carries less burden of fearful superstition than his crew of unlettered countrymen, but Galvin is careful to show that Brendan's faith is still strongly tinctured with the old Gaelic religion and that this hardy monk is, despite himself, also prey to superstition. The poet shows too that the saint's motives are as mixed as his philosophic heritage.

Galvin tells us in a brief foreword that Brendan might have undertaken this perilous sea journey by way of the Hebrides, the Faroes, Iceland, and Greenland to (perhaps) Newfoundland so as to undergo a "blue martyrdom," giving up his "religious brethren, kin, and homeland for a solitude in a foreign country or on an island, the better to contemplate God without distractions." The saint does indeed hunger after God, but he has other impulses too. He tells the story of his voyage to a nameless young scribe and at one point instructs his amanuensis about the attractions of exploring and the active life, the sights to be seen:

shag-defended heights backlit by evening;
rocky stacks; mere humps supporting
washed-up mats of scraw; landfalls of
sheep fat as cattle; egg islands
where, flapping your arms, you drive birds off
and fill your baskets for the change
of diet; treeless anvil shapes without
anchorage; tern-swarmed beaches; skerries;
a narrow stretch between rockfaces
riddled with caves, fast water reeled over
by a dinning stir of gulls, gannets,
puffins, guillemots, skuas—and then
that island you never dream, the one
you'll know only when you wade ashore
and feel, among the bindweed and reddening
ferns, in the silence of lichen-flowering
stones, like a trespasser on some
lump of everlastingness. You'll never know
unless you drop that quill and sail, my boy.

We see that one impetus for his voyage is—adventure. A number of historians have made bold to deny adventure as an important motive during the medieval period, but such an assertion seems just plain dumb. The terms that Galvin supplies to describe the thirst for adventure are apt, completely realistic and unfanciful, but touched with the air of nostalgia that in reminiscence soothes every traveler's recollections.

Brendan strives above all to be a realist, and he is not freshly recounting his voyage to his scribe in *Saints* but instead correcting an account already written. He tells the scribbler to expunge the passage about the voyagers having beached upon a whale's back, to get rid of all the "miracles"—"no dreaming whales / and no gryphons either." He insists on accuracy, and in speaking of an island filled with yelping seals his boat passed, stops to warn his scribe to get his words down correctly.

Yet he has his own superstitions, including the belief that his curragh is animate and intelligent enough to understand his misgivings if he were to voice them aloud. He takes care not to frighten his boat:

> Many's the time, quaking under my cloak
> like a calf who knows he's appointed for meat,
> I admonished my brothers for their fear
> and accused their faith while my own
> turned thin as mist on a wall
> and my resolve melted like snow off ditches.
> Worse, at times I was afraid I'd revealed
> my doubts to that sea-keeping boat.

But if the success of the voyage lies in the hands of the pragmatist, the purpose of the voyage and its profoundest meaning can be revealed only to the mystic holy man. Brendan the Navigator is both kinds of man at the same time, but it is the saint rather than the navigator to whom the revelation comes. At the end of the journey an angel (unrecognized at first) appears to the voyager and fulfills the traditional three functions that angels perform when talking to humankind—prophesying, advising, and revealing a glimpse of the godhead. His prophecy is that later explorers will follow Brendan's trace to this "land beyond the wave": "You are the first I've led here, but others / will sail across centuries to it." His advice is that the holy man think less on his fortune in eternity and be more thankful for the world where he exists in present time: "Smell it, man! Take a deep breath / for once in your life without fearing / you'll spring a rib through a lung / just for falling in love with the world."

For revelation of divinity, the angel turns to the world, to this new world, this latter Eden, that Brendan has discovered. If the angel seems much too pantheistic to be a good Catholic, we can recall that Galvin's foreword to *Saints* notes how Irish Christianity in this period was not constrained by the precepts of Rome. At any rate, the angel is at pains to describe God to Brendan in terms the questing pragmatist can comprehend with mind and hand:

> —Here where no man behind a wall
> has dropped his ear in on his neighbor's
> business yet, for a time the creation
> will please its Maker with original
> birdsong again. He drifts in wild-flower

pollen across your bow and strikes
tendrils from seeds and rain from clouds.
He is there in this startling vine fragrance
and in mud flats edged with rotting fish,
in fish rot and stone damp and rockweed
baking on sand. He's the purple,
blue, and maroon of berries you'll taste
behind that shore.

If Alan Shapiro is accurate in predicting a return of narrative poetry, I would point to *Saints in Their Ox-Hide Boat* as being the kind of narrative I would like to see produced. The story poems that most of us write do well enough, but they lack the scope and immediacy of true narrative verse. I make this remark as a descriptive observation, not as a critical stricture. There are many story poems superior to genuine narrative poems, and there are, Lord knows, plenty of genuine narratives that are execrable poetry. But only reviewers and literary critics have to read those productions. Lousy books of poetry constitute one punishment, at least, that the virtuous among us are spared.

Piecework:
The Longer Poem Returns

It is surprising to discover that the longish poem has made a comeback, that poets are stretching out from the tight metaphysical lyric into broader, less well-charted latitudes. After all, we'd been told (often in supercilious tones) that poetry had lost its audience and now claimed but minimal interest even from readers of belles-lettres. Perhaps these two statements are not contradictory; we might imagine that a small audience would be more intensely devoted than a big one, more prepared to welcome our bards' expansive efforts. But whatever the case may be, it is not true that the lengthy poem has driven contemporary readers off, for the high efflorescence of this fashion seems of recent origin.

In preparing for this essay-review I was able to count well over one hundred examples of longer works published in the United States in the past five years and was able to read through fifty of them. I am speaking not only of book-length poems, though there are plenty of those, but of books that include poems longer than fifteen pages. David Slavitt has designated this length "the longer poem," noting bemusedly that the longer poem is actually shorter than what we think of as "the long poem." I am unwilling to bring strict line-counting to my choices; the extended poem ought to be more genuinely recognizable by its goals than by its bulk.

My reading reveals, however, that relatively few of these efforts are in fact extended wholes; they are usually mosaic structures, different in kind from the strongly grounded earlier lengthies like *The Rape of the Lock* and *Aurora Leigh*. Long poems were the pride of nineteenth-century American literature, and titles like *Evangeline, Snowbound,* and *Song of Myself* enjoyed a prestige that not even the prophetic demurrals of Edgar Allan Poe could damage. But after our Golden Age came Modernism and two key works that redefined the structure of the long poem. Contemporary poetry has still not recovered from *The Waste Land* and *The Cantos.*

"These fragments I have shored against my ruins": this phrase from Eliot's crazed and despairing Tiresias is almost too famous to bear repeating, yet it is too apt to overleap. The collage method that Pound and Eliot instituted has been as influential in poetry as its analogous procedures have been in plastic art and music. Picasso, Braque, Jean Arp, and Kurt Schwitters are but four masters who made their canvases and sculptures littorals of fragments, and Stravinsky described modernist musical structure as the "pulverization" of classical harmony. The fragmentation and subsequent recombination of familiar elements is one of the obvious hallmarks of Modernism.

This particular modernist method has not been discarded. Contemporary poets still find it as useful as William Carlos Williams did in *Paterson,* as David Jones did in *In Parenthesis,* as Charles Olsen did in *The Maximus Poems.* Sometimes our contemporaries claim the same motive as the Modernists, saying that the press and scurry and bewildering confusion of twentieth-century life cannot be adequately rendered in the old-fashioned way, with stories that have beginnings, middles, and endings. Only the continuous rearrangement of small motifs can give an accurate impression of current history. Other poets—Frank Bidart, for example, and A. R. Ammons—have justified their use of fragmentation by calling upon certain conceptions of psychology and physical science.

Whatever the reasons, the mosaic procedure is alive and widespread and capable of producing a startling variety of tones and effects. A number of poets nowadays may adhere to the same general methods of composing longish mosaic works, but these may bear little resemblance to one another as finished poems.

Anselm Hollo is a poet whose allegiance to the high modernist tradition is obvious. His pages look as if they date from the 1930s; his broken phrases are scattered over the paper in a typographical analogy to calligraphy, with parentheses, ampersands, italics, and boldface fonts abounding. The Daddy Bear influence here is, of course, Ezra Pound.

Hollo himself is quite straightforward about this, willing to belong to that chatty tribe of versifiers who refer to Pound in their poems in the most offhand manner as "old Ez." Sometimes these poets say "ole" or "ol'," but in Hollo's sonnet-only-because-it-has-fourteen-lines, "i. m. Ernest Hemingway," he prefers "(old Ez   he wrote it down)." Hollo bobs in the wake of Pound's hydroplane of interests, translating fragments of Greek, turning discourse on classical subjects into slang ("Diog' said Pythagoras / would have liked to hear that"), interpolating diary scraps ("3:30 p.m. the view is / Flatirons above trees & / neighbors across the street"), disguising personalities under nicknames like "Tattered Old Bird" and "Comrade Blank," and running to polyglot ("that doesn't seem too much to wish for / on the way to the old *pulvis et umbra   il faut s'amuser, non?*"). He borrows other of Pound's devices too; almost any page of the middle *Cantos* will furnish usages that turn up in *Corvus.*

Hollo's organization is Poundian too, a collocation of fragments that determines meaning mostly by means of spatial contiguity, rarely by means of logical argument or sustained thought, and almost never by means of narrative continuity. Hollo's reliance on fragments is so assiduous, in fact, that I have had trouble making out which parts of *Corvus* are meant to stand independently and which are pieces of longer works. Sometimes I would decide the whole book was a single poem and then I'd change my mind. It may be that this poet would declare all his work, original and translation, makes up a seamless whole, though if he did so, I'd greet his statement with stubborn skepticism.

But surely pieces like "1991" and "West Is Left on the Map" are wholes, and I am inclined to read "Not a Form at All But a State of Mind" in the same way, even though its separate parts are clearly demarcated and given individual titles. It is even more probable that the series called "Survival Dancing" is meant to be read as a whole, for an endnote refers to it in the singular when it tells us that it is dedicated to the memory of a friend, Joe Cardarelli.

This series is not easy to read in the singular, however; it consists of fourteen sections (or fourteen separate poems) with titles like "Kindly

Water Other Level," "Now on to Ghazal Gulch," and "In the Music Composed by Nutritious Algae." The title of the sequence was found, we are told, "on a laundromat bulletin board in upstate New York, in the early summer of 1994." Though the "found" title alerts us to the casual nature of the poems, I surmise that the several parts of "Survival Dancing" are meant to compose an elegy whose principal topics—besides Mr. Cardarelli—are memory and the art of poetry. If I am correct, then "Survival Dancing" ought to fit squarely into the tradition of "Lycidas" and "Adonais." But never would Milton or Shelley begin their elegies with a stanza like the one that opens "Canto Arastra," the first poem in Hollo's sequence:

> opera creatures   technicolor elves
> love to roam in profusion
> make home in voices   shouting at no one
> dotty shamans   pathos & farce transmitters
> many birds singing waters gardens in Spain

The endnote is little help. The word "arastras" of the title refers to millstones used to grind up ore, and the poet discovered it "on a drive to Central City, Colorado, an old mining town now abandoned to slot machines, with Joe Cardarelli in late April 1994." So the title may be a tip-off to method: the millstones of Time crush memory to fragments and leave the glittering gravel that makes up the first stanza. Or at least I think that's what the second stanza implies:

> but time's grindstone jaws
> surely crunch graybeards
> & smoky lamplit ore
> in fatal history's central city

Fair warning here that the memories alluded to—*not* reported—will be fragmentary and often so personal that there is little way to discover their significance. "Kindly Water Other Level" begins with three puzzling lines ("two found together   construct regard / place comb in hand part knot exactly / look out windows   collect words") and later presents a stanza I take to be a scrap of someone's conversation, since it is set in quotation marks: " 'she went right / clearing fence.' " But who says it—or when or why—we never know.

Such giblets are characteristic of the old-Ez breed of long poem. One reads them rather as one inspects the clues in a detective novel, hoping that they will later connect with other details to bring the whole design into focus. But these particular scraps, like a great many others, turn out to be red herrings; we scan them with an inevitably frustrated curiosity and no emotional engagement. (This reaction also applies, I find, to a great many pages of *The Cantos*.)

Yet, as with Pound's massy confused work, certain passages arrest the attention with a strange mournfulness. Consider the final stanzas of "Now on to Ghazal Gulch":

> Tiny figures
> from the past
> troop by
> in porkpie hats
>
> And why not
> think of them as
> "souls free of the body"

That the porkpie hats here are supposed to recall another dead artist, the jazzman Lester Young, I cannot aver, but the whiff of reminiscence adds to the wistful tone, whether purposefully or not. For myself, I would not doubt that the fleeting allusion is intentional, for Anselm Hollo's loyalty to allusion is fierce. But his allusions are not always easy to recognize and his endnotes are haphazard. For instance, the titles of two consecutive poems ("As Leaves Sweep Past," "& Time Trots By") make up a single phrase, and the first is a quotation from one popular song ("Autumn Leaves") while the second is a variation on the title of another ("As Time Goes By"). It is also possible that the first poem title is intended to remind us of a line in "Canto Arastra": "sweep twenty years from day."

Hints, whispers, wisps, shards, scraps, sighs—whatever can they add up to? Can a poet make an effective poem out of mere echoes? I would submit that Anselm Hollo is sometimes able to do so, and I'll also propose that the final poem in his "Survival Dancing" sequence gives it a fitting closure and constellates many of the elements of the preceding parts. It does not make sense of earlier lines like "dazzled heart thump rhododendron," and I think the interpolation of the cornball invented proverb is a mistake. But this poem does engender a mood that casts an emotional tinge over even his most puzzling sections. I believe that Hollo must think so too, for his endnote is careful to identify the allusions in "At Evenfall" to Edith Piaf, Mallarmé, Rilke, and Edward Dorn:

> recall enormous heave of moment
> *la vie en rose*
> before some Mallarméan blows it into the *vide* or *abîme*
>
>   (but *timing egg in storm*
>   *beats driving car through rock*)
>   —Albanian proverb
>
> sun shadow fields cast loose
> drum vibes in ground moths flutter
> "O Lady Time, summer was great"
>
> but now no house of letters stands
> Elizabethanly enjoying given song
> paradox knots each graduate
>
> yet she'll stay up to read & write long letters
> & on still tree-lined streets attend her musings
> do art   eat well   never please wicked money
>
>   always treat language like a dangerous toy

Anselm Hollo's poems are hard to figure out, though they are not hard to read. But isn't that odd? Surely one of the advantages of writing a long poem is the opportunity offered by its length to make things clear to readers. The lyric has to be compressed, sometimes mercilessly, and ambiguities are bound to inhere. It is the poet's job then to make the ambiguities expressive. In a long poem, no such problem: there is room to clarify and expound.

Yet I have found the contemporary long poem much harder to comprehend than the lyric, and I attribute a great deal of the difficulty to the particulate character of these works, to their showcasing of the fragment. If an old-Ez poet like Hollo relies on little bits of things—puns, allusions, echoes—then Harryette Mullen's *Muse & Drudge* would be blank pages without these devices and others dependent upon even smaller elements: homophones, anagrams, nonsense syllables, fractures of slang.

Muse & Drudge tells no story, pursues no argument, entrains no consecutive thought. It is a rant, of the sort that Allen Ginsberg and Jack Kerouac and their cronies made fashionable forty years ago. When Mullen devotes a stanza to describing her way of writing, it could apply as well to Ginsberg and our other ranters:

> mutter patter simper blubber
> murmur prattle smatter blather
> mumble chatter whisper bubble
> mumbo-jumbo palaver gibber blunder

The stanza is apt and does not stand alone, for though Mullen's book apparently has no narrative and no argument, it does have a subject matter to which she has attached a lot of attitude. Her topic seems to be (and I broach this possibility with nervous diffidence) the situation of a black female poet in the United States who is trying to make a viable modern poetry out of African American speech rhythms and folk forms, attacking traditional materials in a radical but conservative style.

She not only displays attitude but sometimes takes it as her subject. *Muse & Drudge* is the kind of poetry that will gain power from public performance, and Mullen's adoption of a special attitude as a speaker is much like an actor's slipping into a role. This persona is one most of us are familiar with: sassy and savvy, fleet of wit and fluent of tongue, assertive and sometimes combative, daring the audience to back-talk:

> ass can't cash
> mere language
> sings scat logic
> talking shit up blues creek

no miss thing
ain't exactly rude
just exercising
her right to bare attitude

The persona of the impudent mocker of authority is well liked in African American culture, and Mullen alludes to what is probably the most famous example in current oral literature, the Signifying Monkey. But I am at a loss to say what point she makes with the allusions: "monkey's significant uncle / blond as a bat / took off beat path / through tensile jungle."

To be honest, I was lost more than once in this maze of bantering chatter, finding lines where I could not pick up even a glimmer of the intended meaning: "he watches her bio clock balk on seepy time / petals out of rhythm docked for trick crimes." Here I don't know whether I've failed to pick up key references or whether Harryette Mullen is just making noises. Sometimes it seems that's all she is doing:

what you can do
is what women do
I know you know
what I mean, don't you

Usually, though, Mullen's energy and humor and verbal inventiveness carry me along with her, gasping and giggling. Within the boundaries of her special genre, within the limits of her tightly circumscribed form, she is a master technician. Her invariable form is the singsong quatrain, her method improvised variation:

update old records
tune around the verses
fast time and swing out
head set in a groove

felt some good sounds
but didn't have the time
sing it in my voice
put words in like I want them

I warned you about the puns. Here "tune" for "turn" and "head set" are pretty lame. Punchier ones from other stanzas will include "deja voodoo queens," "apocalypso," "hip chicks ad glib," "clipped bird eclipsed moon"—and this one in the last line of a stanza that can mean little unless one happens to remember from a few years back a beautiful African American model named Lola Falana:

> black-eyed pearl
> around the world girl
> somebody's anybody's
> yo-yo fulani

Anagrams abound as well: "a voyeur leers / at X-rated reels," "tomboy girl with cowboy boots / takes coy bow in prom gown," "avid diva," "lemon melon melange." She includes proverbs straight ("sun goes on shining / while the debbil beats his wife") and in elided variation ("the blacker more sweeter juicier"). Sexual signification is everywhere ("jelly in a vise," "hip signals like later," "that snapping turtle pussy"), but the intent is usually humorous as in this quatrain:

> wishing him luck
> she gave him lemons to suck
> told him please dear
> improve your embouchure

Mullen is as allusive as Hollo, but her references are more likely to be to blues lyrics, hymns, spirituals, jazz, and popular songs than to book learning. If one knows the tune "Disorder at the Border," the line "how a border orders disorder" has resonance, but it must be a mere botheration to readers who have never listened to Coleman Hawkins. I assume the allusion in "under the weather / down by the sea" is obvious to most folks, but how many will remember Jimmy Rushing's "Rusty Dusty Blues"—"get off your rusty dusty / give the booty a rest"?

There are other jazz reminiscences throughout, and Mullen's associative usages constitute a kind of verbal jazz, variations on themes that are usually but not unfailingly familiar. She doesn't always succeed because some of her variations are obvious and silly ("get right with

Godzilla"), and sometimes she seems merely to be running the scales, filling in time until a fresh wavelet of inspiration carries her forward. But even the best jazz players may sound perfunctory for a chorus or two.

Muse & Drudge may bear a superficial resemblance to some of the more predictable rap music that spackles our airwaves, but Mullen is a sophisticated mind using unsophisticated tools. Her book is prefaced with a telling quotation from Callimachus: "Fatten your animal for sacrifice, poet, / but keep your muse slender," and her first line—"Sapphire's lyre styles"—erects a paradoxical cultural complexity that foreshadows her main themes. I take this line to refer to the poet herself, an African American Sappho ("Sapphire" was the wife of Kingfish on the old "Amos 'n' Andy" radio and television programs), and its heavy accents and insistent slant rhyme strike up the jazzy sound the ensuing volume maintains. She continues:

> Sapphire's lyre styles
> plucked eyebrows
> bow lips and legs
> whose lives are lonely too
>
> my last nerve's lucid music
> sure chewed up the juicy fruit
> you must don't like my peaches
> there's some left on the tree

Muse & Drudge is a whole; it makes the sound of one speaker standing in one place and uttering in syncopated *Sprechstimme* a long associative sermon. So perhaps it is unfair for me to say that it is made up of fragments even smaller than Anselm Hollo's. Are not these puns, allusions, and asides common rhetorical devices in the service of the large designs of all poets? Yes, of course they are, but because of the static nature of this poem they become the main points of notice, and it is only through them that a reader's interest can be maintained. That's why I'd recommend Harryette Mullen be taken in moderate doses, maybe ten pages at a time, because when one's attention has to focus on language elements as small sometimes as phonemes, it flags and grows dulled.

Hollo and Mullen present some difficulties, but they are quickly out-paced by Richard Kenney. The complexities of *The Invention of the Zero* are so multifoliate that an accurate description of them would devour my entire review space. A simple straightforward account of the book is bound to be inaccurate, but I despaired early on of dealing with much of Kenney's fascinating rococo detail.

The torso of the volume consists of four separate narrative poems. The first is an account of an airman driving his jeep in the predawn New Mexican desert toward the atomic test detonations at Frenchman Flat; the second is the story of a group of Army officers stationed in the Galá-pagos Islands to watch for Japanese aircraft that never appear; the third tells of the great typhoon that nearly destroyed the United States Third Fleet in 1944; the fourth narrates what happened to Navy Seal Lew Elsey on his first parachute jump.

Except for their temporal proximity—World War II—there is no in-herent relationship among these adventures. But Kenney has surrounded them with prologues and epilogues, both general and individual, and has imposed upon the whole a daunting intellectual superstructure which is supposed to underscore consonant elements in each circumstance and tie them all into a conception of history. The central notion is that mankind's destruction of the atom has created a new world in an action analogous to the creation of the universe out of the primordial destruc-tion that was the Big Bang. This conception motivates Kenney's inclu-sion of geological, zoological, military, political, and scientific history at almost every point by means of analogy or associative spark-gapping. The four incidents that make up the central narrative may look like ran-dom happenings without apparent aim, but in the poet's vision they are minor yet necessary passages in a war whose blind final purpose was to bring into being a new world reborn from the radioactive ashes of old ideas.

The overall conception of *The Invention of the Zero* is the most ambi-tious and probably the loftiest of any of the books I investigated. The ef-fort is not entirely an artistic success, and one has to wonder if it ever could have been, given the difficulties of the subject, the grandioseness of design, and the elaborateness of the poet's language.

It may be diction that at last overloads Kenney's huge fragile spider web of metaphors and analogies. He has made his language as ornate and overcharged as that of Gerard Manley Hopkins, but he prefers to use it as decoration rather than as vehicle for his often arcane musings. Sometimes, in fact, Kenney alludes directly to Hopkins:

> But what can I know,
> Father, other
> than that the zephyr's
> first root's
> wrought rain?
> is this the West
> land's last lay?

He points toward the closing line of "Thou art indeed just, Lord," but such clear sources are unusual. Kenney's array of reference also includes a bristling armory of technological hardware, astronomy, American history, childhood rhymes and games, ancient Greek culture and mythology, physical theory, magic—you name it. Here is the passage I chose as a core sample, and I've barely begun to enumerate the starting-chock topics in these few lines:

> Turn off the screen. This dirt's reversible;
> there's software for you! Corse and plot, eternity's
> at hand, friend, and who has terms for that? *Etc.*,
> you'll say? A grease spot on the radar dish, *dah-*
> *dit*, tin phone to the monkey's ear! O sibyl-
> lance of far light, firelight's fiber optics, souter-
> rain to empyrean, Reader!—*blink, blink*, a pulsar's
> hopeless Paul Revering, dictees taken from the dark garden,
> gravity, adumbrated once more by black arts
> into another cursed cosmogonic satyr
> play—
>
>   And this one, too, begun with apples
> falling, the click of billiard balls gone wrong . . .
>   God

ends up verisimilar, steep down the decimal
somewhere, dicing quarks in a heavy water's
wet, hot heaven. That's the text, taken simple.
Make it sing!

Whatever can he mean, "taken simple"? This passage does recapitulate some part of his largest theme—that history drives forward into the ultimate past—so its import is not unprepared for, but what a gumbo of reference it boils up! Here Newton's apple is identified with the one Eve served up; "billiard balls gone wrong" refers to a theory of the reversibility of time in a closed atomic system, which, if true, reduces God to a mere physical entity subject to mathematical analysis and description, so that the God of Deuteronomy becomes only a god of deuterium ("heavy water"), forever dividing matter into smaller indeterminate parts ("dicing quarks"=chopping subatomic particles=playing dice with the universe, a notion Einstein refused to countenance). And so on— *"Etc.,"* as the poem says, a leitmotif term Kenney substitutes for the mathematical symbol *sigma*, implying an additive infinity of meanings and significations. . . . And we didn't even mention puns like "sybil-lance," "Revering," "Corse," "verisimilar," and "far light, firelight's."

So, it ain't simple. But has he made it sing, as he so cheerfully encouraged himself to do? I will equivocate: yes it sings, more often and more steadily than one might expect; no, it often falls flat, maunders, babbles, and bores the reader numb. *The Invention of the Zero* is overdone—and that's an understatement. But Kenney recognized the chances he was taking when he chose this species of diction, and he decided not to change his course:

> *What change?* What change can I recall, or work?
> I'm doomed to overstatement, last as first:
> a sun's reintroduction, new forms of worship, fustian
> as ever: *air, earth, water, fire*—

Still, the poem is just too fancy for its own good. The language is so inspissated that it wraps its subject matter with a dense fog of verbosity. Six times I have read parts nine to twelve of the section called "Lucifer," and I still don't know exactly what happened during Lew Elsey's frightening escapade. Marginal glosses tell me that his parachute failed, that his reserve parachute collapsed and tangled about his feet, that in some undescribed fashion either he got it untangled or it freed itself, and I learn from an endnote that he survived his misadventure. But the climax of the story is so encrusted with rhetoric I cannot make out the action:

> Where now Lew's tangled shroud lines all unknot:
> vines and roots of green earth rising, wrist and ankle,
> cheek and eyelid, rhizomes there in blue veins cool
> as milkweed sap, where the dream takes up again, *in medias
> res:* here feather's vane grows flat, metallic, and the monitor
> takes wing. Here mongoose scurries forth from the domed
> sanctum of the reptile's egg—
>   Kettledrum, please—
>   His meteoric
> moot future mirrored overhead in straked heaven,
> while under all the world begins (O hot premonitory
> hunch!) again, anticipating Kingdom
> Come.

When I suggest that *The Invention of the Zero* fails artistically, I mean only that the complete book produces no single complex of effect, intellectual or emotional. What remains in the mind is the dazzle of it, an incandescence struck for its own sake rather than for illumination. This poem is not a handy lantern but a Roman candle, and its immense self-indulgence is part of its fun. Page to page, line to line, it is for the most part a lark, and it may be that when I thought I discovered letdowns I was only suffering fatigue.

This book is for the reader who enjoys discursiveness, acrobatic word-play, intricate versification, and a wilderness of pedantry. If you like Evan Connell's *Points for a Compass Rose* or Avram Davidson's *Adventures in Unhistory,* then Richard Kenney may be the poet you have been searching for. I remember that Dr. Johnson was so enamored of *The Anatomy of Melancholy* he would rise before sunup to continue reading it. I like to fancy he would enjoy a passage of untamable caprice like the following, wherein the god Neptune makes a personal appearance during the Third Fleet's deadly 1944 encounter with a typhoon:

> Unsettling notion! Here green serpents' jaws,
> jewelled scales coiling: coastwise sailors watched the Pillars
> of Hercules awash this way, once; here we'd
> left our own home waters, I was thinking—
>   Jostled
> from the thought by greater mystery: no pelorus
> but trident's needles swinging wild, in green seaweed
> and not much else, *ex machina,* the god slung
> up a breeches buoy and, piped aboard, bore
> heaven to the deck. Ring-crusted knuckle-
> bones unkissed, he closed two loony hawsepipe eyes, kelp-
> caped and straightening to speak, all barnacles
> and bared teeth, beard aquiver like a Gorgon's scalp,
> his own adjusted with a little coral atoll,
> tipped and jaunty: *now hear this!* Rum eschatology
> professed by One Who Ought to Know! The quorum
> of initiates assembled to a scallop
> shell they'd torch-cut from an oil drum for his throne.
> They blew the conch. He sneezed.
>   The sailors all went prone.

We have been examining works whose building blocks have been tiny ones, so that the resulting structures are unsteady in balance though strikingly baroque in appearance. But Ellen Bryant Voigt resurrects a traditional long form with less wobbly foundations. *Kyrie* is a sonnet sequence concerned with the dread "Spanish" influenza that ravaged the world in 1918–19, taking twenty-five million lives (including a half-million in the United States). Her pages make up a sort of panoramic novel, a little like Defoe's *Journal of the Plague Year,* and at first I thought that for such a subject the sonnet was too small and constricted a form to sustain the poet's design.

I was wrong. It is true that sonnets are so self-contained they cannot produce much forward narrative movement, but Voigt has realized that enough of them, placed in proper order, can produce the illusions of motion and duration. Reading *Kyrie* is a little bit like flipping rapidly through a stack of still photographs to see the figures move. That is how film works, of course, and finally I was reminded powerfully of silent films—especially those of D. W. Griffith, whose talent for making great historical outlines visible by means of small personal detail is almost matched by Voigt.

Like any novel or film, *Kyrie* offers a cast of characters related by the book's subject matter, and like Griffith's *Intolerance* or V. I. Pudovkin's *Mother*, it lifts its regard at times from individual plights to place them in wider scope by means of metaphor. Griffith used repeated shots of a mother rocking a cradle to recall his theme, Pudovkin those of a frozen river thawing, but Voigt employs more than one. The prologue pictures new forest growth after a fire; the first poem offers an eclipse of the sun; "The barber, the teacher, the plumber, the preacher" is a long traveling shot with a nursery-rhyme voiceover; and the epilogue presents the onset of winter. All these metaphors symbolize the spread of the disease. They don't strain the imagination; indeed, they are steadfastly unoriginal. But they are just and moving and comfortable to the time and place.

Voigt's method is for the most part stringently visual, even when her subjects can present no palpable image. That is why she reminds me so strongly of those silent filmmakers who could make mere commonplace objects beautifully expressive. The following sonnet is a picture of the absence of a woman:

> Around the house uneasy stillness falls.
> The dog stiffens the ruff at her ears,
> stands, looks to the backdoor, looks to the stairwell,
> licks her master's shoe. What she hears
>
> must be a pitch high on the Orphic scale,
> a light disturbance in the air,
> like flicks of an insect's wings or a reed's whistle
> distant and brief: he barely stirs.
>
> Out in the kitchen something seems to settle—
> cloth on a dish, dust on a chair?

The animal whimpers now but doesn't growl:
this absence has a smell.
　　　　　　Poor master,
it's touched him too, that shift in molecules,
but all he feels is more of what's not there.

I mustn't leave the impression that *Kyrie* is a book of silent images. It contains characters who are given voice in letters or in interior monologues, and now and again there is actual speech, though usually as indirect discourse. Some characters appear only once, but we might follow others—an enlisted soldier and his fiancée, a minister with prayer book, a heartsick doctor, a young schoolteacher, the mother of a stillborn child—through several poems. The narrative is not rounded with a beginning, middle, and end like a novel, but it does have a novel's progression and does employ fictional techniques like flashback and background exposition.

Exposition is the bane of fiction writer and poet alike. How can the author get necessary information into the pages without setting up a blackboard and lecturing? The problem is more difficult for a poet because information usually isn't "poetic." But Voigt is generally adroit at finding a character—a doctor or undertaker, say—who can broach the necessaries from within a dramatic situation. Occasionally, though, she has no recourse but to tell us something in an unidentified voice, as in these lines about the fact that the influenza once thought finished has returned to rampage again:

Who said the worst was past, who knew
such a thing? Someone writing history,
someone looking down on us
from the clouds. Down here, snow and wind:
cold blew through the clapboards,
our spring was frozen in the frozen ground.
Like beasts in their holes,
no one stirred—if not sick
exhausted or afraid. In the village,
the doctor's own wife died in the night
of the nineteenth, 1919.

Verse can hardly be plainer than in this example, and for Voigt's purposes it really needed only to be serviceable, to fill in some data that would give the succeeding sonnets force and drama. But this poem has its own power; its understatement produces an emotional effect that Richard Kenney's overstatement rarely achieves or tries to achieve. The last sentence is even quieter than the preceding lines:

> But it was true: at the window,
> every afternoon, toward the horizon,
> a little more light before darkness fell.

More powerful, though, are the poems directly concerned with individual figures. In the following sonnet a woman remembers her dead children, contrasting imagined evils with the real ones that befell, recalling a tiny detail like fingernails, crooning out her sorrow in monorhyme:

> After I'd seen my children truly ill,
> I had no need to dream that they were ill
> nor in any other way imperiled—
> no more babies pitching down the well,
> no more watching from shore as my boy rolls
> like a kicked stone from the raft, meanwhile
> Kate with a handful of bees—
>
>   when I was a girl,
> I practiced in the attic with my dolls,
> but Del went out of right mind, his fingernails
> turned blue, and Kate—no child should lie so still,
> her small excitable body held enthralled. . . .
> After that, in order to make it real
> I dreamed them whole.

There is no complexity of characterization in *Kyrie*. The young soldier is brave and naïve, the doctor is weary and disillusioned, the minister is defeated but dutiful, other survivors are either bitter or despairing. These would be clichéd figures in serious fiction, flat stereotypes. Yet one might say the same of the speakers in *Spoon River Anthology*. Poetry has the power to ennoble stereotypes, to give their simplicity a starkness of outline that limns itself upon the mind, causing a reader like me to nod his head unconsciously, acknowledging the truth of the portraiture. In the following poem Voigt glimpses a moment in the psychic life of a widower whose wife has died in childbirth. A welter of feelings moil in him: sorrow, regret, anger, wistfulness, and love. We see him in the process of becoming a different person than he ever was before, and in the last line we find that he is embittered and will remain bitter for the rest of his years, ruining his own life and damaging that of his child. This sonnet tells a fairly involved story, presented mostly in images:

> He stands by the bed, he sits beside the bed,
> he lays his unfledged body on the bed
> where she had lain. If he'd had the right words
> in his prayer, if he'd stayed awake
> all night, if he'd been good, been wise, perhaps
> he could have brought her back, the way she drew him
> out of his dark moods, guitar in her lap,
> her hair lace and shadow on her cheek—
> in the hard-backed book propped open by the lamp
> the shape-notes swarmed like minnows on the page,
> she'd said their lives were scripted there.
> Nearby someone feeds the treasonous baby.
> *She lied* is the first verse of his new life.

Kyrie is not the first sonnet sequence to undertake historical panorama. Gary Gildner's *Letters from Vicksburg* (Unicorn Press, 1976) is somewhat similar, and I'm sure there must be others. I'll wager, though, that mighty few of them surpass Ellen Bryant Voigt's in breadth of understanding or depth of compassion. Without specious self-identification (she doesn't "feel the pain" of these figures), without tear-jerking rhetoric, she recovers for us the wrenching fear and the crushing sadness of this passage in history. Her restraint is so darkly eloquent because she respects the people she writes of and is at pains not to violate their dignity. Yet she fears she has done so, and in the penultimate poem she imagines that the dead as a group reproach her for bringing their sorrow to light once more:

Why did you have to go back, go back
to that awful time, upstream, scavenging
the human wreckage, what happened or what we did
or failed to do? Why drag us back to that ditch?
Have you no regard for oblivion?

History is organic, a great tree,
along the starched corduroy of its bark
the healed scars, the seasonal losses
so asymmetrical, so common—
why should you set out to count?

Don't you people have sufficient woe?

Yes we do. But generally it only perplexes, confuses, and angers us. Poetry like *Kyrie* provides a perspective by which we can measure our own woe against the woe of others, perhaps to discover even in our personal anguish the consoling power of compassion.

In this essay I have looked at long poems which present a rubbly first impression, whose parts appear initially to be discrete, and I was curious whether the particulate method of composition, even with its drawbacks, is capable of producing an apprehendable and aesthetically satisfying whole. But maybe my question is irrelevant. If Modernists like Pound and Williams were correct in their assumptions, the apprehendable whole is an antiquated illusion, a falsity that belies the true character of twentieth-century history.

The trouble with this idea is that it denies validity to palpable successes. Alban Berg's *Violin Concerto* may sound incoherent to the unaccustomed ear, but it is as inexorably unified as a mathematical demonstration. The same is true—or almost true—of *The Waste Land*, whose gnarly details are held together by two interlocked narratives. Because these two works are actually though covertly unified, should we name them counterfeits? Are *Paterson* and *The Cantos* superior to them just because these latter fail at unity?

In the books discussed here, Kenney and Voigt set out to produce unified wholes. Voigt has succeeded in this aim better than Kenney because she has not burdened her structure with a surplus of detail. Hollo and

Mullen probably did not aim at sculpting single rounded shapes, and their poems are memorable only in those fragments that glitter more brightly than the surrounding clutter. The advantage of architecture in the long poem is that each part supports every other and a homogeneity of interest results. With the particulate method, in the "open form," the separate small parts vie with one another for attention, as in a sort of poetic jumble sale. I consider both these kinds of poetry legitimate but am not convinced they possess equal staying power.

The Contemporary Long Poem:
Minding the Kinds

While gathering and reading a largish number of contemporary long poems, I began to give some of the files of specimens fanciful names. I found "The Rant," as practiced by Allen Ginsberg in *Howl* and by Harryette Mullen in *Muse & Drudge;* I found many examples of "Mosaic," such as Anselm Hollo's *Corvus* and Ellen Bryant Voigt's *Kyrie*. I was able to distinguish two types of autobiography. One I called "The Mirror Crack'd" because it offered up the author's life in piecemeal fragments interspersed with distantly related material. Michael Mott's *Corday* (Black Buzzard Press, 1995) was fairly typical: it interrupted an account of the poet's life as a war protestor in the late 1960s with an idiosyncratic selection of events from the career of Charlotte Corday, the woman who murdered the revolutionary figure Jean Paul Marat in Paris in 1793. The other kind of autobiographical poem I denominated "Internal Journal" because it recounted some limited amount of the poet's life with frequent interpolations of cultural, social, and historical musings. Gary Metras's *Seagull Beach* (Adastra Press, 1995) was a genial, engaging example of this sort.

Other classifications pointless to describe here in any detail included "The Narrative Distillate," "Fleetchat," "The String of Beads," and "The Ruminative Ramble," this last a type in which the poet attempted an old-fashioned didactic effort, usually a philosophical argument or a personal essay. A particularly strong example of the Ruminative Ramble is "A Georgic for Doug Crase" in George Bradley's *The Fire Fetched Down* (Knopf, 1996), although it more closely resembles an Ovidian epistle than the Vergilian georgic its title promises.

Three other classifications attracted my attention more steadily than did the aforementioned. These were "The Jigsaw Biography," "The Spiritual Journey," and "The Verse Novel"—for the last of which I distinguished two kinds. I had expected to find numerous verse novels—long poems that told the kinds of stories fiction writers might set down—but it became apparent as I read how forbidding are the difficulties of the verse novel and why they are scarcer than other sorts of the long poem.

A true verse novel ought to possess, I decided, many of the virtues of its prose counterpart: temporal plot, strong characterization, convincing setting and background, coherent incidents. To these it would add some of the advantages of poetry: exciting language, verse design, striking metaphor, and compression of thought. Most long poems do not attempt to include so many prize qualities. If they emphasize the energies of language they are likely to be interior in nature, uninterested in observing the exterior world as fiction is obliged to do. If long poems do present stories made up of objective incidents, they usually break them down into separate intense moments unconnected by chain of circumstance or by supplied transitions.

But Robert McDowell's *The Diviners* stands out forthrightly as being first and foremost a story. It takes place over a period of about two decades, beginning in 1958, and concerns a middle-class American family with father (Al, a boorish wealthy clothes designer), mother (Eleanor, lonely and depressed), and son (Tom, disenchanted with the family's empty bourgeois life). These are the basic materials of many a prose novel concerned with the same period of time, and most of the incidents here might show up in fiction by John Updike or Richard Yates: adultery and divorce, reconciliation of parents, alienation of offspring, Vietnam War upheaval, interracial marriage, psychological probing.

What advantages accrued, then, when McDowell decided to cast his story in unobtrusive blank verse? What qualities make *The Diviners* a poem instead of metrical prosiness? Though it may not be fair to work that offers many other attractions, I would settle on *compression* as its most salient poetic quality. The events recounted are as mundane as those of any local television newscast, but they hurtle by at a speed that gives them sharp impact even while hiding minor details and blurring some important ones.

Here, for example, is a sequence showing what Eleanor does when her infidelity is discovered and she is forced from her home:

> But Eleanor drives southeast, somewhere, follows
> The two-lane desert road through small motels.
> Her room seems always smaller than a car,
> But first things first. She lights a cigarette,
> Then sits down on the bed to count her money.

This is an important scene because its imagery sets the tone of her life for the next six months, yet it occupies only fifteen lines all told. Its brevity precludes its becoming boring but tends to make it flavorless. McDowell's chosen idiom is an extremely tight one; there is no room for digression from the swift story line, so he has to squeeze in expressive thought and detail wherever and however he can. It is almost as if he is chinking a piton into a cliff face when he writes "Her room seems always smaller than a car," a detail of Eleanor's perception that implies a deadly period of boredom, despair, straitened means, and loneliness.

The point of view of *The Diviners* is grasshopper omniscient, jumping from one character to another as thematic economy requires. Sometimes the poet allows theme to dictate overbearingly, so there is (for instance) a jarring shift in point of view in one scene when the castoff Eleanor drinks by herself in a bar:

> The bartender notes the familiar, listless way
> That Eleanor nods her head. He keeps his distance;
> He waters down her refills, and when she goes
> He shrugs and sighs while pocketing his tip.
> It's adequate. He drops her from his mind.

A skilled fiction writer would not plunge us into the perception of this barkeep, a background figure we never meet again, but would find a more graceful way to present an exterior view of Eleanor, the impression she makes upon strangers. But a fiction writer would have more elbow room and could devote a whole scene to the task. McDowell allows himself only these five lines.

If such necessary brevity is sometimes a drawback, it is also sometimes an asset. Just think how many pages of prose a fiction writer might have to scribble to draw the young man's character changes against a five-year historical background. Robert McDowell does it in an octave:

> The decade drowns in violence and blood,
> Conspiracies and unacknowledged coups.
> The nation seems to lie down willingly
> As Tom gets older, filling up with grief.
> The faces and the land ahead look bleak,
> And he begins to hear about the war.
> Desolated, angrier each day,
> He'd like to kill. A war is one good way.

A later passage of only two lines manages a double transition; we move through time and space to a different character's point of view: "A year goes by, and from many miles away / A song Tom favors purls in his mother's sleep."

A poet's brevity can overleap a fiction writer's plodding dog-jobbery in regard to time and space, and it can also make certain psychological observations flare out like flashbulbs. When Tom is told that his mother has contracted cancer, he is sorrowful but not surprised:

> It's then that he thinks of mother doomed in bed,
> But he has always thought of his family
> As cancer patients waiting to be called.
> It hurts to think his mother will be first.

The plot of *The Diviners* has a debatable resolution. Tom, to assuage his father's feelings, takes over the clothing firm but then falls in love with Elaine, an African American writer of popular sociology. After his mother's death he jettisons the business and moves with his wife to Ireland to subsist on the royalties of her books. They have escaped his father's—and America's—brutal materialism, and they expect other young Americans to do likewise:

In bed Tom lies awake to watch the moon,
And sees the great migrations circling back,
The children home in lands their elders fled,
Back home among their births and burials.

This notion of American youth retreating from our native tumult to the peace and security of Europe (Ireland!) seems to me as unlikely as the way the characters in this story always acquire money just when they need it—and with little apparent effort. There are other improbabilities, too, and one of the disadvantages of poetry is that it provides less camouflage for them than prose does. McDowell might have aided himself on this point if his blank verse was only a little less blank, a little more vivid. Its plainness leads not only to clarity but sometimes to a threadbare presentation that ill conceals the gleaming bones of his narrative.

Still, *The Diviners* furnishes much of the weight and complexity of a novel and does so with the impressive swiftness of a poet's thought. I cannot imagine that Robert McDowell will write a long series of books in this manner, but this one shows what wide opportunities are open.

Improbabilities spangle *Middens of the Tribe* too, but Daniel Hoffman has calculated their usefulness and their effects and made them a necessary part of his fascinating design. His story really is a novel, with a larger cast of characters than *The Diviners* sports and with a more complicated plot. Hoffman tries to display the panorama of characters we enjoy in the shorter novels of Trollope, say, or of Edith Wharton.

In the first of the book's forty-three sections we meet—through the eyes of a doctor making house calls—a man who has just been laid off his job in a railyard, a five-year-old child dying of meningitis, an old financier with a tacky but expensive art collection, a businessman's secretary involved in a streetcar accident, the financier's butler, and a woman who has had a stillborn child. In other sections (they ought really to be called chapters) we meet the financier's bitter ex-wife, his son who has taken over the family business, a stage magician and his pretty assistant, a painter of nudes in process of becoming an Abstract Expressionist, and others. Scattered throughout the story are observations about a prehistoric Cromlech People in Wales by an archaeologist who happens to be the second son of the financier; these archaeological notes provide ironic commentary on the contemporary American story as it takes place.

If this latter stratagem seems too easy in its artificiality, it is still hard to count it a fault in the design because Daniel Hoffman seems to be making a point about his narrative: the fact that it is obviously artifice does not make it unbelievable nor lessen its value.

Hoffman's plot is a facture of coincidence much like the plots of Dickens. The girl killed in the streetcar accident turns out to be Wilma, the secretary of the old financier's son; the mother of the stillborn child is revealed to be the magician's assistant, whom he has betrayed; the financier's mistress was the mother of both Wilma and the magician's assistant, and she was also sister-in-law to the idled railroad employee, who has become a security guard where the newly emerged Abstract Expressionist is protesting a showing of one of his disavowed earlier nudes. And so on.

Add to these figures a sprinkling of minor characters like Charles the butler, and nonce characters like the cab driver who transports the doctor to a rundown neighborhood, and you get the idea: Dickensian coincidence, Dickensian complication, Dickensian artificiality. Everyone is connected to everyone else, by blood, marriage, inevitable circumstance, or sheer accident. In *Nicholas Nickleby*, in *Great Expectations* and *Bleak House*, we accept such artifice. If we defer a little our complete engagement with *Middens of the Tribe* it may be because, as with *The Diviners*, the swiftness of pace that poetry enjoins reveals too nakedly the skeleton of the structure. It becomes too easy to discover the necessary coincidences and to point them out. I think that is the reason Daniel Hoffman has laid them on so thickly; he wants us to take the artificiality of his narrative as a donnée and then to focus our closest attention upon the revelations of character this donnée makes possible. These revelations can only be made within his artificial framework, the sequential order in which he reveals the coincidences.

For example, we meet the old financier himself in a third-person-omniscient chapter two; in chapter four we get another picture of him through the eyes of Charles, his butler; in chapter nine the financier's ex-wife reveals her bitter jealousy in the details she gives of his financial dealings. But it is not until twenty-five that her injured pride vents in furious sarcasm, and we have a portrayal of the marriage itself:

Oh, life with him was fun, such fun! Children
growing up with a zombie father, he scarcely
noticed they were there. I felt myself
a widow with three kids and a stranger boarding
who came home sometimes for meals.

Then she tries to remember how it was she happened to marry her be-
trayer in the first place. She decides that his "cocky self-assurance" was
too powerful for her youthful naïveté to resist:

So destined to succeed by his own measure,
so handsome, so intent on sweeping me
off my feet—I mistook it all for love,
didn't I see that I was just a trophy
among the triumphs his ticker tape recorded.

What she cannot make herself comprehend is her recent discovery that
her husband had supported a mistress for many years. She is less wounded
than flabbergasted by this intelligence. He was so dull and unimagina-
tive—

A man untouched by life, uncultured, his mind
a void except for business and the Market—
where would he have had the first idea
of how to find or keep another woman?

That is a perceptive twist on the eternal triangle theme; *Middens of the
Tribe* is alive with psychological acuities. One of the handiest devices
available to fiction writers pressed to reveal the inner lives of characters
is the dream; both McDowell and Hoffman report dreams, but Hoffman's
show more relevance than McDowell's while retaining a fitting aura of
mystery and dread. In chapter eleven we learn that the financier has alienated his daughter so thoroughly that she refuses to speak or write to him.
He dreams about her being born and about how he bungles the emergency—unable to dial the hospital telephone number, unable to drive
the car because he has let the tank go empty, desperately searching for a

quart of gasoline, confused as to directions to the hospital, helpless there before the admissions nurse without his medical insurance card. At last he spots a doctor and accosts him feverishly:

> —Doctor, my daughter's in the car,
> she's sick, and this white cow who's spiteful as my wife
> won't admit the child. You are a doctor,
> you took the Hippocratic oath, for God's
> sake, I'll pay you later, look at her—Doctor
> grasps the car doorhandle, flings it wide,
> peers in and says The seat is empty.
> You have no daughter.

One of the things that makes the dream effective is the inclusion of realistic dialogue. The financier babbles hysterically in his dream just as he would if it were a real emergency.

Hoffman has a good ear for demotic speech. In the following lines the railyard man is giving his version of the day he got fired:

Did I tell that sonofabitch? Did I tell him?
You can bet your sweet patootie I told him where to shove his thumb
                    and when he got it out to chew it, lousy bastard
standing there in his neat coat, white collar like he stole it out of a
                    Arrow ad, his thin black tie
around his neck—I'd like to string him up on his thin black tie. . . .

The whole long speech has the stinging timbre of anger verging on violence. But a mother's lament for her son dead of meningitis is no less accurate, even though couched in tightly formal verse:

> How remorseless is the knowing
> my little son is gone.
> His untouched room's the sepulchre
> of my future. Now I live
> only to dream he's wakened.
> Awake, I am alone;
> my grief, a shell of stone.

Realistic literature must convince by means of verisimilitude, and poetry shoulders this ungainly burden with less ease and often with less
grace than prose. McDowell and Hoffman have largely succeeded in over-
coming the problem, and it is enlightening to note the differences in technique. *The Diviners* is carried throughout by a steady, rather placid blank
verse, while *Middens of the Tribe* exhibits a panoply of styles, from the
proselike dramatic monologues of the artist's model to the rangy free-
verse pages of omniscient narration to the brief observations in very
loose iambic pentameter (almost sonnetlike) of the archaeologist in Wales.

Variety is appropriate for Hoffman's panoramic story line as well as for
his broadest theme. This theme seems to me remarkably similar to Mc-
Dowell's—that the sins of the father are visited upon the children. The
financier's infidelity to his wife, his business partners, his children, and his
friends has desolated those lives and damaged others he knows nothing
of. His businessman son cites his father's transgression as a lack of fealty:

> His depression, he came at last to understand,
> was caused by his long failure
> to honor his ancestors.

The son in *The Diviners* actually returns to the land of his forebears, but
in *Middens* the financier's son can only dream that his father goes back in
time to meet his grandfather and do him homage.

Middens of the Tribe is a book Daniel Hoffman should be proud of, full
of energy and life, though these cannot supply it a happy ending. It closes
with the archaeologist preparing to write his treatise on the Cromlech
People, all unaware that his observations and methods of preparation—
and his dark skepticism about these—apply equally well to a study of his
own family:

> Look, more clues
> than I'll ever use, yet who could get enough
> evidence to verify what inference
> grasps as the only truth? Based on these found things
> spared the depredations of decay or time,
> my study of a culture at a distance
> must, so little known of its inner life, be
> fiction. And now, look into my notes, and write.

The classification I called "The Jigsaw Biography" comprises two kinds: one concerned with historical, the other with fictional, characters. A brilliant representative of poetic historical biography is David Slavitt's exploration of Mozart's librettist, Lorenzo da Ponte, in *A Gift* (Louisiana State University Press, 1996); a classic example of the fictional is William Meredith's *Hazard, the Painter* (Knopf, 1975). The reason I added the adjective "jigsaw" to the noun is that presentation is almost never chronological; poets seem to use every other method of organization, traditional or unheard-of, to tell their stories. Often as not, the author expects the reader to put the story in order, preferring dramatic chiaroscuro to well-lit narrative. This means the author also expects that in the case of history the reader will begin with a pretty fair knowledge of the material, so that the poetic work stands as a variation upon a familiar theme.

Angela Ball's *Quartet* offers not one but four representations of this idea as she gives us brief sketches of Sylvia Beach, Nora Joyce, Nancy Cunard, and Jean Rhys. One thing all these figures had in common was an acquaintance with James Joyce, and it is tempting to think of them as a vocal quartet, altos and sopranos, singing while waiting for the novelist to join them with his proud Irish tenor.

Please forgive my digression. Ball has more-serious themes in view than my fancy has allowed—but it is not always easy to search them out. Her jigsaw puzzle pieces are tiny ones, her separate biographies being so brief. The longest, that of Jean Rhys, runs to fewer than three hundred lines.

This means that chronology will be jammed as well as jumbled. One page of the story of Sylvia Beach flashes dates of 1927, 1944, and three different days of 1941, as well as one other date I am unable to fix. Confusion is inevitable; the question will be whether it is functional, useful, and informative, or merely frustrating.

The larger resemblances among the lives of these four women are their connections with the legendary literary scene of Paris in the 1920s and '30s, their independence of spirit, their amatory freedoms, their betrayals by or disappointments in males, the importance of their work, and the liberating examples their lives set for women of later times. Angela Ball admires each of them independently but seems to admire them more deeply as a group, even though they never thought of themselves as a group and most likely would have rejected violently that notion if it could have occurred to them.

The poet is offering a proposition: four women whose landmark careers bear certain strong likenesses to one another offer an opportunity for unique historical perspective. One of the reasons they might do so is that the differences they made in literary history are measurable: Beach first published *Ulysses;* Nora Joyce sustained her husband and his work "in ways impossible to estimate," according to Ball's headnote; Cunard helped bring African American literature to world prominence; Rhys shone as an example of courage, endurance, and persistence—and she produced brilliant fiction. I don't know whether or not the resemblances Ball has found among these lives add up to a new historical perspective. In fact, I don't know that I am imputing a correct motive to her composition, but I do see it as a strong justification for the book and only wish that the performance were equally strong.

The trouble is that so much material is touched upon in such a short space that some important details and even some of Angela Ball's sharpest insights leave but faint impressions upon the mind. When, for example, Nancy Cunard remembers the heyday of literary Paris, she supplies the same details that you and I, who were not present, might set down:

> There *was,* now I think of it,
> on a summer night, dancing, outside—
> an accordion, violin, piano. Lanterns
> in trees, leaves bright green,
> veneered with light. Bob McAlmon yipping
> like a mad cowboy, Kiki of Montparnasse
> singing slowly of love and abandonment.

I'm sure these details are accurate, but they are also shopworn and have become sentimental clichés. Ball might have chosen fresher materials from Cunard's writing to make her point. In other passages she does find fresh images and the lines are livelier. Here is Nora Joyce, making her first acquaintance with the city of Dublin:

> Winter afternoons at Finn's the bar light
> like smudged drawing paper

sketched with shadows, beards
fit to be scrub brushes. Shoulders
held up by shadows.

Meat stewed on the bone for them
in the ovens their thin wives
warm their toes under.

Down the fine street,
the gray mien of rich houses,
a softness peeked from within,
a nod of pink petals.

Again, it is a question of verisimilitude, the best details chosen to give a real sense of place. Nora Joyce's Dublin is pungently immediate, Nancy Cunard's Paris is blandly nostalgic. There are other unconvincing notes too: Ball has Jean Rhys say "Like always, I should have expected / something different," but "like always" is not a British locution. When Rhys says, "The words 'dry rot' make me laugh / like anything" her words are given no immediate context and the remark stands as a puzzlement. Cunard reports that she poured a libation into a canal "30 years later." Thirty years later than what date? We are not told. These are the kind of niggling little problems—housekeeping chores, as it were—that fiction writers routinely clear up. Apparently, poets sometimes feel privileged, or maybe compelled, to sweep them under the rug.

On the other hand, poetry has a bravura that makes acceptable certain sentences a circumspect fiction writer might shy away from. Cunard reveals a great deal of herself in a dozen words: "Addicted / to the quick gift, I collected loves / without bothering to discard." When Sylvia Beach ponders her relationship to her famous writers she concludes, "They needed me for contrast. / Frugal, modest, clean." When Jean Rhys thinks of happy episodes she slips into the music-hall rhymes she used to perform: "The moon shines down / without a frown." The spareness of poetry isolates such passages, highlighting them for impact; in prose fiction they might well be buried—or blurred, at least—by the mass of verbiage. (Of course, there are some sentences that poets and prosists alike would kill for, as when Nancy Cunard says, "Being in bed with Huxley was like being crawled over / by slugs—interesting, but not addictive.")

I don't need to gabble on about this matter. It is enough to say that poetry is poetry and prose is prose—as long as I am not forced to define the
distinctions. Angela Ball knows that she is making poetry, and I intend it
a compliment to *Quartet* when I say that I believe her poetry would be
better if there were more of it, if she had allowed herself more pages in
which to portray these wonderful women. To be frank, I cannot decide
if I am at last disappointed by a certain niggardliness or left intrigued by
suggestive hints. In the Cunard section there is a redolent passage that
might almost stand as a description of *Quartet,* its excellences as well as
its limitations:

> I've always loved the sweet study
> of fragments: some oddly curved root,
> stick stripped of bark, its wood gleaming,
> fierce sea-green flints, a shard
> of pottery, a small blue
> medicine bottle picked up
> unseen, to look at
> for the first time.

My favorite spiritual journey in literature is *Don Quixote,* but I am
also partial to certain magnificent others: to Dante, John Bunyan, the
tale of Sir Gawain, and *Alice in Wonderland.* In *The Descent of Alette*
Alice Notley has taken Dante's *Inferno* as a distant model for telling
the story of a woman who must descend into an underworld of ghosts
and spirits and defeat its ruler, a figure called the Tyrant. Her story
is nearly as nightmarish as Dante's, its lighting as fitful and murky,
but its logic is not so inexorable—in fact, usually the logic is not even
discoverable, seeming such a product of arbitrary fancy that it lacks
the stern inevitability that chastens and convinces readers simultaneously.

It is unfair to hold a contemporary poet to the standard of Dante, but
it is also impossible to keep the comparison at bay, given the outline of
Notley's narrative. A woman wakes up one day to find herself on a subway headed to a world "of souls," of "Despair & outrage," "Sorrow,"
"darkness," "another's mind," "little dreams," "cars & scenes," "animals," "singers," and "corpses." The creatures she encounters on the

long subway journey—strange human and animal figures—often transform to other shapes, and she herself is continually transformed. Her antagonist, the Tyrant she seeks to defeat, also undergoes transformation, assuming partial identity with many of the separate entities our quester, Alette, encounters. From the world of the subway she descends even lower, to a world of caves, and here too she discovers an array of symbolic images and figures.

The transformations continue, now at a faster pace. The third realm, a world of meadow and forest, is entered through a river and the action becomes more personal, as Alette herself changes in various, sometimes violent, ways as she prepares to confront the Tyrant. In Book Four the long-awaited battle takes place as Alette, now in the form of an owl, slays her opponent and carries his body back to the daylight world, which is wonderfully cleansed and reanimated by her victory.

Laid out in these summarizing terms, *The Descent of Alette* could seem a fairly simple story, allegorical to the point of medievalism. But the outline is deceptive; the oddities of style, the relentless ambiguities of meaning, and the wild quirkiness of incident make the poem confusing. Here, for example, is the beginning of an episode in Book Two that is typical of the others in the volume:

"I entered" "a cave" "in which I instantly" "divided into three"
"separate" "figures," "chained together" "in single file"
"I was most the one" "in the middle" "A man stood watching us,"
"professorial," "in glasses, bearded," "dressed in suit & tie"

" 'Why are there three of me" "in here?' I—we—asked him," "our voices
separate," "out of sync" " 'You are your" "Past, Present," "& Future,'
he said" " 'You divide into" "those components" "in this room' "
" 'But I do not have" "components!' " "our three voices said," " 'My

secret name—" "Time's secret name—" "is Oneness," "is One Thing' "

Yes, I agree with you: the mere look of a page of *Alette* is daunting. An author's note explains that all these quotation marks are supposed "to measure the poem. The phrases they enclose are poetic feet. . . . The quotation marks make the reader slow down and silently articulate—not slur over mentally—the phrases at the pace, and with the stresses, I intend."

Alas, the road to hebetude is paved with good intentions. Maybe other readers will react differently, but I found myself reading fitfully, sometimes dawdling as I speculated about why one phrase or single word was bewigged with quotation marks while another went barefaced, sometimes disregarding the typography and just getting on with the story. After a while, in the interest of reading the entire book, I settled on the latter method of perusal, resigning myself to the possibility that I was missing much of significance and beauty and envying those whose leisure allowed them to experience each quotation mark as the author desired.

I don't want to be dismissive. Alice Notley's experimentation aims at plausible goals, and to affect the pace of reading is not her only purpose. The quotation marks, she claims, "also distance the narrative from myself, the author: I am not Alette. Finally they may remind the reader that each phrase is a thing said by a voice: this is not a thought, or a record of thought-process, this is a story, told."

Seen in this light, the experiment is only naïve. An experienced storyteller knows that the first rule is not to obtrude the teller upon the narrative, not to distract an audience with irritating, or even with beguiling, mannerisms. It seems superfluous to deny that Alette is Alice Notley, since this elaborate fantasy can be no literal autobiography, and here I think the poet is not quite candid. If *The Descent of Alette* does not draw heavily upon Notley's spiritual experiences and discoveries, if it is only an exercise in the manipulation of literary symbols, then it is a hollow poem, without bearing or emotional purpose.

But in truth there are many passages of emotional intensity, even though to fix them in a pattern of stable meanings may be impossible for the majority of readers. The allegorical images usually have strong resonance; the incidents, no matter how puzzling, often offer climaxes and resolutions. In Book Two Alette discovers in one of the caverns a skeleton of a colossal woman. She steps into its giant ribcage and hears the voice of this woman say that before she was banished to the netherworld she was a queen. The quester objects:

" 'I'm not looking for" "a queen,' I said" " 'A

queen is not" "my origin" "Our mother would not" "be a mother"
"of others' poverty," "a mother" "of the subway—" "You are
not her" "are not her' "

Later the search for a mother becomes a search for the biblical Eve, and
the struggle against the Tyrant becomes Alette's effort to slay her father.
But these identifications do not remain in place either, and the terms
"mother" and "Tyrant"—as well as "snake," "owl," "cave," "eyeball,"
and dozens of others—replace their original significations with fresh
ones, then change these in turn. Yet even with all this symbolic spookery,
separate passages can hold narrative as well as thematic interest, as when
in the lines above Alette decries her false mother.

I do not pretend to understand *The Descent of Alette*. In fact, I will surmise that it is not meant to be understood in the way that *The Divine Com-
edy* can be understood. In Dante the allegorical structure is erected upon
and within an elaborate but inflexible system of thought, whose images and
incidents are religious and philosophical concepts in poetic dress. It would
be possible (though very difficult) to find other poetic terms for these
concepts. But in Notley's poem the images point toward meanings beyond themselves only during the time it takes an incident concerning them
to happen. Then the meanings shift. This is the obverse of Dante: there the
root meanings are constant and their symbology might be changed, here
the motivic images—snake, meadow, cavern, tree, mask, lapis, and so
forth—recur constantly but there are no steady root meanings.

We had to expect then that the final conflict for which the poem so assiduously prepares us would reveal only one more ambiguity, even at its
climax. The Tyrant has been identified with a number of ideas in the
course of the story, including quotidian reality, fatherhood, science, and
oppression of women. But when Alette kills him by uprooting a bush
that seems to embody his identity, his question to her is "And do you
not" "kill yourself?" "your own culture . . ." "soul's breath?' " Her reply
shows clearly enough that his function as a figure never reaches beyond
the symbolic, that he possesses an identity only within Notley's colligation of private symbols:

" 'I'm killing no one" "You are not real" "You said so" "yourself,' I
said" " 'Forms in dreams . . ." "forms in dreams . . .' " "I searched
     within"
"for right words" " 'I will change the" "forms in dreams' "

Then from his dead body arises a ghostly tableau of a skeleton woman
tending a dying knight in armor—one more image in a very long pageant
of emblematic images.

The battle is over, the Tyrant slain, and Alette emerges from the subway into the daylit world to discover that everything above ground is
changed for the better:

"it was early" "in the morning" "The sky was jeweled blue, rich blue"
" 'What we can have now,' " "a woman said," " 'is infinity" "in our
     lives"

"moment by moment," "any moment" "He no longer lies" "between
     us & I"
"The light is new now," "isn't it?" "The light has been made new' "

This passage invites a feminist interpretation, as does the poem as a
whole. It also invites Freudian, Jungian, Marxist, Reichian, mythological,
and anagogical interpretations, but none of them alone, and not all of
them together, will clear away the omnipresent perplexities of the work.
In order to be enjoyed, *The Descent of Alette* must be read as mystifica-
tion for its own sake.

There are a few other works that extend so deeply into ambiguity they
must be relished for the play of their terms alone and not for whatever exterior significance they might propose. George MacDonald's novel *Phan-
tastes* comes to mind, and Miguel Serrano's *The Visits of the Queen of
Sheba*. But it is a limited form, I believe, and it may be that Alice Notley's
ambition to write a book-length poem led her to stretch a minor mode of
narrative past its breaking point. Anyhow, I admire *The Descent of Alette*
more for what it attempts than for what it delivers. If a poet must fail—as
all of us inevitably do much of the time—this is an honorable way to do it.

It is no great accomplishment in literary criticism to define and describe
a few examples of form. But the presence of the contemporary long

poem is so insistent and its nature so various I thought some tentative first steps toward clarification might be welcome. If the attempts I have made here and elsewhere are more playful than rigorous, that is because I wanted to emphasize a fact I found out: the long poem is still a viable form, not only readable but enjoyable, and its resilient endurance is a striking manifestation of the superabundant energy that animates the literature of the present day.

Let Me Count the Ways:
Five Love Poets

Poets used to be famous lovers. They were admired, often adored, because they were such willing fools of Venus. Casual as Byron or faithful as Dante, devoted as Keats or prodigal as Burns, the moony midnights kept their passions fierce and their pens restless as they poured out upon the complaisant ear of the world such a symphony of delighted praise and dazzled anguish that one nigh swoons to remember. Romantic love informed not only amatory songs and sonnets but religious and metaphysical musings; it provided motive to wage war and to sue for peace, to found kingdoms and to forfeit them. It was the stuff of life in its sweetest and most refined form. Only a very few writers dared inveigh against love—Lucretius, Stesichorus, de Sade—and curses were laid upon them. For the others it was roses and nightingales all the way. Or, when the fates were against them, yew and ravens.

But among our contemporaries 'tis a subject not long dwelt upon nor thoroughly cogitated. Perhaps romantic love now seems adolescent to us, an embarrassment as unavoidable and unsightly as acne—and no more serious. There is a cornucopia of talk about sex, poetic discussion of every sort from enthusiastic to tepid, from bumbling to expert. But that's not the same thing as love poetry, for no matter how gymnastic it gets or how odd ("mayonnaise and rope"), sex poetry rarely rises to passion. And passion is the real business of lyric poetry, as it is of the emotional life.

There are some good love poems around by George Garrett, James Whitehead, Carolyn Kizer, Galway Kinnell, and others, but they don't seem to loom large in current critical consciousness, possibly because the historical and metaphysical speculations of poets are supposed to be of greater import than their love lives. But this notion may be only vulgar academic superstition.

Not that poets are always wizard lovers, either. It may be that one of the reasons love poetry is in partial eclipse now is that it is so difficult to write. Many a peril awaits the singer of amorous songs, and Samuel Hazo meets lots of them with *The Past Won't Stay Behind You*. A few defeat him; others he overcomes. Some of the dangers of writing love poetry include coyness, obviousness, sentimentality, reliance on cliché, empurpled hyperbole, coarseness, and strained earnestness. These faults also haunt other kinds of verse, but when the subject is love they seem to glow on the page in vermilion neon.

When I find in Hazo's "Lovemakers" phrases like the following I almost feel a need to avert my eyes: "Your very lips are words. / Your hands / speak sentences." These lines are all the more embarrassing because they are heartfelt; no undertone of wit nor sidelong ironic glance undercuts the sententiousness. Not only the baldness of statement embarrasses, but also the obviousness of thought, and this is a weakness not confined to "Lovemakers." In "The Vow We Breathe" we find one of our most ancient human complaints framed in these lines: "And yet to live / together but to die alone / seems so unjust of God / the merciful." The predictable irony of these lines occurs about a third of the way through, and it wreaks such grave injury there is not much chance the poem could recover—and it does not. Here are the final lines:

> I bless
> all love that baffles understanding,
> human or divine.
>   What else
> explains how every mate's
> a lock one key alone
> can open?
>   I'm yours.
>   You're mine.

I repeat: the lover's sincerity is not in question; he means what he says. But does he say all that he means? Doesn't his reliance on cliché imply that he is letting received language muffle some of his thought? If he pursued the course of his feelings more assiduously, wouldn't his language gain in interest?

Perhaps—but it is also possible that Hazo is not interested in impassioned analysis of his feelings, for his focus of observation does not intensify when he turns from love to other subjects. In "Pipedream" he asks a rhetorical question startling in its obtuseness: "What else is Hiroshima but a possible / tomorrow?" To a great many people, and not only the Japanese, Hiroshima represents something much darker than a warning. In "The Night Before the Snow" he looks at a bare maple tree in March and declares: "Leafless or not, / it stays erect, intent, correct / and waits for resurrections / that it knows will come." Like many other direct statements in poems, this one is unnecessary, but Hazo is very much a poet of statement.

Poetry that relies on assertion rather than indirection for its effects runs the danger of platitude. Hazo seems to embrace platitude, to employ it either defiantly or resignedly, as if any novelty of diction might signal a betrayal of his real and earnest feelings. Here is the great problem with love poetry: the feelings it portrays look to be basic, so to induce complexity of thought from them is likely to seem a falsification. Maybe an amorous song ought to say "My luve is like a red, red rose" and shut up. Keep the language direct and the thought simple. No one desires to read a subtle, longwinded comparison that splits metaphysical hairs, demonstrating that the girl is like a rose because she is fresh and fragrant and wonderfully beautiful—not because she stands all day with her feet in compost, attracting beetles.

But this argument against difficulty (which I do not impute to Hazo) will not hold up. "Lovemakers" begins with an epigraph from John Donne, the mention of whose name is enough to remind us that the most passionate love poetry may also be the most subtle, the most ingenious, the most complex of utterance. The closely reasoned, intricately felt lyrics of Dante and Shakespeare, of the troubadours and the metaphysical poets, of Emily Dickinson and W. B. Yeats, embody a warmer and more durable passion than the dithyrambs of Whitman or the pellucid thin lines of Sara Teasdale and James Stephens. Samuel Hazo, in divesting his poetry of intellection, cuts off one source of power.

Yet there is a power in flat statement, too. In "The Courage Not to Talk" occurs a sentence that rises to the level of a proverb: "Since gratitude and love and pain / are languages you learn to speak / by keeping still, keep still." And "One Flesh" has a nifty postcoitus description, "the loll of after-love." Even those clumsy lines about God the unjust and merciful in "The Vow We Breathe" are preceded by a modest and engaging stanza:

> Our rooms
> gaze out on flowers that proclaim
> like flags we're here to be
> each other's counterpart, and that's
> enough.

The use of the pathetic fallacy is as unexpected in this context as it is amiable, and even the characteristic retreat from language in the final phrase has acquired warmth.

In "Two Against the Mountain," a poem that likens marriage to mountain climbing, four lines belabor the obvious aspects of the comparison: "It's waging / both our lives on faith / by pitting all we are against / what cannot be foretold." But these are followed by another quatrain of plain statement scrubbed so clean it is transparent, and the expression of trust it contains shines through as sweet as a candleflame:

> It's falling when we fail
> but knowing that whatever held
> or holds the two of us together
> like a vow will hold, will hold.

This poem too expresses a doubt about the language of love. Marriage partners are connected in a fearful way, Hazo tells us, because their lives depend upon one another. Then he asks, "Who knows / the word for this?" There are too many similar questions in the book. The title of one poem, "The Courage Not to Talk," says perhaps most of what Samuel Hazo has to say about poetry, and particularly above love poetry, but he repeats the sentiment so often it becomes almost reflexive. I think

The Past Won't Stay Behind You disserves its affirmation of the passion that is marriage when it ends with a diffident shrug:

> What's taking shape is never
> > what we planned and not what we expect.
> We call it life because we must.
> We have it just where it wants us.

It is probably impossible to do without rhetoric in poetry or in any other kind of discourse; rhetoric is built into language. In contemporary poetry the claim of rejecting rhetoric has itself become a conventional rhetorical flourish, as expectable as personal confession and fractured organization. Disavowal of rhetoric is intended to assure readers of sincerity of sentiment: "This is not just poetry, this is how I really feel; this is the truth of the matter, these are the facts of the case, the real nitty-gritty. Please don't mistake my phrases for poetry merely because they happen to occur in a poem." Sometimes this maneuver may be pretty successful, if it is disarming in just the right way. For Samuel Hazo the effect is not always fortunate, but Allison Joseph usually attains to happier results.

The third and concluding section of *What Keeps Us Here* contains her love poems, but Joseph's most explicit disavowal of rhetoric occurs earlier on, in "Endurance." Here the subject is her mother's final struggle with cancer. The opening is head-on straight talk tinged with bitterness:

> I am tired of metaphor,
> the lure of the tragic
> making me turn the shadows
> beneath my mother's eyes
> into words like *sullen*
> *gradations of light.*

In these six lines some of Joseph's strengths, as well as her faults, are already apparent. She has a talent for investing the plainest diction with fibrous intensity, and she is able to keep the energy at a high level throughout most of the fifty-two lines of the poem. No easy feat, that. But we also have to note the slovenly misuse of "tragic," and later there is a grammatical error ("loving He who has died and risen"). Even so, the poem finds a strong dramatic closure shadowed by bittersweet ironies. Joseph has attempted to jettison rhetoric in order to portray her mother's situation, yet she knows that the mother herself finds comfort in rhetoric of a very high order:

> I want something real
> as a woman with a Bible
> stopping to rest while climbing,
> sitting on rocks to read
> from Revelation: *Then I saw*
> *a new heaven and a new earth*
> *for the first had passed away*
> *and the sea was no more.*

When Joseph turns her attention to love, she tries hard to maintain her direct gaze and her straightforward tone. She does not always succeed. Now and then a cliché as wan as any that a pop song can muster sneaks in, e.g., "to touch him as I've never / been touched by anyone else" ("Preservation"), and the poem "Immersion" uses its title word to describe the sexual act in a way that is mystifying: "I ride you faster, / conscious of this deep immersion, / this clench of jaws, arms, hands." But when Joseph is able to sustain her concentration, to keep her tone steady and her subject clearly in mind, she is capable of a persuasive eloquence. In "No Ways Tired," she speaks of the strength to be found in the familiarity of making love with one's spouse. The religious trope is a little distracting and probably unnecessary, but the durability of her passion is cleanly presented:

> We have no meager parties,
> no slight get-togethers,
> loving until we're proud,
> the world's benevolence
> shining through. We love
> so much our image stays
> with me, and I close my eyes
> to summon you—fingertips,

lips, chin and chest—
litany for my church,
my sanctified evening,
when the phone, rocking,
won't bother us. Let it ring.
Let mountains rise. Let our bodies
continue their distinct story
of touch, caress, strokes
of sure hands, rites
to keep us live, growing.

For all her directness, though, Joseph is a thorough romantic. "Immersion," "Preservation," and "Inquiry" all make more than oblique reference to the *Liebestod* theme, and though the language is anything but Wagnerian, the physical and emotional passions are at a grand pitch. In "Inquiry," after learning that the French call "each spasm of coming / a 'small death,' " the speaker decides that she would be unwilling to bear the role the male plays in the sexual act. It is unclear why this sensation is confined to the male, but Joseph believes that she would be unable to endure "this continued and continual dying, / proceeding each day like nothing unusual, // nothing you'd call extraordinary." Joy is uppermost in this poem, but there is real fear also; such intensity of delight is a little frightening.

I do not read the feelings portrayed in "Inquiry" and the other two poems as being hyperbolic; the poet convinces me that these descriptions of her joys and fears are accurate. But the contrast of such intense emotion with such plain—even homely—language is a bit distracting, and sometimes I can't help wishing that means and ends were more conformable in her work. Perhaps that is why I prefer the quieter closures of poems like "Penny Candy," "What Keeps Us Here," "In Fear of Sleep," "Late Letter," and "The Swath of Afternoon."

The last of these shows Joseph's talent for employing concrete detail, and a great deal of it, so that each separate item keeps its intensity while still furnishing out a satisfying design and adding surprise to the ending. "The Swath of Afternoon" tells of lovers who are walking through an arboretum with a guidebook, pointing out chokecherry, bramble, frosted hawthorn, and "black oak, red oak, // the rougher slippery elm." This last tree, they learn from the book, has been used to supply a balm to ease sore throats. The speaker admires it as a *"tree of healing,"* and desires for the two of them to experience the tree together:

> I take your hand, not just to feel it,
> > but to hold it to this tree, so we
> may note its quiet legend—red-brown bark,
> > notched leaves, pods like tiny wings.

The way the lovers communicate here is strongly reminiscent of Helen Keller's account of discovering that the tactile universe is not merely a collocation of impersonal objects but a means by which human beings speak their feelings. There is a deep tenderness in "The Swath of Afternoon," and I find it more resonant in character, if rather less exciting, than some of the volume's more explicitly sexual poems.

Some of Joseph's best offerings are not about love; "Dolls," "Penny Candy," "Accomplices," and "Family Life" are especially impressive poems that deal with apprehension, fear, and anger. But *What Keeps Us Here* is animated throughout by sexual love; it is the force that draws most of the poems together and makes this book, not tightly unified by theme or tone, impressive as a whole.

The same cannot be said for Evan Zimroth's *Dead, Dinner, or Naked.* This volume never adds up to make a whole, though there are a number of striking separate poems. One problem is with tone; so many of the pieces are so casually ironic it is difficult to know when the irony leaves off. For example, "Telling Her" is a straightforward and gently moving elegy for the poet's mother, yet it is followed by "Front Porch," a poem that addresses the same subject but takes some unnamed drama critic's stupid remarks as its point of departure: *"Even worse, the critic continues, / someone's mother always has cancer."* The overall tone of "Front Porch" is, then, angry, and this emotion seems out of place when we recall the unhappy subject matter and the other, more serious poem.

A good number of Zimroth's efforts are tinged with anger or exasperation, and she shares with Allison Joseph a distrust of rhetoric—not of poetic rhetoric so much as of the current fashionable intellectual vocabulary. In "Do You Take" she asks us if we comprehend

romantic love
between a man and a woman

as a fragile post-
industrial phenomenon
of an overly-eroticized culture?

Well, I don't, and neither does Evan Zimroth, but she is more sharply irritated by such pseudosociological nonsense than most of us allow ourselves to be. The satire is so keenly barbed that I think she must believe
such gibberish to present impediment to our emotional lives. Or to dis-
color them, at least.

In "Another Trashy Aubade" she declares, "It is the morning / of the
late twentieth century / whose Exhibit A / has trashed us into terror,
its transport- / trucks and boxcars marked *meta phora*, / *the transfer, from
place to place.* . . ." There is an unhappy loss of control here: Zimroth's
continual anxiety about the way language betrays us has led her to an
unfit comparison; the boxcars full of Jews destined for concentration
camps are more dreadful than any fuss about metaphor could possibly be.
Such overstatement signals the presence of an unreasonable annoyance,
which appears again in "Planting Children: 1939," where the children
murdered by Nazis are buried and then "come up storytellers."

Sometimes Zimroth runs to pure bitter sarcasm, whose broadly obvious nature does not usually make it an effective mode for lyric poetry. In
"She Wakes Up," Sleeping Beauty is roused by the Prince and told what
she's missed during her long dormancy: "trench warfare, / pogroms,
mass graves, the names / of all the camps." Her response to this gruesome information is baffling: *"Touch me,* she says, / *You do me, I'll do
you."* This little allegorical narrative might have worked if the proper
terms could have been found; there was opportunity to produce a parable as neat and deadly as any by Karl Shapiro or Randall Jarrell. But Zimroth's bitter anger compels her to try for shock effect and the result is
confusion.

"On Hearing That Childbirth Is Like Orgasm" is another exercise in
heavy sarcasm, and the title tells us the source of the poet's anger. She
pretends to consider this idiotic proposition by following the logic of
whoever said it. According to this theory, no agony is involved in giving
birth: "you don't feel it // anyway / having gone somewhere be-

yond / pain." She compares the experience to sadomasochistic sex ("O / the lush stories to tell! the extravagance! the irresistible / rules!"), and she declares it is "classier even than *The Story of O.*" Her furiousness gives this poem a savage energy, but there is no feasible way to come down, and she ends too mildly: "it's what the good fairy promised / / and the good girls get: / the kiss in the turret, the happy-ever-after."

Zimroth's most elaborate meditation on language and love (or language-as-love) occurs in "Talk, You." The title can be read as an imperative sentence or as a noun followed by an appositional pronoun, defining the person addressed as "all talk." She attempts here a correspondence that doesn't completely work out but is still perceptive:

> At your turning,
> each part of my body turns to verb.
> We are the opposite of
> *tongue-tied,* if there were such an
> antonym; we are synonyms
> for limbs' loosening of syntax,
> and yet turn to nothing: *It's just talk.*

Zimroth's passion stumbles; these final lines come out as mere cleverness, and that is uncharacteristic of a poet whose feelings usually run strong. But in "Cafe" she undertakes a similar subject with remarkable success, looking at her need for affection with cool and rueful wit. The situation is that the speaker has been meeting her beloved for afternoon coffee in restaurants. Their relationship is physically unrequited. The desire between them is powerful, but since they are "forty, married" and "mired" in children, this careful social arrangement is as close as they shall come to fulfillment, and finally the speaker decides to accept the fact:

> Talk, and in a public spot,
> will do as well as sex, and talk
> we can be seen at. It's like a drug
> I take to immunize myself
> against disease: over coffee
> my fever is abrupt, authentic, quickly starved.

All of Zimroth's love poems are edgy, flavored with a sensation of danger. The lovers she portrays will wind up hurting one another, sometimes physically; they cannot be faithful and shall not remain together; impending loss is a central part of the whole experience.

"The Park, at Midnight" compares love to a dog's instinct to chase and retrieve a thrown stick: "some compulsion: like losing love, finding it, / only to ask to lose it again." (It is the phrase "to ask" that contains the most pain and danger.) In "Just Another Love Affair" Zimroth describes an idyllic summer-vacation relationship that is unmarred by such responsibilities as "babies." Yet the fairy tale can have no happy ending: "In other words / theirs was indistinguishable / from many such loves   and not without / disaster   for all that." In this poem, too, Zimroth returns to the theme of language-as-love which so often occupies her sensibility, but here she broaches it with gladness and tenderness: "licking each other's alphabet / from *A* to *Z* and back   and calling out / all the golden names." The tenderness is undercut by the poem's ominous closure ("not without / disaster"), but it is not defeated.

Her most thorough treatment of this theme occurs in "Scripture," a poem almost vertiginous in its ambivalences. It celebrates physical passion while demonstrating its inescapable entanglement with power. Here, love-talk is imbued with sexual cruelties, and part of the alarming but not unwelcome dominance of the male derives from the words he uses and teaches to the female. The emission of the male's semen is seen not only as a physical invasion but also as the more terrifying conquest of the speaker's language, her means of thinking and feeling.

> She lives his words. Everything
> he says comes true. Call it
> a new invasion: flush
> of language, a beachhead
> he never thought
> to take before. *What's the drill?*
> he asks, and
> drills her to the bed, drilling her
> all the while
> in tea-party good manners.
> Say please and thank you.

> She says please, please,
> a hundred-times please
> but forgets the thanks, because
> neither has a shred
> of language now.
> She's swallowed all his words.

There are other poems in which Zimroth tries for shock effect—we have glanced at "She Wakes Up"—but this is the only one where such a ploy is really successful. This poet is usually better when she doesn't try for such effects, because she doesn't need to; her view of love is so thoroughly unsettling that she need only outline her thought in clear language to startle her readers into new recognitions. The elements of her work that at first I regarded as perverse have become, after some disturbed reflection on my part, just and necessary. Zimroth communicates thoughts and attitudes that seem truly feminine, rather than merely feminist. I cannot admire all the poems equally, but *Dead, Dinner, or Naked* is an intriguing book, one from which male readers can learn things of urgent importance.

Reginald Gibbons's *Maybe It Was So* contains only five love poems, but they are memorable enough to warrant inclusion of the volume in this review. The book also has much to offer otherwise: interesting adaptations from foreign languages, imitations of other poets, short and long narrative poems, dramatic monologues, even a touching *paysage moralisé* in "Foreign Landscape."

Not all the poems are winners. "From an Early Train in Spring" reads as if it was too easy to write; it comes within an ace of being propaganda. "Atlantic Incident" begins as an anecdote and remains one. "Retributions" tells the story of an "ambitious, profligate cousin" who bought from the speaker's father a fine pony and then, through inattention, allowed it to starve. Twenty years later, this same cousin stopped on the highway to help another motorist and was "hit by a bus, injured and stupefied for life." These two incidents cause the speaker to ponder the idea of poetic justice, but not in any profound way: "It may be that everything is a coincidence with something else / and we don't notice the other half." That is the kind of fancy tossed out late at night in a sophomore

dorm room, yet Gibbons is not content to offer it casually, but pursues it
to exhaustion:

> And that's how some rancorous deed of my own,
> by me forgotten but linked to some other moment
>
> by coincidences I never even knew, will be thrown at last
> from someone else's on-moving life that somehow I damaged
>
> when under blows I complete the pattern, I stagger
> today or tomorrow: justice hard, deserved, unwitting.

But Gibbons's love poems are thoughtful, passionate, and musical.
They do not declaim, they do not shout; neither do they snigger or mumble. The tone of voice is steady and the themes are clear; the diction is not
elaborate (though the syntax sometimes is), but neither is it starveling.
And though the feelings are complex, the poems manage to resolve them
into gestures single and unbroken.

In "Poem," Gibbons takes up a theme dear to Evan Zimroth, the relationship between love and language. "Poem," though, reads almost as
an answer to an adaptation called "One of César Vallejo's Human
Poems" that appears a few pages earlier. Vallejo contrasts the harsh facts
of existence, as he sees them directly before him, with fancy intellectual
theories and artistic notions; then of course he roundly contemns these
latter vagaries. The sentiment is predictable, but the poem swings along,
jauntily making its point:

> A cripple goes by with a boy, arm in arm,
> And after that, I'm going to read André Breton?
>
> Another man is shivering with the cold, he coughs, he spits blood.
> Will it ever be right to refer to the Inner Me?
>
> . . . . . .
>
> A mason falls from a rooftop, he dies, and he does without lunch
>   from now on.
> And then I'm going to invent new tropes and metaphors?

But in "Poem" Reginald Gibbons declares that there *is* a true relationship between the nonintellectual facts that seem to make up the real

world and the intellectual and spiritual nature of a person. He begins with the early days of a courtship and the uncertainties between the lovers. Next, a specific instance of failure is recounted ("that afternoon I lost my voice"), one reminiscent of Tiresias's empty encounter with the Hyacinth Girl in *The Waste Land*. The speaker then recognizes that it was necessary for him to be remade from top to bottom in order to regain a careful and truthful language: "Now it seems to me that I needed to begin / over again from a time before I could speak." The language he regains is not a tongue confined to protestations of romantic love, but has a broader range than that:

> Maybe it was so I could say to you that I love you.
> Maybe it was so I could say what I meant, to anyone.

These lines are hardly profound in themselves; they are not even as lively as some of Samuel Hazo's statements. Their importance for my purpose here is in their relationship to an ancient doctrine, the ability of love to transform the lover's personality.

This transformation of personality was a favorite theme of Renaissance poets who saw romantic love as a lower rung on the ladder toward Platonic perfection. Chaucer, Petrarch, Dante, and all the magnificent others treated the theme numerous times; it drew from them some of their strongest and sweetest words, and they remarked it not only as a psychological change but also as a physical one. Love was an experience that cleansed the senses and heightened the powers of perception: the colors and flavors of existence focused themselves more forcibly upon the sensorium, and the whole being was made more receptive.

In "Hark" Gibbons reports the same phenomenon. His syntax sometimes fumbles as he struggles to fit the experience into a single sentence, but the poem still manages to be warm and intimate, awed by revelation:

> Stars in the clear night sky more silent than any other silence,
> even a cave's; and yet at each star the noise of fusion
> blasts to beggar rockets massed in the millions, a roaring
> multiplied to futile infinity out there, in the silent sky
> over us, as we lie close listening to each other breathe,

hearing each other's heartbeats, sensing the smallest
candle wick of each other's noiseless warming desire.

Of his erotic poems, Gibbons's "Lovers" is probably the best, a tender and humorous lyric containing, as its final line tells us, "Mischief,
happiness, sorrow, desire." "Analytical Episodes" is also fine, a mosaic of
tangentially related fragments that presents a picture of love defining itself. In a passage where the poet lists things that are so good they ought
to stay forever occurs the best line: "Old clothes on a hook, an open summer window." It is a sentimental line, and the best love poems in *Maybe
It Was So* are sentimental.

So are those in Christine Garren's *Afterworld*. This is a book I would not
ordinarily review, since its author lives in my hometown and took a graduate degree in creative writing at the university where I teach, though she
did not study with me. But in preparation for this essay-review I examined more than sixty volumes of mostly American contemporary verse
and found only eight with a significant number of love poems, and of
these only five offered much interest as poetry. The best of these was *Afterworld:* that is my most careful judgment, unsullied by any personal interest, but it is only fair to alert readers of my proximate connection with
the author. I would not speak of the book here if I did not think it truly
remarkable.

It is not a perfect collection. Its infelicities include allegorical effects
that are sometimes too obvious, sometimes too opaque; now and again a
pronoun without clear reference muddies the meaning; and "The Fountain" is cruelly disfigured by a dangling participle. But for the most part
these quietly spoken, intensely experienced poems glow with an ardency
that causes the lines to throb.

Let me pursue my earlier thought about the possibility of love poetry
gaining strength from intellection by offering "Solarization" as an example. The title is a term that refers to the effect of overexposure upon
a photograph, where the image comes out almost as white as porcelain
and contrast is largely lost. The context is that the reader has been examining a selection of snapshots of her marriage or courtship and pauses
to consider one:

This is where we stopped, in the metallic garden
by the shoelace ferns.
You were laughing so fully I think you drank the music
of a silver tuning fork
to make you that beautiful.
This time we look more white than black and white,
all the wine drained onto the sugary grass.
Count the leaves around us, bullet-tipped,
white too, the hundred irons of the fence.
And the half-bitten apple, the laid-out grapes
a white like cooling coals;
this is the only honest picture of how we existed
loving so thoroughly, living so closely against the other
we were almost erased.

It's true that the eighth line would benefit from a semicolon at the end
and I think "that" in the fifth line should be "so," but these are hairline
flaws. The important thing about the poem is its brilliantly original,
fiercely passionate vision. Romantic love has not only changed the phys-
iology and psychology of the poet, it has transfigured the whole landscape, turning it into a place that is intensely physical and at the same time
burningly transcendent. Love has created an Otherworld—a spiritual
realm which admits the physical and depends upon it for existence, a
world so filled with radiance that only an overexposed photograph can
suggest its qualities. A poet needs not ingenuity but an exceptionally
rare talent to find in such a homely object, a photograph that most of us
would regard as spoiled, an emblem of enduring ecstasy. And after that
the poet needs talent and application to make the idea clear, dramatic, and
graceful.

I am happy to admit that "Solarization" and Garren's other love poems
are sentimental, because this enables me to pursue a point I asserted when
discussing Reginald Gibbons. Love poetry is *supposed* to be sentimental;
romantic love is as sentimental an emotion as patriotism, hero worship,
reverence for parents, intellectual vanity, and mania for baseball. This
love comes out sappy in poetry when the writer retreats from its full articulation, when he or she refuses to give soul, body, and mind com-

pletely over to it, when the poem is too bashful or embarrassed or vain or frightened or cool-tempered to tell all the heart.

Sentimentality can betray the poet by distracting her from technical necessities that help to make a poem excellent; being in love is not an excuse to dangle participles. But imperfections of rhythm, syntax, diction, and so on can be remedied. What cannot be mended is fear of passion, lack of dedication. One of the best ways to overcome sentimental excess is to accept it wholeheartedly and go on from there to the other genuine feelings that give rise to it and legitimize it. Clichés, sententiousness, coarseness, and all the other sins result from going only halfway. When applied to love poetry, William Blake's proverb is gold sterling: "The road of excess leads to the palace of wisdom."

"Flowers," the poem that gives Garren's volume its title, is closely related to "Solarization"; its trope for being in love is again that of a transcendent plane of being. Here, though, the passageway is not a visual image but an olfactory one. The major conceit is that the speaker now inhabits an afterlife, having metaphorically died in the earlier crisis of falling in love. The specific metaphor for this crisis is near-death brought on by the surfeit of the sweet smell of flowers, and it recalls Alexander Pope's line from the *Essay on Man*, "Die of a rose in aromatic pain." The speaker then drifts through an afterlife of dazed contentment:

> Gas flames, those dahlias, those and all the crane-
> and heron-colored flowers blooming on the hill.
> This house, within the plaster rooms, must be the afterworld
> where the living have been put away. Because I could not breathe
> the fragrant air, I almost died last year one day
> among the flowers' perfumed wreaths. Now I go
> from room to room dusting the pleated vase;
> I look beyond the window's well-cleaned panes.
> And I believe this is the afterworld, feeling
> the green of my first want for you
> as you kneel in the garden below, planting
> the verbena, so fondly I cannot stand it.

It is very difficult to write poems like this one, verses that engage so fully both heart and mind. The mistakes that are likely to be made are the same kind we may find occasionally in Góngora or Cowley or even in Donne, when the metaphors become so elaborate or extravagant that they distract attention from a comparison that needs to be held clearly in mind. Some of Garren's poems suffer from such imbalances. In "Folly" the speaker compares a suitor's voice to "a vase of longing / tipped forward like a planetary marking / defining its kingdom," which may be no more than a too-fancy way to say that the sound of a voice was seductive because it was quite striking. And although "Pre-Nuptial" pursues a remarkable metaphor throughout ("a bowl of roses I carry all day in my arms / even after the flowers have blackened and the water stinks"), the poem never makes entirely clear what the metaphor refers to.

Which is only to say that if you go all the way you may go too far. But a real love poet knows this truth, counts on it, and is willing to suffer the losses for the sake of the intoxicating gains. That so many of the poets I've noted here are anxious about problems of language is not accidental; even the less successful understand that writing a love poem is not solely a literary act, is not separate from being in love. When we write love poems we are making love, and our small errors in the process are usually as forgivable as overeager caresses or mistimed kisses. Unforgivable are the true sins of deception, falseheartedness, playacting, and feigned passion; one of the major frauds in contemporary love poems— especially those by young American males—is the faked orgasm.

But let us turn from such poseurs and piddlers to celebrate those who have copied from their smitten hearts and stricken senses, those who cried, "Take, oh, take those lips away" and "Go, lovely rose!" and "Had we but world enough and time" and "Helen, thy beauty is to me" and "Wild Nights, Wild Nights!" It is toward these poets that Christine Garren directs her gaze. Not daring to count herself one of them, she pictures them with a glowing admiration undimmed by envy, and she calls this group portrait "The Romantics":

> Save them from dreaming
> though already, I can see, their diaries have been opened.
> Already they carry lutes into the mandolin fields.
> How can they not hear the ferrying beneath them,
> Charon's keel in the sand, the oar lifted?
> I know the fields are too beautiful to stop them:

it is true, come to them once, the gold, the hot rushes,
and you are ruined. Look how the silos, the white dairy
vanish before them—the blacksmith stops hammering—
and still they believe.
What are they thinking, what are they waiting for
when they lean back, like gods in the grass,
with wine on their tongues,
their fingers drowsy with the fields' bright clay?

The shortest line in this poem states an observation that might serve as manifesto for the whole of *Afterworld* and for all other real love poets elsewhere and elsewhen: "and still they believe."

Wise Saws When Last Seen

Chaucer liked his Clerk of Oxenford and admired the way he talked:

> Noght o word spak he moore than was neede,
> And that was seyd in forme and reverence,
> And short and quyk and ful of hy sentence;
> Sownynge in moral vertu was his speche,
> And gladly wolde he lerne and gladly teche.

By the phrase, "hy sentence," the poet meant, first of all, signification or meaning, but also *pithy statement, maxim,* and *apothegm.* The Clerk's "sentences" would have come from Seneca, Horace, Vergil, Statius—poets who wrote *sententiae,* lines that encapsulate in few words wisdom gained from observation and patient thought and sudden insight.

Poets used to take pride in their sententiae. Longfellow and Oliver Wendell Holmes were pleased to find phrases from their poems become common currency. In our century the undoubted American master of the sentence is Robert Frost. "Something there is that doesn't love a wall"; "Earth's the right place for love"; "We love the things we love for what they are"; "I sha'n't catch up in this world, anyway"; "Something you somehow haven't to deserve"—we can recall dozens of such lines without breaking a sweat. Other modern poets whose lines stick separately in our heads might include A. E. Housman, W. B. Yeats, W. H.

Auden, Wallace Stevens, Howard Nemerov, Richard Hugo, Richard Eberhart, and—in a special way—T. S. Eliot. Of course, we remember X. J. Kennedy and Dorothy Parker too, but epigrams comprise a different species; an epigram is a complete context, but here we are concerned with lines that, however apt dramatically, leap out of context and fasten to us like refrigerator-door magnets to knights in armor.

It is no easy feat to write phrases that detach from their original settings to fit comfortably into casual conversations about subjects entirely different from those the original poems broached. Yet the sententia, like many other poetic traditions, has fallen out of favor; it has become an object of distrust.

This distrust is founded upon some sound reasons. One of the secondary meanings of the adjective *sententious* is "given to pompous moralizing." But poets moralize continually about the environment, gender equality, abortion rights, and so forth; they just don't do so memorably. They are often enlisted these days for political causes—but their poems are not. Many contemporary poets avoid creating apothegms because they sound wise and poets no longer wish to sound wise. They want to sound like their neighbors, especially their blue-collar neighbors. They fear falling victim to what we might name the Polonius Syndrome; that father figure was full of "hy sentence"—but was also obtuse and fatuous.

May Sarton began her career before the avoidance of maxims became so assiduous, and her poems early and late plenteously display them. *Collected Poems (1930–1993)* shows her to be infrequently swayed by fashion. Now and then new voices claim her attention: here a tinge of Auden, there an echo of Frost or Roethke. But for the most part her work has been consistent, maybe a bit too consistent. She writes solid and sturdy poems, rarely surprising but generally satisfying, earnest and well intentioned. Some of her work is stolid, with the air of the dutiful twenty-lines-a-day, and her uses of the sententia show both its attractiveness and its dangers.

Looking at "A Hard Death," we may understand why young poets turn away from this rhetorical figure. Sarton has written moving poems about the passing of both of her parents ("My Father's Death, Forethought"), but "A Hard Death" ends with a line so flat it almost makes trivial the poet's genuine feelings: "Only the living can be healed by love." A sententious line often injures poems where they are most vulnerable, in openings and closings; the last stanza in "Of Grief" consists of four apothegms in a row which blunt the impact of the strong preceding stanzas. Another temptation is the pavonine; once having discovered a wise line, the poet may find it hard to resist worrying it to extinction, like a concerned father discussing with a teenage son his style of haircut, as in "My Sisters, O My Sisters":

> And now we who are writing women and strange monsters
> Still search our hearts to find the difficult answers,
>
> Still hope that we may learn to lay our hands
> More gently and more subtly on the burning sands.
>
> To be through what we make more simply human,
> To come to the deep place where poet becomes woman,
>
> Where nothing has to be renounced or given over
> In the pure light that shines out from the lover,
>
> In the warm light that brings forth fruit and flower
> And that great sanity, that sun, the feminine power.

When the last glimpse we have of a poem is a bumper-sticker message, it usually means that the whole vehicle was propaganda, which no closing slogan can make interesting. Here the final preachment—"that great sanity, that sun, the feminine power"—is just silly.

Note that all the nouns and adjectives in this passage are abstract. Our contemporary poets have learned that abstractness is a plague to be avoided at interstellar distance. "No ideas but in things," said William Carlos Williams, joining two abstractions to create his most memorable sententia.

In a strong poem about the loneliness of aging, "Gestalt at Sixty," Sarton uses abstractions to convey hard knowledge she has taken from experience:

> I can tell you that solitude
> Is not all exaltation, inner space
> Where the soul breathes and work can be done.

> Solitude exposes the nerve,
> Raises up ghosts.
> The past, never at rest, flows through it.

The thought is clear and bitter, but there is nothing striking about the language. Then the first lines of the next stanza sum up these feelings and project them forward with an observation cogent but modest, sad but disarming:

> Who wakes in a house alone
> Wakes to moments of panic.

My personal preference is for those sententiae that seem to occur inevitably within the narrative line or reflective processes of a poem, lines which call little attention to themselves at first but then linger after the poem has been put aside. Sarton's "In Suffolk" contains a middle stanza comprised of generalizations that the two preceding stanzas justify and the concluding two develop intensively. The subject is memory and the poet wonders, "To what have I been faithful in the end?" Never to her lovers, it seems, nor to all her friends—but she has kept faith with her art and she has always believed in nature. Her trust in the earth itself has brought her through some dark hours:

> All lovers sow and reap their harvests from
> This flesh ever to be renewed and reconceived
> As the bright ploughs break open the dark loam.
> Whatever the cost and whatever I believed,
> Only the earth itself, great honeycomb,
> Gives comfort to the many times bereaved.

The poem ends with another sententia—"What had to grow has been allowed to grow"—but it is less effective than those of the middle stanza. Its import is self-evident; it has been too obviously prepared for.

Context must be strong enough, or else the wise thought appears contrived, manufactured for the occasion. Or worse: it may seem sometimes that a poem has been composed merely as an excuse for the felicitous phrase. "It is but a trick poem and no poem at all if the best of it was thought of first and saved for the last," cautioned Frost in "The Figure a Poem Makes." I surmise (dangerously) that this is the case with Sarton's "New Year Poem," a chatty meandering effort that concludes with a bromide:

> Unless the gentle inherit the earth
> There will be no earth.

When the device fails so utterly, it is easy to see why poets might decide to give it up in favor of an image—and May Sarton herself has a fine touch with images; "Evening Walk in France" is but a series of them and is one of the most charming poems I have read. "My Father's Death" is a full-blown conceit, its dominant image of ship-launching both proud and melancholy, and "Baroque Image" and "A Parrot" are allegories in which closely rendered images are interpreted. Sarton is a good picture-painter, and it may be the case that her more imagistic poems are her better ones.

But I admire the courage of the sentence-maker. Almost nowhere else in poetry composition is there such opportunity to look so dogfaced foolish, so emptily pontifical, so stuffed-shirtish. I am willing to suffer the dolors of this stanza from "A Winter Notebook": "I lift my eyes / To the blue / Open-ended ocean. / Why worry? / Some things are always there." I can suffer them because I may turn to a different page to read a poem like "Humpty Dumpty," sad and knowing, natural in tone and diction, and with an ending sententia that transforms anticlimax into sudden sorrowful recognition:

> Pain can make a whole winter bright,
> Like fever, force us to live deep and hard,
> Betrayal focus in a peculiar light
> All we have ever dreamed or known or heard,
> And from great shocks we do recover.
> Like Wright's hotel we have been fashioned
> To take the earthquake and stand upright still.
> Alive among the wreckage, we discover

Death or ruin is not less impassioned
Than we ourselves, and not less terrible,
Since we nicely absorb and can use them all.

It is the small shock, hardly noticed
At the time, the slight increase of gloom,
Daily attrition loosening the fist,
The empty mailbox in the afternoon,
The loss of memory, the gradual weakening
Of fiery will, defiant to exist,
That slowly undermines the solid walls,
Until the building that withstood an earthquake
Falls clumsily among the usual days.
Our last courage has been subtly shaken:
When the cat dies, we are overtaken.

If we say that most contemporary poets eschew the sententia, we are not entirely accurate. It is true that they distrust the authoritative, overbearing tone of such direct statement. But the figure is a powerful one, and poets do not easily give up sources of power for their work. Those who loudly decry end rhyme will compensate for its absence with internal rhyme and assonance; those who abandon regular meter are often demons for cadence. In the same way, poets have found methods of disguising the sententia so that it is barely noticeable, almost unrecognizable, yet still lends its force to poems.

One technique for doing so is in a canny use of the epigraph. The poet prefaces a poem with a quotation from someone else; the quotation is a short passage full of wise thought, but the poet is not directly responsible for the thought; it is attributed to Plato or Elvis, Gandhi or Mickey Mantle. The poem then comments upon the quotation or ridicules it or illustrates it. A sententia is employed; the poem cannot stand without it—but the poet has escaped its onus. A good example of this usage occurs in "Grief," one of the shorter poems in Andrea Hollander Budy's strong first book, *House Without a Dreamer*.

"Grief" makes an instructive example because the epigraph so deliberately strives to impart wisdom and because Budy agrees with its import. None of the complex ironies that often attend the use of an epigraph is present. The quotation is from Isadora Duncan: "The most terrible part of a great sorrow is not the beginning, when the shock of grief throws one into a state of exaltation which is almost anaesthetic in its effects, but afterwards, long afterwards, when people say, 'Oh, she has gotten over it.' " I think the observation is sound, and Duncan's life gives it the ring of authority. Andrea Hollander Budy only adds sensation and immediacy to its abstractions:

> It is the cave you visit
> in your dream. There are
> no stars, no moon; and so
> you swim naked, knowing
> you cannot be seen.
> You move down, down
> through the black water,
> and there is no end.
> You see nothing, feel
> only small waves passing
> through your ears
> as you descend.
> It is not different
> from other caves
> in other dreams:
> a secret place,
> and you have learned
> to breathe in it.

If we strip away the epigraph and the title, the poem could be about almost anything; it is presented as a dream within which a series of simple actions takes place and a quietly dramatic conclusion is reached. It might be a parable about solving a problem in advanced mathematics or acquiring religious faith. But when it is read whole it dramatizes the proposition of the quotation. The poem averts the personal; Andrea Hollander Budy does not declare, *I have suffered grief and have come to tell you about it.* The poem only says, *If Isadora Duncan's description is correct, then this is what the process of an assimilation of grief might be like.* Yet the latter statement implies the former. The poet has managed to embrace the sententia and to use it without having composed it.

Another instance of this strategy occurs in "What You Find." Here the epigraph is from a poem by William Stafford: ". . . it is better / than gold, if you learn to accept what you find . . ." Again, the poem consists in a series, this time a series of images that are related to one another only by means of the epigraph: first a racehorse cantering in a field, then the light that weaves through a young girl's hair, then words and phrases the girl said, and a concluding image of the girl's mother watching her sleep. I have to surmise that the young girl met a tragic death and that these remembered images, if accepted by the speaker and the mother, will have the power to console. One of the auditory images, a sentence the little girl uttered, becomes an occasion for Budy to include a definition of poetry:

> *The horsey tickled in my hand,* she said,
> as she drifted into sleep and clenched
> the memory. But mostly it is not
> the words at all, but something unsaid,
> something poems try to net
> when we haul them into the dark
> hours of morning when nothing yet
> is spoken or lit.

This is not a grandiose definition; it is deliberately provisional, fleeting, suitable for this one situation and perhaps for no other. But for all its diffidence, it is still one sententia which has been suggested by another. It is possible too that Stafford's sententia was suggested by the famous one that opens Pindar's first Olympic Ode (here in C. M. Bowra's translation): "Water is the best thing of all, and gold / Shines like flaming fire at night, / More than all a great man's wealth."

My suggestion brings us to the ironic use of quoted sententiae, and Budy's "Beginning and Ending with Lines from Shakespeare" revels in its ironies. Once more, the poem illustrates the quotations with a concrete example and vivid imagery, but the example is one that Shakespeare could never have thought of: "Whoever made us believe that all the world's a stage / must have known we'd drive as slowly as the car would go / past the aftermath of the accident. . . ." The lines then describe the results of a traffic accident—a man bleeding on the pavement, a woman with an injured shoulder in the car, a dazed woman walking randomly about with her two children, the bone jutting from the leg of the downed man. The speaker insists that we consider such scenes as theater, as a kind of event that "cannot really happen to us":

> This is a game, we insist,
> the next car we hear will be his pulling in,
> this is only a stage
> and all the men and women merely players.

Earlier lines make it clear that the car pulling in belongs to a husband or lover, someone the poem refers to as being "more important" than the accident victims because they have no personal connection to the speaker and so are thought of as being "merely players." Budy offers a violent reinterpretation of Shakespeare's lines with the incident and images she supplies. She disagrees with the sentiment of the quotations but finds a context that makes them true for her, though only in a special and limited sense.

I can also recommend *House Without a Dreamer* for poems like "When She Named Fire," "Firmly Married," "Just," "This," "Because We Have Been Married a Long Time," and others not obviously involving sententiae. Budy, like most contemporary poets, prefers to avoid the appearance of overt sagacity. One poem, however, pretends to wisdom and proclaims its intention with its title, "Advice." The poem is addressed to a male "you" and takes the form of a reply. Evidently, the male has tried to explain why he is attracted to certain kinds of women, but his motives are rejected by the speaker: "First, / you've mistaken the crazy / for the mysterious." Fancy women with layers of feathers or lace are not truly mysterious; it is better to pursue more mundane activities, or to search out some woman—a poet, perhaps—who is willing to tell everything about herself. The mystery that attracts, the poem avers, is not in the women but in yourself:

> Or look at that mirror.
> The clue that lures you
> lies between the glass and
> the silver, between the shadow
> and the ice. Do not move.
> Open your eyes.

Again, the strategy is ironic because the advice offered is only half-serious. The speaker knows that her advice will not—cannot—be taken, that the male will prefer the illusion of sexual mystery to the real mystery of his own psyche. This irony, along with the gnomic quality of her formulations, lightens the burdensome freight of Budy's maxims. But sententiae they remain, nonetheless.

Of the poets discussed here, Gerald Costanzo and John Haines seem the least likely to employ the rhetorical device under consideration. Haines is famous as an oblique nature poet, his poems filled with animals and trees and stones; his human figures almost always are solitary, and his poems seem often to talk to themselves as they describe landscapes and objects, rarely addressing the reader or any other particular figure. *The Owl in the Mask of the Dreamer* collects poems from nearly thirty years' labor and exhibits a sober consistency of tone and imagery. But even here, in the heart of wildernesses stony or icy, now and again resounds the sententia, one of the most sociable of poetic figures.

"Yeti" is a case in point. A poem in two parts, it begins by defining the Abominable Snowman as a creature that people, driven by the fears of society, need to imagine, a monster, an emblem of blood, "in the sleep of reason." The Yeti is then described as "a maimed and shaggy captive" climbing among its icy mountains. The second part of the poem is a reflection upon, an interpretation of, this image:

> In this world we think we know,
> something will always
> be hidden, whether a fern-rib
> traced in the oldest rock,
>
> or a force behind our face,
> like the pulse of a reptile,
> dim and electric.
>
> A possibility we hadn't
> thought of, too tall
> and thick to be believed.

The first clause of the first sentence is a good example of the sententia; it addresses the reader directly and tells him or her something the poet has discovered about our existence. The third stanza elaborates upon the opening observation, expatiating upon the nature of our belief. It is, however, a characteristic of Haines's poems that they will conclude with an image rather than a generalization, and "Yeti" is no exception:

> Its face like a wise ape
> driven to the snows,
> turns at the starry ford,
> gives back one burning
> look, and goes.

The image is forceful and haunting, this look of betrayed innocence, of bewildered resentment, but without the passages of explanation it would be merely puzzling. In fact, a number of Haines's poems are puzzling because the poet tries to make images do *all* the work of interpretation. I come away mildly frustrated from such poems as "Cranes," "Smoke," "The Tunnel," "The Rain Forest," and a good many others.

I am, of course, making no special plea for the sententia. A poem like "Marigold" would be hobbled, if not ruined, by unnecessary intrusion:

> This is the plaza of Paradise.
> It is always noon,
> and the dusty bees are dozing
> like pardoned sinners.

I am only pointing out that poets do not casually abrogate sources of verbal power and will strive to preserve them in whatever disguised and modified forms they can come up with.

We have noticed the use of the epigraph as the sententia in disguise, but Haines—when he is on his game—is able to use his talent for imagery so adroitly that he can obliterate almost any telltale sign of sententiae. Yet they are still there under the surface, giving sharp order and strong meaning to the pictorial elements. The highly specific final images of "The Way We Live" almost hide the generalized statement, "a man may long for nothing so much / as a house of snow," tucked away in the center of the poem:

Having been whipped through Paradise
and seen humanity
strolling like an overfed beast
set loose from its cage,
a man may long for nothing so much
as a house of snow,
a blue stone for a lamp,
and a skin to cover his head.

The sentiment is unremarkable, a restatement of primitivist fantasy that Rousseau so persuasively presented. Here it is the camouflaging imagery, along with the disgusted ironies of the term "Paradise" to describe our affluent civilization, that give the sententia strength and charm.

It may be that a proficient skill with imagery ill fits a poet for offering up well-weighted adages. Sometimes Haines's employment of sententiae is clumsier than that of most other poets of our time. The opening of "Foreboding" is needlessly portentous, the opening of "On the Road" flat; the final stanza of "Listening in October" is overwritten, and a great deal of the long poem, "In the Forest Without Leaves," is tubthumping. From this last poem, one section in particular seems overbearing in its use of sarcasm, with these parodistic bromides imputed to a small-minded populace:

Say after me:

That freedom was weight and pain,
I am well-parted from it.

Earth was too large
and the sky too great.

I believe in my half-life,
in the cramped joy
of partitions,
and the space they enclose.

Other passages of equal lugubriousness might include lines like these: "Life was not a clock, / why did we always measure / and cramp our days?" and "Those who write sorrow on the earth, / who are they?"

and "The key that winds the clock / turns a lock / in the prison of our days."

But such lines are exceptions. John Haines is a genuine poet and an earnest thinker, and my favorite of his long philosophical reflections is complex and moving and beautifully clear. "Meditation on a Skull Carved in Crystal" includes sententiae to which the poet has given drama: "Put death aside, / there is nothing to fear / from the sleep-walk of spirits / in this darkness / not wholly of the night." One maxim—"death is the last confusion"—is lame without its context, but Haines establishes a pervasive background for all 183 lines of the poem with a potent quotation from Martin Buber about the afterlife: *"After* is the wrong word. It is an entirely different dimension. Time and space are crystallizations out of God. At the last hour all will be revealed." It is hard to make a poem live up to an epigraph like this one, but Haines succeeds almost completely. His conclusion is, once more, a collection of images that are transcendental without being forced:

> Intelligence is what we find,
> gazing into rock as into water
> at the same depth shining.
>
> Mirror, glazed forehead of snow.
> Holes for its eyes, to see
> what the dead see dying:
>
> a grain of ice in the stellar
> blackness, lighted
> by a sun, distant within.

It is probably otiose for me to recommend to readers *The Owl in the Mask of the Dreamer.* John Haines is a poet well known and widely acclaimed. But as he is a poet celebrated for his reticence as well as his sincerity, it is instructive to find the sententia at work in his lines; it is an unexpected element.

If the detachable adage is hard to discover in the work of Andrea Hollander Budy and John Haines, it is well nigh invisible in Gerald Costanzo's. *Nobody Lives on Arthur Godfrey Boulevard* is highly idiosyncratic, a wry and quirky sequence of poems that portrays America as the fever dream of a media network stoned out of its mind. Costanzo offers parables, fables, jokes, and put-ons—and yet his book is serious in intention and memorable in expression. It is great fun to read.

"Excavating the Ruins of Miami Beach" takes place in the far future when a team of archaeologists begins digging up the ancient resort city. They discover omnipresent representations of a figure called Big Daddy, who seems to serve as a tutelary deity to such historical figures as Dr. Erwin Stillman, Patty Duke, Shecky Greene, Norm Crosby, Totie Fields, and Jerry Vale. ("This in the midst of something // called a Hot Dog Stand / in the fallen United States.") In order to preserve something of their own history, the archaeologists prepare these relics for a museum. And, of course, they begin to make a theoretical reconstruction of this vanished society. The poem ends with a stanza that seems to have no appearance of a sententia, being only an interpretive development of the narrative, but its compact statement of skepticism about the theories of scientists gives it some of the force of a maxim:

> And since this was *all* they knew—
> all this much—
> they assumed they knew it all.

The poem is a neat and pointed parable, but it is preceded in the book by a poem called "The Story" that throws disturbing light on its stylish fabulation. In "The Story" the speaker tells how he journeyed through the South with his children and his wife, whom he has temporarily rejoined after a bitter separation. In Miami Beach the man and his son drop into a lunch counter named Big Daddy's:

> On the walls hundreds of group portraits
> of the proprietor and his family alongside
> celebrities, all their names stamped out
> in tape-gun plastic and affixed
> to the frames: Big Daddy, Mrs. Big Daddy,
> and the kid—Big Daddy, Jr., posed among
> Tiny Tim, Johnny Weissmuller, Henny

Youngman, Roland LaStarza, Troy
Donohue, and Dr. Joyce Brothers.

This display case causes the speaker to daydream that he is an archaeologist, and he decides to write a story about the incident called "Excavating the Ruins of Miami Beach." The poem called "The Story" is in two
parts, the first an informal prologue that sets the scene, telling of the
narrator's past history and of his distress. It is a particularly bleak period
for him, "one of those times when living / becomes a cruel parody / of
our intention."

"Excavating the Ruins" is a clean-cut fabulation, but it was drawn
from a dreadfully messy and painful situation, and Costanzo is careful to
insist on this irony, as well as upon the many other ironies that attend
these companion narratives. The skepticism that informs "Excavating
the Ruins" is made even more thorough by "The Story"—and, extreme
as Costanzo's attitude is, I do not find it an anomaly in contemporary poetry. The absence of certainty in personal life and about philosophic and
scientific and historical endeavor that "The Story" implies would draw
agreement from many contemporary poets. With dubiety so deep and so
broad, poetry will find it hard to come up with the nifty mot, the chiseled
adage. It will offer image and incident in plenty but will refrain from
drawing conclusions; it will be information rich, pith poor. Yet even in the
midst of such turmoil some sentences strike with the force of the traditional practice. When the speaker of "The Story" remembers the motives
of his damaged family's Southern odyssey, he says ruefully:

> I think now
> we were lucky to live in a country
> where you can become someone
> else so easily.

Nobody Lives on Arthur Godfrey Boulevard is surely the slyest of the volumes considered here. A great deal of Costanzo's eccentric japery is
throwaway, and readers should keep a close eye on such fables as "The
White Experience in America" and "Dinosaurs of the Hollywood Delta."
One thinks about some of these pieces that, if Martin Mull wrote poetry,

it would probably sound like this. But at the center of all this *blague* is serious—sometimes darkly serious—purpose.

And now and again Gerald Costanzo will drop his guard just a little
and offer a poem like "Braille," a lyric whose gentle but well-pondered
ironies are given clarity and force by its final, highly didactic sentence:

> The blind folding their dollar
> bills in half. Giving the fives
> a crease on each corner; leaving
> the tens smooth as a knuckle.
>
> There are ways, even in trust
> among the rank and file
> of the seeing,
> not to be bilked.
>
> The blind leading the blind
> is not so bad—
>
> how it is lost on us every day
> that you can learn all
> of the world you need to know
> by tapping it gently
> with a stick.

One of the most familiar methods of disarming *sententiae* is the use
of the persona. When the wise saw is put into the mouth of an invented
character the poet is not directly responsible for the saying. This strategy
circumvents reader disagreement; some things the speaker meant to sound
wise are really pretty dumb, but that's all right—the dumb remark helps
to characterize the speaker and move the narrative along; it is part of the
design. Frost is a past master of the proverb-spouting persona: "Mend-
ing Wall" ("Good fences make good neighbors"), "The Death of the
Hired Man" ("Home is the place where, when you have to go
there, / They have to take you in"), "Blueberries" ("It's a nice way to
live, / Just taking what Nature is willing to give"), "The Self-Seeker"
("Pressed into service means pressed out of shape"), "The Bonfire"
("War is for everyone, for children too"), and scores of others.

Miller Williams is fond of the persona poem. His *Adjusting to the Light* contains thirty-seven poems (counting a series of epigrams called "Rubrics" as one), and by my estimate seventeen of them are persona poems. There is nothing unusual about this for Williams, who has always written these. Nor is there anything unusual about the high quality of the volume; Williams, one of our most dependable poets, seems to know his strengths, and he stays with them. One of his consistent qualities is that his lines, especially those spoken by personae, are reminiscent of Frost, partly because they are in blank verse, partly because Williams too is willing to embrace the sententia.

But the characters and situations he draws are not the kind that Frost would draw. In "The Art Photographer Puts His Model at Ease," the photographer is trying to woo his subject out of her clothing, and it strenuously taxes the imagination to think of a Frost persona saying, "I hope you remembered about the underwear. / The lines from all the elastic and the straps / can take an hour or two to go away." But when the photographer attempts to explain his own motives to the model, his generalizations—reductive and almost fatalistic in tone—may recall some of the dourer of Frost's New Englanders. The photographer makes art, he claims, because he is compelled to do so:

> No artist creates art because it's art.
> An artist makes what people may call art
> because, whatever you call it, it has to be done.

He seems to think, though, that even this low-key motto is rather too grand, for he follows it immediately with a personal, highly pragmatic observation: "You must be needing money pretty badly."

Closely related to this dramatic monologue is another called "The Stripper." Again the person the speaker addresses is a young woman whose job requires her to shed her clothes and who is feeling jittery at the prospect. The speaker is an older stripper now aging out: "It seems like every day I hang looser. / I look in the mirror, I can't believe it's me." She talks to her junior colleague sometimes like a fellow worker ("You need to have your lips a little surprised, / your fingers playing the air like an instrument"), sometimes like a Dutch uncle ("Let me ask you something. What would you do / if one of your family wandered in here?"), sometimes like an older sister ("You're pretty as anything I ever saw").

The dramatic situation of the experienced hand giving tips to the tenderfoot is ready-made for adages—"Every man wants his woman a secret"; "Once in a while somebody beats the odds"; "Pretty soon you won't know yourself." Like Polonius, the seasoned stripper is full of sage advice, but unlike Shakespeare's busybody, she has come by it the hard way. She is not mouthing maxims by rote; she has observed and cogitated:

> Don't share the stage with anybody ever.
> Scores every night are going to climb up here
> in their imaginations. That's crowd enough.

Another poem, "To a Friend, an Unhappy Poet," also offers sage advice, but here no persona is supplied and I believe we are justified in assuming that Williams speaks in his own voice. He reports how his friend complained that contemporary verse lacks popularity: "You fret how few now read what's hard to write." He replies that serious literature has rarely been popular, that eighteenth-century London slum-dwellers did not read Blake or Milton, that those who resided in Mansfield Park never read Jane Austen. The last stanza makes a statement that many poets and schoolteachers might disagree with, though those of a libertarian cast might see it as an evident fact:

> Because millions can say the printed word
> you think they should read
> not signs and menus and scores and labels but us.
> They know what they need.

That is a proposition that a literary critic, or more particularly a poetry reviewer, may find discouraging, since it obviates his or her labors. But the line that precedes this stanza—the line that is a sententia—throws a different light on the quoted stanza, for it is more aristocratic than libertarian: How many millions have ever avidly read fine literature? According to Williams, "The question was never how many but why and who."

"A Short History of the Game" ends with an aphorism I have not managed to puzzle out. The lines consider the nature of fame and scandal in the twentieth century by looking into the biographies of well-known actors and athletes and singers. These figures do not present us the most wholesome of examples, it seems, but, after all, they "deserve neither credit nor blame / for how human beings behave." Next, the biographies of mathematicians and poets are examined for clues about the nature of their times, but they too lived flawed lives and, like the others, should not be held up for praise or censure on this score: "They didn't devise the game." The final stanza reflects upon the nature of modern fame:

> Acclaim while you live is a thing
> they give you for being forgotten
> increasingly after you're dead.
> Esteem after death is quiet
> but faithful in the bed.

The first three lines here are clear enough in their statement that those who are famous now will be forgotten after they are gone; the point is reminiscent of Heinrich Heine's remark about a poet of his time: "He was immortal until he died." But the concluding lines are perplexing. Is fame after death quiet because its possessor cannot know of it? Because we, the present generation, cannot know about it? Because "esteem" is a quieter condition than fame? If we take "the bed" to mean "the grave," why is esteem faithful there? Because it cannot promiscuously transfer to others? Because it comforts only its dead cynosure? One of the problems with the lapidary motto is that it may sometimes be as opaque as marble. When that is the case, the result is frustration, and a poem's immediate dramatic effect is damaged, if not ruined.

But such perplexity is unusual in the poetry of Miller Williams. His work is widely known and, I hope, warmly admired for its clarity as well as for its wit, characterization, broad knowledge, and humor both dark and bright. His career has been long and crowded, and it shows, by the evidence of *Adjusting to the Light*, no sign of slackening. I read each new volume of his with full confidence that I am in safe hands, but also with anticipation, knowing that no matter how familiar his excellences are to me, I shall find occasions for surprise.

The sonnet "Things" illustrates the tension between context and independence in regard to the sententia. This elegy for the poet John Ciardi (1916–1986) is, as its title indicates, thick with detail. Yet Williams uses detail not to hide his concluding generalizations, as John Haines does, but to provide a sort of backdrop that will set off his abstract thought. The last line of "Things" rises inevitably from a strong context, but one can easily imagine it acquiring a career of its own and being applied to situations where feelings other than rueful resignation are in play, where revelations other than the recognition of inescapable but false emotional projection are under discussion. There is such fitness in the expression that it could become a convenient one to quote, the elegiac sadness wearing off with much handling. And then, when returned to its original setting, it would reclaim its first signification—but with added force:

> The day we went to visit the house of the poet
> I sat in the chair he sat in when he died
> to look at the last things he looked at:
> the cribbage board; the blue wall; the clock,
> the slow brass pendulum; the deck of cards;
> the small Picasso, slapdash black on white,
> almost oriental, one foot by two;
> the black round telephone with the circular dial;
> the rug with wine roses; books on the floor.
> I sat until the pendulum took my attention
> to feel what he might have felt, sitting there.
>
> For nothing, of course, for all my foolishness.
> The dying gave the room its brown meaning.
> When he sat down, the chair was just a chair.

"A Million Million Suns":
Poetry and Science

Scientists number the streaks of the tulip—which Dr. Johnson told us poets must not do. Others, too, have been diligent in warning poets off the perilous grounds of analysis and abstraction. Thomas Campbell's 1819 poem "To the Rainbow" includes this stern admonition:

> When Science from Creation's face
> Enchantment's veil withdraws,
> What lovely visions yield their place
> To cold material laws!

And one of Poe's earliest poems, his "Sonnet—to Science," complains that the materialist discipline has "torn the Naiad from her flood, / The Elfin from the green grass, and from me / The summer dream beneath the tamarind tree." In course of time, however, Poe recognized science as a most powerful source for his hallucinatory art. An entry in the *Journals of Edmond and Jules de Goncourt* for 16 July 1856 limns his achievement in brief but masterly fashion, and prophesies the tenor of the art of the future—that is, of our own time:

> After reading Edgar Allan Poe. Something the critics have not noticed: a new literary world, pointing to the literature of the twentieth century. Scientific miracles, fables on the pattern A+B;

a clear-sighted, sickly literature. No more poetry, but analytic fantasy. Something monomaniacal. Things playing a more important part than people; love giving way to deductions and other sources of ideas, style, subject, and interest; the basis of the novel transferred from the heart to the head, from passion to idea, from the drama to the dénouement.

A more accurate and suggestive representation of twentieth-century literature would be hard to come by, for no amount of sage admonishment was going to keep poets away from science. Its images, its discoveries and missteps, its prodigies and wonders, its theories and heuristic powers were and are too attractive. Poets flock to this plunder like cows to a salt lick.

Such bardic attention has not always pleased scientists, and some of the grumpier used to tush-tush quite freely, despising any presentation of data less stringent than scientific demonstration. The famous quantum theorist Max Born even regretted having to publish his own lectures. In a prefatory note to his *Natural Philosophy of Cause and Chance* (1949), he says, "I did not like replacing rigorous mathematical reasoning by that mixture of literary style, authority, and mystery which is often used by popularizing and philosophizing scientists." But literary style and mystery are what poets are all about, and authority—especially the authority of science—is something they often lust after because it lends an air of authenticity to products of fancy.

Is it possible to imagine a twentieth-century poetry without science? I suppose our poetic history would not suffer a mortal blow if Erasmus Darwin and Loren Eiseley were lost to it. But I would miss them. I would miss too Ronald Johnson, William Harmon, Amon Liner, Mae Swenson, A. R. Ammons, Diane Ackerman, Robert Morgan, Elizabeth Socolow, Kelly Cherry, and others. Many, many others. Science has become as inescapable a presence in our literature as in our daily lives; poetry, which had such a difficult time learning to assimilate science, now has difficulty thriving without it.

Even so, the task is not easy. The vocabulary of science is sometimes arcane, uncouth, and even downright ugly. There ought to be prizes for poets who can use the term *quantum* correctly and the word *xylocarp* gracefully. Poetry celebrates visual appearance while disciplines like chemistry and particle physics plunge below appearance into a universe often impossible to visualize, a void punctuated by brief pulses and intermittent bleeps of electromagnetic energy. There is, besides, the dread problem of accuracy: those of us who are forced to learn our science from popular texts, films, and lectures are likely to garble details and overleap stages of thought, impatient to come to the grandiose images of astronomy and the intriguing paradoxes of subatomic theory.

Finally, there is the simple fact that most contemporary poetry takes the form of personal lyrics in which the main effect must be emotional rather than intellectual, subjective rather than objective. Thus science will infrequently show up as subject matter; its role is often to be ornamental—to furnish simile and diction, image and illustration. When employed as a structural element, it is likely to be used as an old-fashioned conceit, an elaborate and highly detailed metaphor. Sometimes, indeed, science appears in poetry as little more than intellectual wallpaper, a background chitchat about phenomena in front of which a personal drama takes shape.

In her first and often quite charming collection, *Light at the Edge*, Devreaux Baker uses what seems to be a genuine but casual knowledge of science in a casual manner. Her usage is simply a part of the normal range of reference in her poems, and a reader has the feeling that she might broach the same references in conversation. In "Measuring Time," for example, she tells of her five-year-old daughter's illness, a fever that bloomed in her cheeks "like damp roses." During the period of anxious waiting the poet finds that the usual ways of counting time have been invalidated, that terms like "yesterday" and "tomorrow" and "five days from now" no longer have meaning, and she searches for a new kind of measurement: "I tried to divide time up into moments / thinking, this is the purpose of numbers / to order the universe, to fulfill the prophecy of motion / based on measurement." She then recalls different methods of measuring, from the pie chart she learned in fifth grade to Roman mensural counting to Egyptian calculations of the periodic Nile floods. Finally, though, only the most personal and immediate method proves viable:

> The placing of the cloth upon her head
> became our one dependable measurement.

Then, as "the last bit of fever" subsides, ordinary ways of telling time return to the mother, and she is able to make a promise: "Tomorrow or the day after / we should ride the ferry from Sausalito / straight across the Bay."

Other poems in *Light at the Edge* also point out the differences between objective and subjective methods of time counting. "Witness" begins with these sentences: "I am marking time and circumstance with borders. / The alarm clock that cannot be broken / wakes us before the sky has warmed / to the color of flesh." "Sentinel" is a poem about the legacy of a piano from the death of a young relative, and the subsequent discovery of a piano book in which time is found to have been measured by the departed pianist's mastering of pieces: "The soft lead of your pencil / thinner now, the letters upright / at the end of the book, 'Played!' " This way of measuring is compared to the more objective method of counting tree rings. As the speaker traces "the spheres within the wood," she silently imagines the history of the tree: *"see here, where the circle draws in, / too tightly pressed against the other one. / Here there was less water, look, it goes on, / a drought for several years."* The analogy—years of unsuccessful practice leaving their marks like drought years in tree rings—is ingenious, fresh, and unexpectedly moving.

Baker's references are not insistent, and most of her poems do not resort to scientific vocabulary or metaphor. Her love poems are perhaps her best. In her elegies she sometimes strains, and the result is bathos, as in "Remember Richard": "When Richard's mother came driving up, / she knelt down on the pavement and beat her fists / until they bled, but it still didn't bring her son / to life again." Yet this awkward passage and a few similar ones are strongly overbalanced by quiet lyrical moments of wistful beauty. Here are the final stanzas of "In a Distant Place":

> I think if we are meant to live like this,
> etched into the world of sleep,
> someday our two bodies will be found
> mine grown large as a harbor, filled with the two of us,
>
> curving from the past into a distant place,
> silent and still as forgotten speech

where the unspoken words fill our heads
with their dark syllables and their soft tongues
are waiting to speak.

I have noted that Baker's use of science is often casual. Sometimes, as in "House of Rain," it is merely decorative. In "Einstein's Space or Van Gogh's Sky," the scientific element is confusing because neither of her points of reference helps to illustrate the central conceit of a love relationship deteriorating like seams of clothing coming apart. The poem itself admits that Einstein is unhelpful, but when it turns instead to van Gogh, the result is still fruitless:

All day the turning of things inside out has worried me
growing larger than life.
Is this what Einstein meant by the relativity of space?
What is relative being determined by when or where or how?

I think it is more what Van Gogh had in mind, mixing the
color red with yellow, hatching crows in a field of corn.

The encapsulation of Einsteinian thought makes no sense and the connection with van Gogh is merely willful. However, the conclusion of the poem is strong: to an outsider a relationship may appear to be whole and sound, but a participant understands the fact of its dissolution; "the gradual letting go of what we see / for what we know." Baker's observation is just and would have more power if Einstein and van Gogh were jettisoned.

Happier are the astronomical references in "Rowing Across Night." In this poem a woman is awakened by the sound of her truck-driver lover grinding his gears on the last downgrade before he arrives home. Half-asleep, she imagines that he is steering his big truck through the night sky: "the sky is radiant / where licks of stars burn themselves out / at the far edge of the universe." She is like the earth, she thinks, and her lover like all the sky that surrounds her: "The world spinning with her great red fever / takes in the black universe like a lover / discovers the body of his one true love is unknowable." Baker's sentence construction is unfortunate, but the fancy is so engaging that the poem recovers as the woman

imagines rowing down the highway as down a river, then off the edge of
the horizon into the night sky, following her lover in his celestial semi:
"The grinding gears of your echo float thin-edged / as a layer of light
escaping in leaks / from the mouth of moon, / drifts unprotected across
my body." At the edge of outer space she halts poised as her lover—now
become a skyrocket or comet or thundercloud—gathers energy for a
beneficent explosion:

> I am transfixed at this brink of earth and air
> sleeping at the edge of things,
> waiting for the fall-out of you
> to sprinkle my body with explosions of rain.

Devreaux Baker is not yet an accomplished poet, and though I don't
like to pin upon her work that curdled adjective "promising," here it provides a just description. Her casual use of scientific matter points toward
major strengths as well as a major weakness: she has breadth of knowledge and a talent for unusual association, but she lacks logic and consistency. The confusions of "Rowing Across Night" are justified by the
trancelike state of the speaker, but there are similar confusions in other
poems ("The Explorer's Prayer," "Interlude Between Stations") that lack
dramatic justification. Still, the personality in her lines is distinctive and
pleasing, her love poems are warm and sexy, and her emotion is usually
unstudied. Her later work will very likely be more resonant and more
graceful, but *Light at the Edge* is a noteworthy beginning.

The history of science would seem a highly advantageous field of subject matter for poetry. Here as in few other areas of human endeavor are
passion and intellect so closely allied, and almost no other kind of history
presents such clear and verifiable outlines. There is a colorful attractiveness about even outmoded or discarded scientific concepts such as the
aether, phlogiston, light pressure, Ptolemaic astronomy, and so forth. In
the efforts of science, the differences between folly and honest error are
especially striking, and our intellectual strivings are stained with pathos
and humor in equal measure. If Montaigne were alive today, I think he
might become a historiographer of science.

These are some of the reasons that David Young's *Night Thoughts and Henry Vaughan* is a disappointing book. Too many fine opportunities are missed, and a reader is bound to feel that the author began his work more with wishful thinking than with careful planning. The volume opens with a suite of five poems spoken by the persona of the seventeenth-century Welsh poet, and one difficulty with this plan is immediately apparent: already having a considerable amount of verse by Henry Vaughan, we may well suppose that he has delivered what he desires an audience to know about his thoughts and feelings. It seems unlikely that David Young will write verse that can compete with Vaughan's own "The Retreat" or "Peace" or "The World," the last with its famous opening: "I saw Eternity the other night / Like a great Ring of pure and endless light, / All calm, as it was bright."

Why, then, has Young so rashly invited a comparison in which he would inevitably come off second best? "Mountain Hare," the first poem in the sequence, begins with these lines: "I rise as the moon sets / and dawn beats up confusion." The construction "beats up" is puzzling, and a look into the *OED* discovers no seventeenth-century usage that would make the phrase clear. The dictionary does show a couple of sixteenth-century instances of the adjective "thirdhand," a word that occurs in Young's line, "the thirdhand light of the pond-moon," but these are so widely scattered the adjective must be counted an anachronism.

But, really, the whole sequence is anachronistic, and I expect we have to accept that it is purposely so. The jacket copy tells us that the "Henry Vaughan" sequence serves as "gateway" to the much longer "Night Thoughts" sequence, which takes place in Young's backyard during a Perseid meteor shower in August 1991. Yet it remains unclear how the first poems introduce the latter and why the figure of Henry Vaughan was chosen. It is true that Vaughan was a scientist of a sort—a doctor who wrote a treatise on medicine and who seems to have engaged in some alchemical experiments. He is best known as a poet and mystic, an adherent of natural theology, the doctrine which held that the nature of God is revealed, to however remote a degree, in His handiwork, "The great Chime / And Symphony of nature," as Vaughan puts it in "The Morning-watch." Young echoes the tenor of that thought in stanzas like this one from "The Weather Cock":

This is a world where soul-shine
blows through the clouds and trees,
where spirit bubbles in springs
and beats in lonely wells.

Such passages are unobjectionable but cannot allay our suspicion that we might be better occupied in reading Henry Vaughan than in perusing summaries of his ideas and intentions in contemporary terms. There is also the embarrassment of "Night-piece," in which Young causes Vaughan to hear God speaking to him directly in order to compliment his poetry: "And I swear I heard him whisper / 'One of your poems made me weep,' / but he never said which one."

I would like to justify Young's pages. Let us say that the persona of Henry Vaughan was never intended as a serious portrait of the man or his ideas. The sequence signifies only a casual homage, a recognition that earlier poets—especially those of seventeenth-century England—were as warmly exercised as our contemporary poets about the problem of absorbing scientific knowledge into poetry. John Donne's formulation is well known: "And new philosophy calls all in doubt." Young's "Henry Vaughan" sequence is purposely anachronistic because it offers a contrast. Henry Vaughan thought about science and physical phenomena in the manner of his time, and now in "Night Thoughts" Young gives an illustration of the way a poet at the end of the twentieth century thinks about these matters.

But this justification might well lead to the conclusion that not only were seventeenth-century poets superior to those of today as poets, they also had a surer grasp of science. We may find it quaintly amusing to read in Vaughan's medical treatise, *Hermetical Physick*, sentences like "Imagination is a Star, excited in the firmament of man, by some externall Object" or the pronouncement that "men are frequently inclined to vomit, when they look earnestly upon those Ejectments which another hath cast up." But taken in suitable context such statements are no more quaint than David Young's description of a famous theorem of modern physics:

Heisenberg's uncertainty principle—

delta times delta p is more or less h-bar:
arid formula, fun to repeat,

halfwit whisper in the billowing dark,
this whole summer these have been
my talismanic words,
my bumper-sticker science.

The poet's disclaimer is humorously disarming, but it is also an admission of surrender. The Uncertainty Principle is just too complex to versify in this context.

"Night Thoughts" is rife with such defensive admissions: "I'm / probably failing, repeating / what others have said"; "I fumble for my little verbal amulet"; "Let me talk on in this starlight / these meteor streakings of nonsense"; "I don't know genetic drift from Adam. / I gaze at a woodpecker or an azalea / and the whole mess makes me glad." Young is, like the majority of us educated folk, scientifically half-literate. His recognition of the fact is cheerfully rueful ("Am I a middle-class shaman—?") but leaves in question why he decided to compose the sequence.

Night Thoughts and Henry Vaughan is by no means a bad book, is pleasant to read through. Young's verse offers few difficulties and maintains a well-bred chatty tone that springs no surprises. He has been reading books and looking at the sky above his backyard, that's all, and we overhear his restless reverie. "A mind gets encumbered / with memories, objects, ghosts," he tells us, and in this sequence he alludes to dozens: John Constable, Freeman Dyson, Wallace Stevens, Edward Young (the seventeenth-century poet who wrote the original *Night Thoughts*), Rilke, Orpheus, and Hamlet. The only connections between them are as figures in Young's consciousness. He offers no plan, no structure, no hint of design to draw them together. Instead, he simply enjoys and celebrates, offers no conclusions, and is satisfied to tease with easy paradox:

You think you make the night again in words.
They just as much make you.
That's what the fireflies are signaling.

Your system is and isn't metaphor.
It lives, you live,
among the hidden structures of the night.

Such defensiveness is not always warranted. If poets are forced to be content with half-knowledge (as Coleridge contended they ought to be), then so are scientists when topics at hand begin to range outside their individual fields of expertise. Science has become so broad in its investigations and so specialized in its methods and terminology that a biochemist who wishes to learn about fractal geometry must resort to a popular or semipopular book, like the rest of us. Of course, experts being what they are, it may be tricky to get a biochemist to own up to ignorance—as W. H. Auden noted in "Shorts II" (from *Epistle to a Godson*):

> Knowing artists, you think that you know all about Prima Donnas:
>   boy!, just wait till you hear scientists get up and sing.

It may well be that the scientist's job is only to ask *How?* and the poet's only to shout *Wow!*, but neither of them seems satisfied with exercising only the one function. Scientists don't often shout *Wow!* because it makes them look naïve. Poets tend not to delve too deeply into *How* because, like David Young, they fear making foolish mistakes. Gary Fincke, however, is successful with a different attitude: he throws caution to the winds. *Inventing Angels* is filled with all sorts of wacky facts and nonfacts gleaned from the annals of science, and Fincke delights in pushing absurdities to their limits—and beyond, as in "The Habits of Eating," which derives a wild space-program scenario from linking a recent crackpot astronomical theory with the notion of spontaneous generation as advanced by Aristotle:

> He thought he saw insects birthed
> By mud; he wrote it down and landed
> On a list of fools, one notch below
> Bill Pickering, the astronomer
> Who said, in this century, the spots
> On the moon are huge swarms of insects,
> Maybe he let his garbage grow wings
> Instead of flushing his cans with spray.
> Maybe NASA filmed the astronauts
> In Nevada like the skeptics claimed
> Because they feared the lunar surface
> Writhed with grubs.

Fincke is fearless, willing to take metaphors from science fiction as well as from science, to illuminate accurate physical data by posing them against fantasy, and to collect the most-obscure facts and colligate them into utterly unexpectable patterns of significance.

"Behind Glass" is a poem that typifies *Inventing Angels;* it exhibits Fincke's wide spectrum of reference, a quirky humor that spices his serious purposes, and his tendency toward allegory. The poem begins in ordinary anecdotal fashion with the speaker watching, from the top-floor window of a glass-walled resort hotel, an airplane spraying insecticide to kill the caterpillars "who want these woods for food." He is safe behind his glass—though he feels extremely vulnerable—and he remembers other situations where he has observed men-under-glass: the television quiz shows of the 1950s with their booths for sweating contestants, the pope waving from his bulletproof glass box as he rides the streets, Adolf Eichmann and the Mafia kingpins from Sicily "listening, / We think, to the unedited language / Of their public trials." These glassed-in figures are secure from the dangers of their immediate environments, but they are as exposed as laboratory mice in their glass cages. Perhaps, in effect, that is what they are—experimental animals used to test the environment. This notion leads Fincke to recall certain old cornball sciencefiction movies and to reflect that not even protected isolation is always truly safe:

> And what of those B-film space helmets,
> The fishbowls the commanders removed
> Like white lab rats on remote planets?
> They'd inhale once and tell their nervous crews
> "It's OK to breathe," though there was no sign
> Of plants, nothing but rocks and the rubber
> Monsters which flourished on every new world.
> And we knew what happened when the captain
> Didn't chance the air: One helmet was flawed.
> Some spaceman would clutch, suddenly, his glass,
> And we'd see his mouth working for answers.

I admire Fincke's flash and dazzle and the nonchalance of his tone. Scientific subject matter in poetry seduces a lot of writers to profounder-than-thou attitudes, to becoming new William Blakes and Annie Dillards eager to show that they too can find the universe in a grain of sand. That is, of course, a legitimate stance for a poet to take, but it has its dangers; principal among these is self-deception, the temptation to believe oneself a lot smarter than is the case.

Fincke avoids this error; in fact, I think it is not a strong temptation for him. He is bound to make errors sometimes, though, given the verve with which he attacks his themes. In "Learning Cursive" the comparison of handwriting to a neighbor dog's daybreak barking is silly, and in the third part of the poem a child's mistake in spelling her name receives a highly dubious explanation: "As if some blink in the genes / Had turned wide-eyed from prenatal / Air or a wish or despair." Fincke is always stretching, and sometimes his reach is just a mite short.

That problem is inevitable, I suppose, with any poet who has in him such a broad streak of Robert Ripley's "Believe It or Not!" Fincke as a poet is like those other contemporary collectors of strange instances and grotesque facts, Charles Fort and Avram Davidson. Unlike these odd polymaths, however, he constructs no elaborate Rube Goldberg theories to develop new cosmologies or secret world histories. He takes the oddities as clues and indices to our interior states of fear, longing, and desire.

"The Hollow Earth," for instance, treats us to a notion broached by William Symmes, Edgar Allan Poe, Adolf Hitler, and Edgar Rice Burroughs—that our planet encloses inside itself another world which can be reached via a hole in the globe near the South Pole. For Fincke it is not important that this hypothesis has been exploded, only that it seemed necessary for someone to think of it in the first place:

> All of these myths we long for from inside
> The ghost-land of our basements, of wide pipes
> We can walk the water with, expecting
> The road to Shamballah or an entrance
> Guarded by a flaming sword, plunging toward
> That land always lit by a central sun.

It takes an outré curiosity to recover these forgotten theories and addlepated notions, and a truly strong talent is required to make them expressive and emotionally salient. All science, legitimate or illegitimate, is meat for Gary Fincke's gourmet menu, and I believe that he prefers to draw little distinction between what contemporary scientists approve and what they reject. "The Developer's Landscape," a sequence of poems about different scientific constructs, begins with two straightforward queries: "How does it feel at the end of science? / What's important the day after closure?" *Inventing Angels* is intended at least partly as an answer to these questions, though a provisional one to be sure.

Louise McNeill's posthumous *Fermi Buffalo* demonstrates admirably the attractiveness of science to poets. In her eighty-first year this West Virginia laureate was at work on this final, unfinished volume in which she undertook such subjects as cyclotrons, Planck's constant, optical theory, Schroedinger waves, and geologic history. She made a good job of it too, all things considered. Her ambitions were not as high as David Young's nor so eccentric as Gary Fincke's, but of the poetry considered here, hers is some of the most charming, perhaps because of a certain modesty of motive and intention.

Her forte is wit, and her ability to turn a piece of scientific data into a telling personal simile is a source of fresh pleasure. "Neutron Stars" is rueful in tone, but the paradox of its last line expresses a wry cheerfulness:

> Burned and black to the neutron bone,
> Dwarf stars stand in the night alone—
> Dead black stars with their firestorms still—
> I am burning and growing chill.

The dark echo of Landor's famous "Dying Speech of an Old Philosopher" ("I warmed both hands before the fire of Life; / It sinks; and I am ready to depart") serves this epigram deftly, but a reader innocent of Landor can enjoy it as is.

McNeill is quite direct in her appropriations; she makes no attempt to detail the tangled complexities of her scientific subjects nor to find delicate nuance in them. She simply broaches her topic (often in the form of simile and metaphor), speaks plainly about it, and constructs a sometimes ingenious but almost always solid poem. Now and again a poem is *too* plain and solid: "The Octave" is a pithy statement about the range of colors available to human eyesight, yet makes no advance on the same thought as we find it in Pope's 250-year-old "Essay on Man."

But in a poem like "Quadrille of the Naked Contours" her antic humor is broadly displayed. The title reminds us of Lewis Carroll, and the poem deals with the quantum theory in a sprightly Carrollian manner. It is too long to quote whole, but here is the rigadoon first stanza:

> At the end of night, at the end of day,
> When the substance burns till it burns away,
> And nothing stands by our burned-out seas
> But some birches stripped to the soul of trees;
> And nothing hangs in the upper zones
> Of the crystal clear but electron bones
> Of the white dwarf stars, like a ring of stones—
> Then the Absolutes in their lucent cords
> Will rise and dance on the burned-out swards.

François Villon and Christian Morgenstern could have no acquaintance with the scientific theories that color this apocalypse, but they would recognize immediately the clackety rhythms and marimba timbres of the *Galgenlied*.

McNeill is best known as an Appalachian poet, her usual subjects the sort that academics classify as folk material. *Fermi Buffalo* includes poems that obviously lie centrally in the Appalachian tradition—"Ballad of Lasha Watson," "Granny's Old Ballad," "Old Man Loar," the lovely and touching "Blue and Brown"—but it is easy to tell that the aging poet found her thought quickened by the science she must only recently have learned. The poem "Granny Fanny" is an elegy for a friend recognizably Appalachian, "An old mountain woman in a black dress / And checkered sunbonnet." The first stanza speaks of Granny Fanny losing her life gradually; it is like losing pennies from a pocket with a hole in it. But these familiar-seeming lines include an adjective not familiar in the least: "a hole in its pocket / To let out the pennies of life / Falling down from the quasar meadows." Perhaps McNeill's choice is not successful—"quasar" is a bit of a jolt in this context—but it demonstrates how thoroughly scientific concepts came to permeate her habits of thought.

She is not only surprised and gratified by the revelations of science but also keenly aware that she has come into possession of a new kind of cognition, a sort of knowledge so novel it is almost alien to her old-fashioned traditions. In "Mother and Son" a woman remarks wryly upon the different ways in which she and her young lad have perceived the world: "For you the fireflies flash their bulbs, / For me, they lit their candles." Sometimes this realization makes her gently melancholy. In "Grace" she reflects upon the differences of experience that such knowledge brings about:

> I know a million million suns
> Expand the womb of space
> Where all the burning webs
> of time and distance interlace.
> My mother only knew the sun upon her lifted face.

The use of the old fourteener measure for the last line neatly underscores her mother's oldfangled ways of knowing, dear but irrecoverable.

In her title poem McNeill clashes old American traditions with new scientific knowledge to produce a raw dissonance that projects a horrific conclusion. "Fermi buffalo" are what she calls the animals grazing the plain above the underground Fermi Nuclear Accelerator in Illinois. The conjunction of two objects—one symbolizing American past history, the other representing global future history—gives rise to a wild vision:

> E, Energy in the fat hump roasted on the chip-fire—
> The juices run blood where the spit turns it—
> Turning in the rings of fire—American time turning:
> Wagon wheels—windmills—turbines—truck tires—
> cyclotrons—silver dollars spinning on the marble,
> And where the lariat whirled in the rimmed sunlight—
>
> At Batavia, Illinois, where the bison feed above the electron-spin
>   in the steel walls
> Accelerate—Accelerate—the speed of light under the slow bull
>   as he lifts his head to the wind-tang—
> The radioactive scent blowing east from Hiroshima—

Other poems too ("Coal Grate Song," "The Long Traveler," "At the Beach") use this montage method to portray what the poet sees as a head-on collision of traditional values and ways of life with scientific advance. This technique is difficult to employ because it offers so much possibility for the kind of naked editorializing that ruins "Fermi Buffalo," which ends with a nightmare about a little pioneer girl "crisping" in a nuclear fallout—a closure garishly overwritten. Restrained black humor serves this poet better than jeremiad, as in these last lines from "Moonflight—Apollo":

> Then Armstrong put his foot down on the moon,
> Endymion woke from his immortal swoon,
> Diana died, and up in all the trees,
> The rats were nibbling pieces of green cheese.

Montage is a method often preferred by poets dealing with science, and a reader can appreciate its advantages. It gives swiftness of presentation to data and images, offering a way to make them appear related even when no close relationship is logically perceivable. Conversely, such conjunctions can lend the impression of phantasmagoria to facts and notions that might appear unremarkable when considered in sober isolation. All the poets discussed here engage in montage to some extent, but the most sophisticated usage is found in *Science and Other Poems* by Alison Hawthorne Deming. She seems alert to its perils as well as its attractions, and in "Letter to Michael" she addresses the point specifically. This verse epistle is intended for a friend facing death, and Deming hopes to offer solace and also to aid in his visualization practice of picturing the cancer cells being destroyed in the bloodstream:

The new thinking suggests I send images. Voracious shrews consuming
twenty times their weight each day. Quasars in the bloodstream
emitting high-pitched wails that dematerialize the killer cells.
A master microbial sleuth which identifies the aliens and turns them in
to Immune Central. Take that with your visionary meal of garlic,
mu tea and brown rice. And promise to let fly your finest rage—
nature's an imperialist expanding its ego at your expense.

The difference in the motives for montage in "Letter to Michael" and Mc-Neill's "Fermi Buffalo" is important: in the latter the reader sees the poet at work, choosing montage as one technique from among others; in the former the exigencies of the situation determine the usage and give it solid dramatic justification.

But Deming also remarks upon the drawbacks of montage, specifically in "Staying over Nature," a poem dedicated to the painter Myron Stout. The second section of this intelligent longish work tells about Hans Hofmann, the German immigrant who served as mentor to so many young American painters. He was one of those artists who believed "in science, / the headlong train that promised everything." This was in the 1950s when "everyone was excited about unity." Soon enough, however, artists understood that the promise of science was not to be fulfilled. Deming uses montage to show that their dream was wistful and quixotic:

> Some things
> the mind isn't good at, like trying to picture
> the proto-universe—that everything's-nothing
> tumble of stars, baboons, and symphonies—
> as a speck one billionth the size of a proton.
> The mind's better at a fractured view,
> though, little satisfied, keeps hunting
> for what it can't see.

"Staying Over Nature" had begun with a description of Myron Stout as he appears in a photocollage entitled "The 10th Street Painters." Collage, montage, catalogue: science in poetry seems to invite "a fractured view," images arrayed in confusion or in orders not easily discernible, images swiftly skimming by to suggest a dizzying breadth of data and relationships that proximity implies but does not reveal.

We usually think of montage as a film technique, perfected by D. W. Griffith and described theoretically by Sergei Eisenstein. Film gives fluidity and forward motion to fragments, and in "Fiber Optics and the Heart" Deming applies film technique directly. A fiber-optic lens delivers images to a television monitor in a traveling shot that "threads the ventricle," then passes "wet tabs of muscle" and "semi-lunar valves" and "membranes shaped like teacups" until it reaches "the junction of iliac arteries." Here the light in the blood vessels changes to a glow "like the mouth of a cave / seen from within." The source of trouble, the blood clot or artery blockage, has not yet been found, and the optic tube must keep on searching:

> so that the wand reaches
> back to the walls of Lascaux
> where painting the bull's
> charcoal head
> kept the hunter alive
> by capturing first
> the image
> of what could kill
> or sustain.

This is reversed time-lapse photography with a vengeance. It could be objected that the poem is a little too patly made, its point telegraphed by making "the heart" part of its title. But these are a reviewer's afterthoughts. On first reading I found the closure surprising yet just, and repeated reading has only caused me to enjoy more warmly the accuracy of detail and the narrative design.

Like Devreaux Baker, David Young, and Louise McNeill, Deming feels alienated from science even when she admires it. Science for these, as for a large number of other contemporary poets, is a seemingly unnatural mode of thinking, a way of perceiving nature that must be acquired with some effort and which rarely lends comfort and never feels quite customary. In "Searching for the Lost" Deming tells of a helicopter scanning the ocean surf for the body of a young man drowned. She begins to muse on the methods the searchers use:

> There must be a science
> for conducting a search—the same start-and-halt improvisation
> as modeling a molecule's structure. How long does it take
> for a lean body to surface? How does wind counter
> the drift of the tide?

Then she catches herself up; she shouldn't be thinking in these terms. Science is too analytic, too unengaged, too cool in temperament for this occasion: "But that's cruel—to think of science / when the night throbs with the death of a young man." One of the major ambitions mounted by modern poets is to overcome this supposed dichotomy between scientific and poetic modes of thought. It is the same one Thomas Campbell spoke of in 1819 with his contrast between "lovely visions" and "cold material laws," and since then there have been valiant attempts at synthesizing these outlooks by such philosophers as Alfred North Whitehead and Michael Polanyi and such poets as Conrad Hilberry and A. R. Ammons.

The posing of an easy opposition between scientific and artistic endeavor is really intellectually untenable and naïvely sentimental when held up to the light of reason. Curiosity too is a human motive, at least as valid as rage and disgust, and an informed admiration of nature is surely as honorable as one that is uninformed. The scientific imagination has become as habitual and perhaps as natural to our organism as the artistic imagination. In fact, these two modes of imagination are not, and perhaps should not be, easily separable.

In "Mt. Lemmon, Steward Observatory, 1990" Deming points out the necessity of metaphor in all attempts at description, including the scientific:

> A scientist
> can say *NGC 5194/5* to another
> and the other says *Ahhh*,
> picturing the same massive whirlpool, its
> small companion galaxy eddying by its side.

The great observatory telescope, its mirror expensive and tediously constructed ("two years to polish / the surface to digital perfection"), can dismiss our ancient legends about the heavenly bodies ("Here are those gods and goddesses / seen for what they are—battered rock / and frigid gas, sulfur boiling out / into murderous air"); it can correct the "map of our misunderstanding" about the moon, upon whose arid surface we have imagined "dew or rivers" and "Sea of Rains, Ocean of Storms."

These fancies astronomy may have destroyed, but our sense of the marvelous remains:

> The wonder is we still can see
> the way it pours liquid pearl
> over the earth's dark waters
> after we know its windless surface,
> that implacable dust the moon travelers said
> smelled like cap guns, is cratered
> with a wire-braced flag, two lunar jeeps,
> and footprints no weather will arrive to erase.

Alison Hawthorne Deming is a brilliant poet, and *Science and Other Poems* a thoughtful, honest, probing, and classy book. With the best will in the world she goes to science for the matter of her poetry. She is not quite at ease with it, yet that can be said not only of her and other poets but also of philosophers, mathematicians, laymen, and many scientists themselves. All the poets spoken of here have made honest efforts to address the presence of science in contemporary thought and experience. Some, of course, succeed better than others, but it is important to have tried, to desire a broadening of poetic idiom so that it may welcome whatever new insight a new knowledge can afford us. In her observatory poem, Deming phrases it this way:

> Describing *is* imagining—
> knowing, not knowing but
> having the language
> to convey, to *be* the water carrier,
> Aquarius, to quench another.
> I saw it with my own eyes.
> Seeing is believing.

Afterword

One needn't agree with W. H. Auden's statement in "In Memory of W. B. Yeats" that "poetry makes nothing happen" to admire his delicately descriptive phrase for the art—"a way of happening." It might even be possible to argue that the two phrases are in some senses mutually contradictory.

At any rate, I do believe that the way in which things happen is important to the nature of those things and my purposes in criticism have been to laud the ways I found beautiful and truthful and to censure, as gently as conscience allowed, the ways I found faulty and unfaithful. Neither my praise nor my censure has met with complete approval by the poets under examination or by readers whom I take in all earnest to have been impartial. If the poet makes mistakes, how many more must the critic commit! The poet gets off easy by comparison; his blundered poems are soon forgotten. The critic's inept judgments show him a fool for as long as the poems he has wronged may live. Because I have tried my best to do right, I am willing to live with this prospect.

But I don't look forward to it.

List of Books Reviewed

"Purple Patches, Fuddle, and the Hard Noon Light"

The West Door. By Alfred Corn. New York: Viking, 1988.
Fictions from the Self. By Michael Burkard. New York: W. W. Norton, 1988.
Annonciade. By Elizabeth Spires. New York: Viking, 1989.
Shores and Headlands. By Emily Grosholz. Princeton: Princeton University Press, 1988.
The Way Down. By John Burt. Princeton: Princeton University Press, 1988.
Stopping by Home. By David Huddle. Salt Lake City: Gibbs M. Smith, 1988.

"Attempts upon Delight: Six Poetry Books"

Once Out of Nature. By Jim Simmerman. Baltimore: The Galileo Press, 1989.
A New Path to the Waterfall. By Raymond Carver. Boston: The Atlantic Monthly Press, 1989.
Groom Falconer. By Norman Dubie. New York: W. W. Norton, 1989.
Balance as Belief. By Wyatt Prunty. Baltimore: Johns Hopkins, 1989.
Eden. By Dennis Schmitz. Urbana: University of Illinois Press, 1989.
Blues If You Want. By William Matthews. New York: Houghton Mifflin, 1989.

"Family Matters"

Playing for Keeps. By Donald Junkins. Amherst: Lynx House Press, 1991.

Days Going / Days Coming Back and Other Poems. By Eleanor Ross Taylor. Salt Lake City: University of Utah Press, 1991.

Forgiveness. By Dennis Sampson. Minneapolis: Milkweed Editions, 1990.

Moon in a Mason Jar. By Robert Wrigley. Urbana: University of Illinois Press, 1986.

The Makings of Happiness. By Ronald Wallace. Pittsburgh: University of Pittsburgh Press, 1991.

"Every Poet in His Humor"

Narcissus Dreaming. By Dabney Stuart. Baton Rouge: Louisiana State University Press, 1990.

The Past, the Future, the Present: Poems Selected and New. By Reed Whittemore. Fayetteville: The University of Arkansas Press, 1990.

Distance from Loved Ones. By James Tate. Hanover, NH: Wesleyan University Press / University Presses of New England, 1990.

Popular Culture. By Albert Goldbarth. Columbus: Ohio State University Press, 1990.

Why We Live with Animals. By Alvin Greenberg. Minneapolis: Coffee House Press, 1990.

Collected Poems: 1939–1989. By William Jay Smith. New York: Charles Scribner's Sons, 1990.

The Death of Cock Robin. By W. D. Snodgrass. Newark: University of Delaware Press, 1990.

"Brief Cases: Naked Enterprises"

The Bicycle Slow Race. By Claire Bateman. Hanover, NH: Wesleyan University Press / University Presses of New England, 1991.

The Really Short Poems of A. R. Ammons. By A. R. Ammons. New York: W. W. Norton, 1990.

Heroes in Disguise. By Linda Pastan. New York: W. W. Norton, 1991.

"Maiden Voyages and Their Pilots"

When Last I Saw You. By Patricia Claire Peters. Lewiston, NY: The Edwin Mellen Press, 1992.

Learning to Dance. By William Aarnes. Greenville, SC: Ninety-Six Press, 1991.

Somewhere in Ecclesiastes. By Judson Mitcham. Columbia, MO: University of Missouri Press, 1991.

Crucial Beauty. By David Scott Ward. College Park, MD: SCOP Publications, 1991.

The Love That Ended Yesterday in Texas. By Cathy Smith Bowers. Lubbock: Texas Tech University Press, 1992.

Under a Cat's-Eye Moon. By Martha M. Vertreace. Bloomington, IL: Clockwatch Review Press, 1991.

"Five New Southern Women Poets"

At Every Wedding Someone Stays Home. By Dannye Romine Powell. Fayetteville: The University of Arkansas Press, 1994.

Ceiling of the World. By Alice Rose George. New York: Spuyten Devil, 1995.

Dangerous Neighborhoods. By Marnie Prange. Cleveland: Cleveland State University Poetry Center, 1994.

Old & New Testaments. By Lynn Powell. Madison: The University of Wisconsin Press, 1995.

A Garden in Kentucky. By Jane Gentry. Baton Rouge: Louisiana State University Press, 1995.

"An Idiom of Uncertainty: Southern Poetry Now"

Lessons in Soaring. By James Applewhite. Baton Rouge: Louisiana State University Press, 1989.

Sigodlin. By Robert Morgan. Middletown, CT: Wesleyan University Press, 1990.

The 18,000-Ton Olympic Dream. By T. R. Hummer. New York: William Morrow, 1990.

The Center for Cold Weather. By Cleopatra Mathis. Riverdale-on-Hudson, NY: The Sheep Meadow Press, 1989.

The Erotic Light of Gardens. By Bin Ramke. Middletown, CT: Wesleyan University Press, 1989.

"Taking Sides: Six Poetry Anthologies"

Against Forgetting: Twentieth-Century Poetry of Witness. Edited by Carolyn Forché. New York: W. W. Norton, 1993.

A Gathering of Poets. Edited by Maggie Anderson, Alex Gildzen, and Raymond Craig. Kent, OH: The Kent State University Press, 1992.

The Rag and Bone Shop of the Heart: Poems for Men. Edited by Robert Bly, James Hillman, and Michael Meade. New York: HarperCollins, 1992.

Men of Our Time: Anthology of Male Poetry in Contemporary America. Edited by Fred Moramarco and Al Zolynas. Athens: The University of Georgia Press, 1992.

Fast Talk, Full Volume. Edited by Alan Spears. Cabin John, MD: Gut Punch Press, 1993.

African-American Poetry of the Nineteenth Century: An Anthology. Edited by Joan R. Sherman. Urbana: University of Illinois Press, 1992.

"Figured Carpets: The Collected and the Selected"

What I Think I Know: New and Selected Poems. By Robert Dana. Chicago: Another Chicago Press, 1991.

A Last Bridge Home: New and Selected Poems. By Dan Gerber. Livingston, MT: Clark City Press, 1992.

New and Selected Poems. By Stephen Berg. Port Townsend, WA: Copper Canyon Press, 1992.

If I Had Wheels or Love: Collected Poems. By Vassar Miller. Dallas: Southern Methodist University Press, 1991.

The Path to Fairview: New and Selected Poems. By Julia Randall. Baton Rouge: Louisiana State University Press, 1991.

"Once upon a Time: Narrative Poetry Returns?"

Covenant. By Alan Shapiro. Chicago: The University of Chicago Press, 1991.

The Black Riviera. By Mark Jarman. Middletown, CT: Wesleyan University Press, 1990.

Autumn Eros and Other Poems. By Mary Kinzie. New York: Alfred A. Knopf, 1991.

The Gathering of My Name. By Cornelius Eady. Pittsburgh: Carnegie Mellon University Press, 1991.

Saints in Their Ox-Hide Boat. By Brendan Galvin. Baton Rouge: Louisiana State University Press, 1992.

"Piecework: The Longer Poem Returns"

Corvus. By Anselm Hollo. Minneapolis, MN: Coffee House Press, 1995.

Muse & Drudge. By Harryette Mullen. Philadelphia: Singing Horse Press, 1995.

The Invention of the Zero. By Richard Kenney. New York: Alfred A. Knopf, 1995.

Kyrie. By Ellen Bryant Voigt. New York: W. W. Norton, 1995.

"The Contemporary Long Poem: Minding the Kinds"

The Diviners. By Robert McDowell. Calstock, Cornwall, UK: Peterloo Press, 1995.

Middens of the Tribe. By Daniel Hoffman. Baton Rouge: Louisiana State University Press, 1995.

Quartet. By Angela Ball. Pittsburgh: Carnegie Mellon University Press, 1995.

The Descent of Alette. By Alice Notley. New York: Penguin Books, 1996.

"Let Me Count the Ways: Five Love Poets"

The Past Won't Stay Behind You. By Samuel Hazo. Fayetteville: The University of Arkansas Press, 1993.

What Keeps Us Here. By Allison Joseph. Bristol, RI: Ampersand Press, 1992.

Dead, Dinner, or Naked. By Evan Zimroth. Evanston, IL: TriQuarterly Books (Northwestern University Press), 1993.

Maybe It Was So. By Reginald Gibbons. Chicago: The University of Chicago Press, 1991.

Afterworld. By Christine Garren. Chicago: The University of Chicago Press, 1993.

"Wise Saws When Last Seen"

Collected Poems (1930–1993). By May Sarton. New York: W. W. Norton, 1993.

House Without a Dreamer. By Andrea Hollander Budy. Brownsville, OR: Story Line Press, 1993.

The Owl in the Mask of the Dreamer: Collected Poems. By John Haines. St. Paul, MN: Graywolf Press, 1993.

Nobody Lives on Arthur Godfrey Boulevard. By Gerald Costanzo. Brockport, NY: BOA Editions, 1992.

Adjusting to the Light. By Miller Williams. Columbia: University of Missouri Press, 1992.

" 'A Million Million Suns': Poetry and Science"

Light at the Edge. By Devreaux Baker. Albion, CA: Pygmy Forest Press, 1993.

Night Thoughts and Henry Vaughan. By David Young. Columbia: Ohio State University Press, 1994.

Inventing Angels. By Gary Fincke. Cambridge, MA: Zoland Books, 1994.

Fermi Buffalo. By Louise McNeill. Pittsburgh, PA: University of Pittsburgh Press, 1994.

Science and Other Poems. By Alison Hawthorne Deming. Baton Rouge: Louisiana State University Press, 1994.

List of Authors and Editors Reviewed

Page numbers indicate references in passing to author, editor, or his or her work; italic page numbers indicate review of author's or editor's work.